MOMENTS OF SILENCE

Moments of Silence

Authenticity in the Cultural Expressions
of the Iran-Iraq War, 1980–1988

Edited by

Arta Khakpour, Mohammad Mehdi Khorrami, and
Shouleh Vatanabadi

NEW YORK UNIVERSITY PRESS
New York

NEW YORK UNIVERSITY PRESS
New York
www.nyupress.org

References to Internet websites (URLs) were accurate at the time of writing.
Neither the author nor New York University Press is responsible for URLs
that may have expired or changed since the manuscript was prepared.

Library of Congress Cataloging-in-Publication Data

Names: Khakpour, Arta, editor. | Khorrami, Mohammad Mehdi, editor. |
Vatanabadi, Shouleh, 1955- editor.
Title: Moments of silence : authenticity in the cultural expressions of the
Iran-Iraq war, 1980-1988 / edited by Arta Khakpour, Mohammad Mehdi
Khorrami and Shouleh Vatanabadi.
Description: New York : New York University Press : New York University Abu
Dhabi Institute, [2015] | Includes bibliographical references and index.
Identifiers: LCCN 2015025923| ISBN 9781479841585 (cl : alk. paper) | ISBN
9781479805099 (pb : alk. paper) | ISBN 9781479883844 (e-book) | ISBN
9781479803248 (e-book)
Subjects: LCSH: Iran-Iraq War, 1980-1988—Literature
and the war.
Classification: LCC PK6412.I73 M66 2015 | DDC 891/.5509358550542dc23
LC record available at http://lccn.loc.gov/2015025923

CONTENTS

ACKNOWLEDGMENTS

This book is based on the papers presented at a conference entitled "Moments of Silence: The Authentic Literary and Artistic Narratives of the Iran-Iraq War (1980–1988)" which was held at New York University in Abu Dhabi in March 2011. It is certainly natural to first and foremost thank our contributors who initially accepted our invitation to be part of that event and then agreed to make necessary modifications to their presentations and prepare them for inclusion in this volume.

We also thank our colleagues at NYUAD's offices in New York and Abu Dhabi. Putting together the conference and addressing intellectual and organizational challenges would not have been possible without the constant assistance of these colleagues. We would like to specifically thank Ms. Sharon Hakakian-Bergman, Ms. Gila Waels, and Professor Philip Kennedy.

When we started working on the conference proposal, we realized very early on that the intellectual integrity of this project is very much dependent on the materialization of its interdisciplinary and intra-regional components. This fact required us, from the very beginning, to acknowledge the significance of the collective nature of this project and to hope that this requirement would be fulfilled with the generous help of many colleagues. Indeed, we were extremely fortunate to have worked with scholars who did not hesitate to go beyond the call of duty in helping us define and stay true to the intellectual integrity of the project. We would like to specifically thank Ms. Marjan Riahi, Professors Farhad Kazemi, Dina Khoury, M. R. Ghanoonparvar, Michael Beard, and Zachary Lockman. There is no doubt that without them this conference and this volume would not have become a reality.

A number of the chapters have used materials that have already been published; also one essay and one short story have appeared in other publications. We would like to thank Random House, Mazda publishers, and *Journal of Research of Applied Linguistics* for giving us their permission to include these materials in this volume. In particular, we are grateful to Dr. Kamron Jabbari, president of Mazda Publishers, and to Professor Paul Sprachman, who allowed us to include the translation of Habib Ahmadzadeh's short story, "A Letter to the Saad Family" in this book. This text first appeared in a collection of stories, *A City Under Siege: Tales of the Iran-Iraq War*, which is a collection of nine short stories by Habib Ahmadzadeh, translated by Paul Sprachman, published in 2010. Also, we are thankful to Dr. Alireza Jalilifar, the editor-in-chief of *Journal of Research in Applied Linguistics,* where Professor Fazaneh Farahzad's essay was first published in 2013.

We are also grateful to colleagues at NYU Press. Their suggestions enriched this book, and the whole team made this process seamless. It has been a pleasure working with them.

Last, our most heartfelt thanks go to Mr. Amir Moosavi, one of our contributors, who in addition to presenting a paper and providing the corresponding chapter, helping with the selection and translation of a number of texts of Arabic literature, also agreed to put together the bibliography section of the volume. Given the underresearched nature of this topic, finding relevant primary and secondary sources is an extremely difficult task. We are grateful to him.

* * *

This publication is supported by a grant from the NYU Abu Dhabi Institute, a major hub of intellectual and creative activity, and advanced research. The institute hosts academic conferences, workshops, cultural events, and other public programs, and is a center of scholarly life in Abu Dhabi, bringing together faculty and researchers from institutions of higher education throughout the region and the world.

Introduction

ARTA KHAKPOUR, MOHAMMAD MEHDI KHORRAMI,
AND SHOULEH VATANABADI

The term "Gulf War" never achieved an equivalent level of media sat-uration and buzzword ubiquity when employed to refer to the 2003 invasion of Iraq and subsequent events as it had a decade prior, when it referred to Operation Desert Storm and irrevocably conjured a cer-tain set of wartime "documentary" images (Apache gun camera footage, Tomahawk missile launches) that Jean Baudrillard famously called an "atrocity masquerading as a war," war's simulacra.[1] What the termi-nology of the 2003 war did achieve, however, was the anointing of the 1990–1991 war as "First Gulf War," a title hitherto held by the Iran-Iraq War of 1980–1988.[2]

This *first* First Gulf War did not lose its salience in governmental and media narratives as it lost its name, however: it was instrumentalized as precursor, lesson, counterpoint, cautionary tale by various agendas. Military analysts used it as a textbook on Iraq's defensive capability,[3] war opponents bearing images of Donald Rumsfeld and Saddam Hus-sein smiling and shaking hands pointed to it as an example of foreign policy hypocrisy,[4] war advocates used the conflict as evidence of Iraqi aggression and war crimes.[5] Not long after, the Iranian regime, which had long referred to its conflict with Iraq as a "holy defense" and an "imposed war," found its own "victim" narrative of the war echoed in unlikely places. In the interests of defusing hostilities between the United States and Iran and preventing yet another war in the regime, various permutations of the supposed truism that "Iran has not attacked a neighboring country in 200 years" were spread by antiwar advocates,[6] uncritical of Iran's own culpability for the war, particularly after the state unilaterally rejected an Iraqi peace accord in 1982. In keeping with this narrative, efforts to portray the war as a by-product of malicious foreign intervention tended to emphasize Western support for Iraq and its criminal chemical weapons program while deemphasizing Iran's own foreign support (a reversal of the situation decades prior, in the days of the Iran Contra scandal), Iran's war crimes, and the fact that Henry Kissinger's famous statement most accurately summed up the cynicism of many of the backers and suppliers of both Iran and Iraq: "It's a pity they both can't lose."

The facts of the war have remained, nonetheless. One million or more soldiers and civilians dead, millions more permanently displaced, countless disabled, a generation of prosthetic implants and teenage martyrs. The facts have remained—to be instrumentalized by agendas foreign and domestic, but also to be aestheticized, defamiliarized, re-addressed, and reconciled by artists, writers, and filmmakers, speakers of Arabic, Persian, Kurdish—Shiite, Sunni, atheist—Iranian, Iraqi, internationalist.

Following their particular agendas, official discourses naturally have tried to dominate the process of production and distribution of war narratives. In doing so, they have attempted to ignore and silence voices that transcend borders further demarcated by war. In order to hear these voices, then, one should be alert to the fact that in the context of this general background of discursive confrontation, there are more subtle elements that generate multiple narratives, each of which attempts to authenticate and legitimize itself and its discourse. The Iran-Iraq War (1980–1988), with the multifaceted efforts of the dominant discourses to control the narratives of that war, provides one of the best cases for a study of the formation of these narratives. Dealing primarily with the literary and artistic expressions based on the Iran-Iraq War developed in these two societies, these expressions allow for a better understanding of the complexities of underrepresented narratives that go beyond those produced by official and conventional discourses. The material in this collection attempts to identify systems of meanings that are behind the multiple narratives of war. They explore the genre of war literature as reflected in Iran's and Iraq's contemporary writings by situating them in their historical contexts, while demonstrating how official efforts to appropriate the narratives of war have created the problem of authenticity for these narratives. Indeed, the more efforts have been made to authenticate these narratives, the more spurious they have become. This even includes works that have tried to dissociate themselves from the official discourse. The material in this collection underlines the fact that the above-mentioned problem has indeed contributed to the creation of a literary and artistic phenomenon in which the most successful war discourses are those in which war stories are placed in the background or are deliberately absent. In particular, this latter has led to the emergence of "sites of silence" which effortlessly contribute to the formation of the most expressive accounts of war experience. The collection therefore includes theoretical studies based on the idea that "silence is full of unexpressed words" as significant elements in reading war literature. They identify these moments of silence as one of the major sites of intraregional and global conversations.

The subtitle of this volume, and the conference that preceded it, may be read as an implication that these narratives—*these* and not *those* narratives of governmental and partisan agenda—are, unequivocally, the authentic ones, but the reality is rather more complex. The literary and artistic narratives that are gathered and studied here were brought together not because they naively represent an authenticity lacking in the—official, hegemonic—discourses of the war, but precisely because they call into question the notion of authenticity—within their own narrating act, within that of a regime or party bulletin, within *any* such act—itself.

A common thread that emerges in this material is the notion that the facts of the war, even when agreed upon, do not translate to simple truths. Donna Pasternak notes the sense of futility Tim O'Brien describes when discussing his attempt to create a "true war story" out of the past—when, in his words, that past is "so intertwined with the present and the future that the truth is only created, represented by, the constant entanglement and expression of all the perceptions that occurred, are occurring, will occur."[7] When O'Brien writes, then, that he "wants you to know why story-truth is truer than happening-truth,"[8] it is less a validation of literature's place as a "realer" reality, a revisionist account of the "dark areas" of history,[9] but rather an assertion that the never-complete *process* of getting at the truth, and the revision, skepticism, and subjectivity that come along with it, has an actual, honest existence that challenges the idea of a non-mediated truth to which we all have access. The fault in the official discourse, then, lies as much in its cynicism as in its denial of its own narrated and mediated nature.

Is this a "secret history," then, of the kind that Peter McInerney believes Vietnam War literature played a unique role in narrating? He writes, "Vietnam is as much a state of mind as a place or event. It is a kind of mystery which cannot be represented or even adequately named by straight or exterior history."[10] If so, this secret history's greatest claim to authenticity is the fact that, unlike "straight" history, which creates truth by erasing deviation, it is self-conscious in its pursuit of truth and in its representation of this pursuit as unending, ambiguous, often self-contradictory. Finding, deciding upon, creating a language that can convey any sort of truth at all—collective, national, private—is a major preoccupation of the texts and critiques in this collection.

The conference "Moments of Silence: The Authentic Literary and Artistic Narratives of the Iran-Iraq War" was conceived as a space where this language and its diverse dialects could be explored by a group of scholars and artists working in equally diverse dialects: linguistic (Persian, Arabic, Kurdish, Khuzi, Gilaki) and disciplinary (from social history to the political history of cinema to literary criticism). Held from March 15 to 17, 2011 at NYU Abu Dhabi, the conference represented the first comparative, interdisciplinary symposium dedicated to studying the cultural production of the Iran-Iraq War as a multifaceted and transnational phenomenon. In this respect, the emphasis of the symposium was to give priority to voices that represent intraregional conversations beyond nationally contained ones. Although it is undeniable that in the current globalized world vehicles of knowledge and research are so fluid that it is practically impossible to identify them within particular geographies, it is also a known fact that, for various historical reasons, including Orientalism and Colonialism, many of these vehicles carry the mark of literary and historical traditions which are not necessarily informed by literary, linguistic, and, in general, analytical characteristics of Southern (i.e., regional) traditions. Therefore, one of the premises of this conference was drawn based on the argument that different disciplines in different geographies have traversed various paths; thus, concepts formed in fields such as history and historiography, literary criticism, aesthetics, and philosophy have particular genealogies, which then necessitates mindfulness when one attempts to create the appropriate ground for the cross-cultural and transnational dialogues.

The chapters gathered here are presented in four parts, representing the major methodological preoccupations and thematic considerations of the conference: (1) transnationality as a phenomenon of war, (2) new theoretical paradigms for studying wartime cultural production, (3) visual culture, and (4) literary culture. They are accompanied by an appendix representing some of the literary texts that were read and discussed at the conference's conclusion. There is also a short bibliography, prepared by Amir Moosavi, which includes only those primary and secondary sources that we believe to be indispensable for those who are interested in working on this extremely underexplored topic.

The chapters in part I, "Transnational Contexts: Interconnected Histories, Geographies, and Languages," are an effort to defy traditional nation-oriented approaches to war and its cultural production. Ella Shohat's chapter considers language and geography as two dimensions of an "exilic mode" of writing and examines their interaction in memoirs involving the war. The very possibility of an "Iraqi" or "Iranian" response to the war is complicated by the nature of these works, written in French and narrating a life in Iran (Marjane Satrapi), written in Hebrew and narrating the life of an Iraqi Jew (Shimon Ballas), or written in English and narrating the life of an Iranian Jew during and after the Revolution (Roya Hakakian). Shouleh Vatanabadi's chapter discusses works that challenge the notion that the only (or most relevant) wartime border was that between the nation-states of Iran and Iraq. Films like *Bashu: The Little Stranger* and *The Night Bus* are shown to use language to create spaces and tensions that defy nationalist fictions: the former envisioning a heteroglossic Iran with mutually unintelligible dialects and languages, including the Arabic of the "enemy," and the latter creating a multilingual microcosm within a bus, whose passengers bear transnational linguistic and cultural subjectivities—the Kurdish, the Iranian Arab, the Arab Iranian—which defy the war's attempt at assimilation.

The chapters in part II, "Theorizing Cultural Expressions of War," involve an intervention in the methodological framework for studying the war and its cultural products. Each makes a powerful argument for the inclusion of such material in any broader study of the Iran-Iraq War, and each draws upon various disciplinary frameworks (trauma studies, social history) while acknowledging their limitations when applied to a still understudied and undertheorized event. Kamran Rastegar's chapter involves a theorization of the "sacred defense field" in Iran and the ways in which its cultural production has interacted with distinct paradigms of memory discourse and trauma production. A comparison with Lebanese postwar cultural production provides an opportunity to examine narratives that fall outside the paradigmatic boundaries of this field. In the first chapter to focus directly on works produced by combat veterans, M. R. Ghanoonparvar examines how these stories, novels, and films have grappled with official discourses and government propaganda in their interpretation of the very character of the war itself—its material reality, its inception and motivation, and the characterization of its combatants.

Dina Khoury's chapter is a potent reminder that constructing a binary opposition between official discourses of the war and the "authentic" narratives of victims and veterans is as tenuous an endeavor as uncritically accepting the truth claims within those discourses. The prisoner-of-war narratives that she examines do not readily accept themes like victimhood, resistance, or "truth to power" any more than they do nationalism, patriotism, or battlefield heroism. POWs who "converted" (or indeed were made to convert through coercion, torture), emblemize the complexities of a situation in which a victim's victimization is inseparable from his own victimization of others. Amir Moosavi's chapter introduces a comparative framework between Persian and Arabic war narratives as well as a shift of focus from the battlefield to the "home front," examining the ways in which authors working in both languages complicated the "war cultures" that were created by both state and non-state institutions within their societies. Finally, Michael Beard's chapter completes this section with a meditation on language and violence, presenting an argument that language, and possibly all aesthetic representation, fails to represent violence with any accuracy or neutrality and yet acquires a persuasive capacity through the deployment of such aestheticized violence that is unquestionably powerful as an exhortation to fight, to defend, to act.

The two chapters in part III, "War through Visual Representations," focus on the visual and cinematic, two elements of Iran-Iraq War cultural production that are particularly salient considering the visual spectacle of one of the most massive wars in recent memory, which anticipated the spectacle that accompanied the two Gulf Wars to follow. Peter Chelkowski's chapter examines the role of graphic arts during the war—posters, murals, commemorative art, patriotic ephemera—as a continuation and development of the themes of self-sacrifice and righteous revolution that accompanied their deployment during the Iranian Revolution of 1979. Marjan Riahi's chapter is a thorough history of the development of Iranian war cinema as a political and cultural phenomenon from the outbreak to the conclusion of the war, analyzing the role of the state in fostering war film as a component of wartime morale-building, and the limits of the filmmaker's agency in operating within the established framework of patriotic cinema.

In part IV, "Literary Narratives of War," each chapter considers new paradigms for studying the literary production of the war, be it original prose, poetry, or translation. Mardin Aminpour's is the first chapter to focus exclusively on literary representations of the Kurdish experience of the war, and the myriad ways in which the narration of this experience rejects nationalist, statist, and patriotic tropes and places an emphasis on civilians, rather than combatants, as the perennial victims of military conflict. Farzaneh Farahzad's chapter, meanwhile, focuses on the politics of editing and linguistic nationalism: a phenomenon that, in the Iranian context, is mostly associated with pre-Revolutionary politics, but in Farahzad's analysis, played a significant role in the editing of translated texts in Iran during the war, and was part of the discourse of nationalist opposition to the Enemy—in this case, conceived of as the linguistic Other. Finally, Mehdi Khorrami's chapter finds in certain works of modernist Persian fiction a response to the war that, while rejecting the staging and simulacra of state-endorsed war "memoirs" and documentaries, does not supplant an "anti-discourse" of truth and authenticity in their stead, but rather deploys silence as both a strategic and an aesthetic device to open a new space, home to neither hero nor victim, neither combatant nor "home front" civilian.

This volume ends with a selection of translated literary texts—poetry and prose by Sinan Antoon, short stories by Habib Ahmadzadeh and Marjan Riahi—that were among the works read at the writers' roundtable of the Moments of Silence conference. It is the hope of this volume's editors that these texts, as well as myriad other heretofore unstudied texts of the Iran-Iraq War, can be read in concert with new methodologies and comparative frameworks that can bring us closer, if not to a singular, secret truth, then to a secret history of the war and to moments of silence brought about not by state-mandated rituals of remembrance, nor by the elision of time's passing, but by the act of criticism itself.

NOTES

1 Jean Baudrillard, *The Gulf War Did Not Take Place*. Bloomington: Indiana University Press, 1995.

2 See for example: "From Gulf War to a Gulf Peace?" *Sydney Morning Herald* (Australia). (July 20, 1988): 576 words. LexisNexis Academic. Web. Date Accessed: May 17, 2013.

3 See for example: Stephen C. Pelletiere and Douglas V. Johnson, *Lessons Learned: The Iran-Iraq War*. Carlisle Barracks, PA: Strategic Studies Institute, U.S. Army War College, 1991.

4 See Stephen Green, "Who Armed Saddam? Who Armed Iraq?" Counterpunch.org (February 24, 2003). Web. Date Accessed: May 17, 2013.

5 See "Kanan Makiya's War Diaries," New Republic Online (April–March 2003). Web. Date Accessed: May 17, 2013.

6 See Juan Cole, "Bush Sets Preconditions for Iran Syria." Juancole.com (December 8, 2006). Web. Date Accessed: May 17, 2013.

7 Donna Pasternak, "Keeping the Dead Alive: Revising the Past in Tim O'Brien's War Stories." *Irish Journal of American Studies* 7 (1998), p. 48.

8 Tim O'Brien, *The Things They Carried*. Quoted by Pasternak, ibid., p. 49.

9 See Brian McHale, *Postmodernist Fiction*. New York: Methuen, 1987.

10 Peter McInerney, "'Straight' and 'Secret' History in Vietnam War Literature." *Contemporary Literature* 22.2 (1981), p. 191.

PART I

Transnational Contexts: Interconnected Histories,
Geographies, and Languages

1

Narratives of Borders and Beyond

SHOULEH VATANABADI

War, however, is the friend of binarisms, leaving little place
for complex identities.
—Ella Shohat

In a previous piece I wrote on the Iran-Iraq War (1980–1989)[1] I argued
for the necessity of looking at this event not as an isolated moment fixed
in time but as an experience within the continuum of temporality as
formulated by Walter Benjamin, to point to the shifting and fluidity of
times that connected the Iran-Iraq War with the U.S. invasion of Iraq.
My argument in that paper also included the usefulness of cultural texts
both literal and visual in narrating the experience of war as "a collective
experience to which even the deepest shock of every individual experience constitutes no impediment or barrier."[2]

I think of this chapter as a continuation of the same attempt through
the lens of shifting spatiality and the diversity of geographies of identity
involved in the experience of this war. My take on the meaning of spatiality in the context of this chapter is through an understanding of space
as a social construction relevant to different histories of human subjects
and to the production of cultural phenomena.[3] My emphasis here is on
the utility and importance of space as an analytical and representational
mode for culture and identity formations that can defy the imaginations
of "nations" as fixed, isolated, and disconnected. Here I find it particularly useful to focus on the site of "borders." Borders are paradoxical
points in space, whereas they delineate divides in between imagined
communities of nations; they expose the overlaps and intersections
between, across, and beyond the constructed dividing marks of nations.
The paradoxical performance of borders as a representational category,
I will argue, draws attention to the competing discourse involving war
and, in particular, the experience of the Iran-Iraq War.

A view from the border highlights the contradictions, paradoxes, and imperfections in the grand narratives of nations and states. At the moment of war, this view spotlights the problematic of "nation" at its very edge, for it is at this very edge where nationalizing policies are regularly subverted. Borders as they represent imperial, colonial, masculinist, and nationalist impositions of power have the potential to open a bottom-up perspective to expose individual and collective border narratives and experiences reflecting the ways in which borders impact the daily life practices of people living in and around them. Borders as zones of instability can point to the ways in which ethical, political, cultural, and national discourses are negotiated, dialogized, intersected, and collided. Borders can shift the analysis and understanding of socio-spatiality away from the static world of container-borders to the complex and varied patterns of both implicit and explicit bordering and ordering.[4]

Let's not forget that the borders of "nation-states," Iran and Iraq, are the workings of nearly five centuries of "bordering and ordering" and conflicts over "territory," with its players as the Ottoman and Persian empires, European colonial powers, as well as neocolonial and postcolonial nationalist authorities. The long history of shifting maps of inclusions and exclusions across fluid borderlines involving a myriad of different ethnicities, languages, cultures, and religions, brings into question essentialist notions of uniform, homologous, and fixed constructions of nations and the binary discourses of war between them.

Much has been written by way of political and historical analysis of the centuries-long shifts of border involving the geographies of Iran and Iraq.[5] On the subject of the Iran-Iraq War, whole bodies of work have concentrated on the descriptive history of contestations over the formation of borders involving these areas. Yet the information on border formations has not been adequate to point to the intricacies of life experiences across, in-between, and beyond these borders. It is perhaps on the site of cultural production, where the borders of politics and poetics intersect, that narratives of these life experiences as they encounter more intensification at the time of war are communicated.

In what ways do narratives of spaces that lie within zones of conflict (borderlands of war) provide an alternative perspective on the experience of war by the inhabitants of these zones? In what ways does an interpretive lens on spatiality expose the complexities of geographies of identity involved in the experience of this war? How would this lens shape alternative readings of the experience of this war as it dialogizes and overlaps with domestic spaces such as the home front, communal spaces such as nations, and the wider transnational landscapes? How are power relations expressed through the lens of spatiality? How are these relations inverted and contested? In what ways do narratives informed by the space of the borders expose the competing discourses of officialdom that construct the space of "nation" as monologized and monoglossic containers? In what ways does the dialogism of a polyphony of geographies of identity subvert the unitary notions of a "nation"? In what ways do the border zones of this war perform to foreground the paradoxes involving the contested power configurations? In what ways do narratives of borders communicate the experience of this war beyond the divisions imposed by imagined "nations" which undermine the "overlapping territories and intertwined histories"?[6] In what ways do cultural products, visual media, and literary texts, informed by borders in both their physical and metaphoric senses, bring to purview the paradoxical and competing discourses of war?

Literal and visual texts on the Iran-Iraq War (1980–1988) can provide a practical forum in which one may examine the individual experiences, collective memories, and their connections with local/global interactions as they relate to that event. Of course, cultural production is one of the primary sites appropriated by the official discourse of the war as well as by the non-official counterdiscourse. In this respect, war stories function around the binaries of war to promote the nationalist official discourse, while at the same time they provide the possibility of changing and countering the binaries produced by the discourses of war, raising other issues immediately impacting the societies involved.

There are numerous examples of films and literary texts on the subject of the Iran-Iraq War. In both Iran and Iraq from the outset of the war, the media of literature and film were active loci for both official and non-official expressions regarding this event and its impact on society. Many cultural works serving the national homogenizing projects emphasized the dichotomous discourse of war as officialdom drew on past symbolisms to produce meanings for a meaningless war. In Iran, the officialdom drew on the moment of consolidation of an Islamic state and named the war "Defa'-e Moghaddas" (the Sacred Defense). In Iraq, the Battle of Qadessia (the AD 637 defeat of the Persian Sassanid by the Moslem Arab army) became the official name of this war in order to emphasize the Arab nationalism of the Iraqi state. Though a whole body of cultural texts falls under this rubric, many literary and visual texts produced in both Iran and Iraq drew on the experience of this war to find ways to collapse the exclusivist discourses of nations and national divides while critiquing the hierarchies within these nations as well as articulating the multilayered complexities of their respective societies. A great number of works with this critical and subversive attribute revolve in different ways around the space and subject matter of "border" in the form of national boundaries, points of crossing, points of in-between-ness and even war fronts. Examples of these works include films like *A Time for Drunken Horses* (2000) by Bahman Ghobadi; *A Place to Live* (2005) by Mohammad Bozorgnia; *Kilometer Zero* (2005) by Hiner Selim; as well as literary works such as *Don't Take Me to Baghdad* (2006) by Nahid Kabiri; *At the Border Line* (2003) by Sherko Fatah; *The Umbilical Cord* (1990) by Samira Al Mana.

Whether the story of these works involves the home front or the Iran-Iraq War, the border becomes a common force of narrative in all of them. The border in these works functions as the paradox to demonstrate the experience of the war as the diverse geographies and identities of Arabs, Persians, Turks, or Kurds, and many more whose intertwined lives, histories, and geographies defy the boundaries constructed by discourses of nation. In what follows, I will examine two films, each demonstrative of war as experienced either at the "home front" or at the epicenter of action, the "war front." In all cases, "border" points to the fluidity of the notion of space to subvert the official discourses of war.

Borders of the Home Front—Bashu: the Little Stranger

Bahram Beyzai's film, *Bashu: Gharibeh-ye Kuchak* (*Bashu: the Little Stranger*), is perhaps one of the earliest films made during the war; it was produced in 1986 and shown only at the end of the war in 1989. Where the central space of the film's action is a tranquil village in Gilan in the Caspian region in northern Iran, far from the stages of combat of the Iran-Iraq War, the central force of the narrative destabilizes the seemingly calm and in many ways linguistically and culturally uniform population of the village who are Gilakis who speak a distinct local dialect of Persian. Yet the core of the narrative in the film is initiated at the epicenter of war—the border region between Iran and Iraq in Khuzestan in the south of Iran. Bashu, a ten-year-old Arab Iranian boy who witnesses his family's death in a fireball of Iraqi bombs and who climbs on a truck to escape, emerges a day or two later in the totally different linguistic, ethnic, and physical geography of Gilan. This is a foreign land to Bashu, who speaks Arabic, while those now surrounding him and rejecting him as a dark-skinned outsider speak Gilaki Persian.

When Bashu emerges from his hiding place in the truck still in a state shock from the explosions and tragedy he has witnessed at the southern border, the primary stage of the war, he runs into the rice fields and is discovered by two children who alert their mother Naii of the stranger's presence. Naii is a single mother in charge of the family and their farm; her husband, a war veteran who has lost his right arm, is away in search of work. Not having had any exposure to any other Iranian outside her village, Naii is astounded by Bashu's darker skin color, and thinks he has been in a coal mine. She takes him in and protects him against the xenophobia and racism of the villagers. Following the story of Bashu's crossing into Iran's cultural borderlands and the initial encounter with unfamiliar zones of identity and geography, the story develops into a bond between Naii and Bashu through a process of negotiation and coming to terms with their culturally informed differences that eventually lead to Bashu's inclusion into the family and the new geography.

Like many stories involving the border, Bashu's is a story of crossing, a crossing that involves his traversing across and within the boundaries of Iran. But, as the film makes clear, the boundaries within are not the safe zones of familiarity, uniformity, and homogeneity. This is what the dominant official discourse of "nation" imposes with a particular emphasis on the time of war. Indeed, Bashu's traverse within the national boundaries lands him in an indefinite zone of cultural, linguistic, and racial differences. Bashu is indeed a stranger in this zone; he is a Gharibeh (an outsider, with negative connotations in Farsi).

The breaking point in opening a path toward Bashu's inclusion is a highly significant scene in which Naii and Bashu surmount their linguistic divisions by engaging in a dialogical relation through translation.

Pointing to different objects, Naii mentions the name of the object in her Gilaki Persian dialect, encouraging Bashu in return to identify the objects in his Arabic dialect. The scene is not free of its own ironies, for in the process of naming the objects, the past colonial connections of constructing this linguistic identity are revealed as well. For some objects, it turns out Naii uses the Russian word, whereas Bashu uses the English terms—a reference to the colonial division of northern and southern Iran under the influence of the Russians and the British. It is after this dialogic moment that Bashu is gradually taken in by Naii to become a new member of her family.

Though taken in by Naii, Bashu continues to remain "a stranger" to the community outside Naii's family. Even the husband with whom Naii stays in touch is adamantly opposed to Naii's determination to take Bashu into the family. It is only at the end of the film when it becomes clear that Bashu can be an invaluable helping hand with their farming that the disabled husband yields to Naii's insistence.

The various connections created between Naii and Bashu point to the ways in which each of these characters undermines the established discourses of nation, community, and family structure. It is through Naii's agency that the patriarchal structure of her family is subverted to pose a challenge to the masculinist power informing it. The communities' discomfort with Bashu's inclusion and its constant challenge with Naii's insistence are also in many ways related to her gendered position as a single woman, a subtext that in an interesting yet subtle way exposes the interconnections of race, gender, and cultural divides. If the immediate space of Naii's actions of resistance is within the parameters of the village and community, Bashu's story and his character move the field of defiance to the broader areas to destabilize notions of spatiality and counter the fixed discourses of national unity and homogeneity.

In a highly significant scene, when Bashu is bullied by the children of the village who think of him as mute and stupid, Bashu picks up a school text and reads a passage from it in Persian with his Arabic accent: "We are all children of Iran." This official line of the state as expressed in the school textbook is sharply countered by the divides, differences, and hierarchies within the nation as experienced by Bashu. Above all, what Bashu's crossing through the internal borders destabilizes is an understanding of the geography within as fixed and rigid. Bashu's ever-present flashbacks, nightmares, and memories of his experience on the front line of war (the borderlands of Iran and Iraq) create overlapping scenes of two different physical and cultural geographies of the south (informed by its Arabic connections) with that of the distant north.

The Iran represented in this exemplary film of the home front during the Iran-Iraq War is anything but a uniform country. It is indeed an imagined community with many others within it that need to come to terms with its cultural, linguistic, gendered, and racial asymmetries.

Through Bashu, an Arab/Iranian who stands culturally in-between Iranian and Iraqi borders, the enemy is indistinguishable.

Borders of the Front: The Night Bus (Otobus-e Shab)

If the film *Bashu: the Little Stranger* exposes the national contradictions and the paradox of the notion of the border in the space of the home front, where the story of war involves the story of a family and a small community, *The Night Bus* (*Otobus-e Shab*) *2007* by Kiumars Pourahmad is built around the typical stories and events taking place on the front line. In contrast to the film *Bashu: the Little Stranger*, this story speaks of the universe of men with a typical role assigned to its only woman character as the wife waiting for her husband to come back from the war. Unlike *Bashu*, the film takes place in the war zone where the constant explosions and devastations of war provide the backdrop.

The film has a simple story line: a twenty-four-hour-long journey of two young Iranian soldiers (*Issā* and *Emād*) and a civilian driver (*Amu Rahim*) transporting thirty-eight Iraqi prisoners of war, taken from behind Iraqi lines, to a garrison inside Iran.

Shot in black and white, from the outset the film represents the discourse of war in a binary of color, with no grey areas in between. Yet against this monochromatism, as the film progresses, alternative and in many ways subversive elements are gradually introduced into the narrative to counter the sharp dichotomies of the warring nations of "Iran" and "Iraq," exposing the complexities and diversities involved across and within these nations.

The film opens with a worn out, almost broken-down bus, driven by an old civilian who has served as a transit driver for years. Once the prisoners of war are on the bus, all blindfolded, the night-long journey begins toward its destination on Iranian soil. This seemingly straight path is complicated by several interruptions due to the lack of direction as the bus moves into a nowhere-land where it is not quite clear to the driver whether they are on the road to Iran or headed to Iraq. The unknown landscape, marked by the constant bombing and explosions, never clear from which side they are coming, destabilizes the marked geographical line of the border to create an ambiguous background landscape through which the bus travels.

With this fluid landscape as its background, the bus ride and the bus itself become the setting in which the story of the film unfolds. If the film starts with the passengers on the bus divided into Iraqis and Iranians, the overlapping of languages, cultures, and ethnicities among them all surfaces to the point where, once the bus finally arrives at its destination, the dividing lines between the two groups are blurred. When one of the Iraqi soldiers experiences an epileptic seizure, another Iraqi soldier who is a physician comes to help and has his blindfold lifted, at which point he is recognized by one of the Iranian soldiers as his old friend, a fellow Kurd whom he met during another journey, on a train from London (where they have been studying) to Istanbul on their way to return to their respective homes at the beginning of war. Following the moment of recognition, the Iranian Kurd and the Iraqi Kurd become involved in a warm conversation (in Kurdish). As the story progresses another Iraqi soldier is revealed to be the son of an Iranian mother and an Iraqi father who speaks both Arabic and Persian fluently; he takes up the task of a translator for the others. From his linguistically and culturally mixed position he has a lot to say about the Iraqi soldiers on the bus to the Iranians pointing to the multiple geographic, linguistic, and religious elements in their composition. For the Iraqis as well, he becomes a link to Iran with his nostalgic stories of the times when the border was open and he would cross back and forth with his family. "My brother had a dream of building a bridge across the Gulf for Iraqis and Iranians to go to each other's area on day trips" he says. In reaction to the events unfolding on the bus, the civilian bus driver (whose son, it seems, is a prisoner of war in Iraq) has this to say to Isa, the juvenile Basiji soldier who is completely sold on the sacredness of the war:

Listen kid, each of these POWs is as close to us as the Kurds of this side, Kurds of that side; Arabs of this side, Arabs of that side; Turks of this side, Turks of the other side, They are not each other's enemies, of course the story is different when it comes to fanatic officials and party leaders.

In sharp contrast to the battle over boundary acted outside the bus, the interior of the bus becomes a space of heteroglossia, where the sharp dichotomies of the two nations at war are brought into question. The bus becomes a metaphoric microcosm of ethno-linguistic diversities and hybrids. The bus and the interaction among its passengers become a contrasting zone revealing cultural overlaps, dialogism, and interconnections among the "enemies."

The shifting, overlapping, and destabilized notions of spatiality with borders as a powerful representation in the two films facilitate a view of the experience of war as lived from the bottom up. The border is a presence to mark the line between the two "nations" at war, but, paradoxically, it also blurs this line by exposing the overlaps and interconnections of subject positions scattered around the borders and the beyond of the seemingly fixed spatialities of Iran and Iraq.

NOTES

1 Vatanabadi Shouleh, "Stories beyond History: Translations beyond Nations," *Critique* 18:2 (2009), 177–83.

2 Walter Benjamin, *Illuminations*, Hannah Arendt (ed.), Harry Zohn (trans.) (New York: Schocken Books, 1978), p. 102.

3 Barney Warf and Santa Arias, eds., *The Spatial Turn: Interdisciplinary Perspectives* (New York: Routledge, 2008).

4 Henk Van Houtum, "The Geopolitics of Borders and Boundaries," *Geopolitics* 10 (2005), 674.

5 See for example: Efraim Karsh, *The Iran Iraq War 1980–1988* (Oxford: Ospray Publishing 2002; Edward Willet, *The Iran-Iraq War* (Rosen Pub Group 2004); Farhang Rajaee, *The Iran-Iraq War: The Politics of Aggression* (Gainesville: University Press of Florida, 1993); Dilip Hiro, *The Longest War: The Iran-Iraq Military Conflict* (New York: Routledge, 1990).

6 Edward Said, *Culture and Imperialism* (New York: Vintage Books, 1993), p. 3.

2

Lost Homelands, Imaginary Returns

The Exilic Literature of Iranian and Iraqi Jews

ELLA SHOHAT

When I first contemplated my participation in the "Moments of Silence" conference, I wondered to what extent the question of the Arab Jew / Middle Eastern Jew merits a discussion in the context of the Iran-Iraq War. After all, the war took place in an era when the majority of Jews had already departed from both countries, and it would seem of little relevance to their displaced lives. Yet, apart from the war's direct impact on the lives of some Jews, a number of texts have engaged the war, addressing it from within the authors' exilic geographies where the war was hardly visible. And, precisely because these texts were written in contexts of official silencing of the Iran-Iraq War, their engagement of the war is quite striking. For displaced authors in the United States, France, and Israel, the Iran-Iraq War became a kind of a return vehicle to lost homelands, allowing them to vicariously be part of the events of a simultaneously intimate and distant geography. Thus, despite their physical absence from Iraq and Iran, authors such as Nissim Rejwan, Sami Michael, Shimon Ballas, and Roya Hakakian actively participate in the multilingual spaces of Iranian and Iraqi exilic literature. Here I will focus on the textual role of war in the representation of multi-faceted identities, themselves shaped by the historical aftermath of wars, encapsulated in memoirs and novels about Iraq and Iran, and written in languages that document new stops and passages in the authors' itineraries of belonging.

What does it mean, in other words, to write about Iran not in Farsi but in French, especially when the narrative unfolds largely in Iran and not in France? What is the significance of writing a Jewish Iranian memoir, set in Tehran, not in Farsi but in English? What are the implications of writing a novel about Iraq, not in Arabic, but in Hebrew, in relation to events that do not involve Iraqi Jews in Israel but rather take place in Iraq, events spanning the decades *after* most Jews had already departed en masse? How should we understand the representation of religious/ethnic minorities within the intersecting geographies of Iraq and Iran when the writing is exercised outside of the Iran-Iraq War geography in languages other than Arabic and Farsi? By conveying a sense of fragmentation and dislocation, the linguistic medium itself becomes both metonym and metaphor for a highly fraught relation to national and regional belonging. This chapter, then, concerns the tension, dissonance, and discord embedded in the deployment of a non-national language (Hebrew) and a non-regional language (English or French) to address events and the interlocutions about them that would normally unfold in Farsi and Arabic, but where French, English, and Hebrew stand in, as it were, for those languages. More broadly, the chapter also concerns the submerged connections between Jew and Muslim in and outside of the Middle East, as well as the cross-border "looking relations" between the spaces of the Middle East. Writing under the dystopic sign of war and violent dislocation, this exilic literature performs an exercise in ethnic, religious, and political relationality, pointing to a textual desire pregnant with historical potentialities.

The Linguistic Inscription of Exile

The linguistic medium itself, in these texts, reflexively highlights violent dislocations from the war zone. For the native speakers of Farsi and Arabic the writing in English, French, or Hebrew is itself a mode of exile, this time linguistic. At the same time if English (in the case of Roya Hakakian and Nissim Rejwan), French (Marjane Satrapi), and Hebrew (Sami Michael and Shimon Ballas) have also become their new symbolic home idioms. In these instances, the reader has to imagine the Farsi in and through the English and the French, or the Arabic in and through the Hebrew. Written in the new homeland, in an "alien" language, these memoirs and novels cannot fully escape the intertextual layers bequeathed by the old homeland language, whether through terms for cuisine, clothing, or state laws specifically associated with Iran and Iraq. The new home language, in such instances, becomes a disembodied vehicle where the lexicon of the old home is no longer fluently translated into the language of the new home—as though the linguistic "cover" is lifted. In this sense, the dislocated memoir or novel always-already involves a tension between the diegetic world of the text and the language of an "other" world that mediates the diegetic world. Such exilic memoirs and novels are embedded in a structural paradox that reflexively evokes the author's displacement in the wake of war. The dissonance, however, becomes accentuated when the "cover language" belongs to an "enemy country," i.e., Israel/Hebrew, or United States/ English. The untranslated Farsi or Arabic appears in the linguistic zone of English or Hebrew to relate not merely an exilic narrative, but a meta-narrative of exilic literature caught in-between warring geographies.

Roya Hakakian's *Journey from the Land of No: A Girlhood Caught in Revolutionary Iran* and Marjane Satrapi's *Persepolis* both tell a coming-of-age story set during the period of the Iranian Revolution, partially against the backdrop of the Iran-Iraq War. Written by an Iranian of Muslim background (Satrapi) and by an Iranian of Jewish background (Hakakian), both memoirs are simultaneously marked by traumatic memories as well as by longing for the departed city—Tehran. Although the Jewish theme forms a minor element in *Persepolis*, Satrapi's graphic memoir does stage a meaningful moment for the Muslim protagonist in relation to her Jewish friend, Neda Baba-Levy. More specifically, it treats a moment during the Iran-Iraq War when Iraqi scud missiles are raining down on Tehran, and where neighborhood houses are reduced to rubble, including the house of the Baba-Levy family. While forming only a very brief reference in the film adaptation, the chapter in the memoir, entitled "The Shabbat," occupies a significant place in the narrative. Marjane goes out to shop and hears a falling bomb. She runs back home and sees that the houses at the end of her street are severely damaged. When her mother emerges from their home, Marjane realizes that while her own house is not damaged, Neda's is. At that moment, Marjane hopes that Neda is not home, but soon she remembers that it is the Shabbat. As her mother pulls Marjane away from the wreckage, she notices Neda's turquoise bracelet. Throughout her graphic novel, Satrapi does display "graphic" images, showing, for example, the torture of her beloved uncle by the Shah's agents and then by the Islamicist revolutionaries who later execute him. Here, however, the Neda incident triggers

Figure 2.1. The *recusatio in Persepolis*. Image courtesy of Marjane Satrapi, *The Complete Persepolis* (Pantheon, 2007), p. 142.

a refusal to show what is being expressed in words. After the destruction, Satrapi writes: "I saw a turquoise bracelet. It was Neda's. Her aunt had given it to her for her fourteenth birthday. The bracelet was still attached to . . . I do not know what." The image illustrates the hand of little Marjane covering her mouth. In the next panel, she covers her eyes, but there is no caption. The following final panel has a black image with the caption: "No scream in the world could have relieved my suffering and my anger."[1]

Of special interest here is precisely the refusal to show, a device referred to in the field of rhetoric as *recusatio*, i.e., the refusal to speak or mention something while still hinting at it in such a way as to call up the image of exactly what is being denied. In *Persepolis* it also constitutes the refusal to show something iconically, in a medium—the graphic memoir—essentially premised, by its very definition, on images as well as words. Marjane recognizes the bracelet, but nothing reminiscent of her friend's hand, while her own hand serves to hide her mouth, muffling a possible scream. In intertextual terms, this image recalls an iconic painting in art history, Edvard Munch's *The Scream*. While the expressionistic painting has the face of a woman taken over by a large screaming mouth, here, *Persepolis* has the mouth covered; it is a moment of silencing the scream. Satrapi represses—not only visually but also verbally—the words that might provide the context for the image, i.e., what Roland Barthes calls the "anchorage" or the linguistic message or caption that disciplines and channels and the polysemy or "many-meaningedness" of the image.[2] In this case, the caption also reflects a *recusatio*, in that no scream could express what she is seeing and feeling. As a result, there is a double silence, the verbal silence and the visual silence implied by the hand on the mouth, and then by the hands on the eyes culminating in the black frame image. The final black panel conveys Marjane's subjective point of view of not seeing, blinded as it were by the horrifying spectacle of war.

Moving from a panel deprived of words to a panel deprived of image, the device goes against the grain of the very medium that forms the vehicle of this graphic memoir. Here, *Persepolis* evinces a refusal to be graphic in both a verbal and visual sense. We find complementary refusals: one panel gives us the image of a hand over face, of a speechless protagonist where the caption relays her thoughts at the traumatic site of her friend's bracelet; another gives us covered eyes but withholds the text; and yet another offers no image at all, but gives us a text that relays the impossibility, even the futility, of a scream to alleviate her suffering and anger. The panel that speaks of Neda's hand shows Marjane's hand, thus suggesting a textual / visual continuity between the protagonist, whom the reader sees, and the killed friend, whom the reader cannot see. Neda's death is subjectivized through Marjane's shock at the horrific sight, allowing the reader to mourn the loss of Neda as mediated through Marjane's pain.

Although the story of the Baba Levy family is marginal to *Persepolis*, the intense mourning of the Muslim, Marjane, for the Jewish Neda does not merely represent a traumatic moment for a protagonist; rather, it is crucial in the *Bildungsroman*. The loss of her friend forms a moment of rupture in the text, which underscores a transformed universe and catalyzes Marjane's departure and exile. But it is also linked to another traumatic moment in the following chapter, "The Dowry." In this case, Marjane does not witness but is told by her mother about the loss of another adolescent girl from their family circle, Niloufar, who is taken to prison. As a cautionary tale about the dangers inherent in Marjane's rebellious actions in school, Satrapi's mother reminds Marjane that the same Islamic regime that tortured her uncle—just as the Shah regime did—is also the culprit for Niloufar's fate. The horror of the unfolding story is accentuated by the gesture of whispering: "You know what happened to Niloufar? . . . You know it's against the law to kill a virgin . . . so a guardian of the revolution marries her . . . and takes her virginity before executing her. Do you understand what that means???"[3] Through the three dots of the blank space, of the unsaid, as well as through the three question marks for highlighting a rhetorical question, Satrapi implies the de facto rape prior to execution. The fear and love for Marjane lead her family to send her away to Vienna, the only place that would offer her an entry. Marjane's exile from Tehran and home begins at this critical moment. Between Iraqi scuds over Tehran that make all Iranians vulnerable, and the regime's war on its citizens, exile becomes the only sensible itinerary for a rebellious adolescent.

"The Shabbat" chapter, which consists of a short sequence of panels revolving around the traumatizing death of Marjane's friend Neda, precedes "The Dowry" chapter, which relates the death of her communist acquaintance, Niloufar. Both young women are killed—the Jewish friend by Iraqi missiles, and the Muslim communist at the hands of the Iranian regime. *Persepolis* makes several references to sexual violence. Already in the section entitled "The Trip," Satrapi relates this gendered dimension of the memoir at the inception of the revolution and its implementation of the veil. Her mother arrives home distraught after having been stopped while driving without the veil and threatened with sexual violence if she does not obey. Here, Satrapi calls attention to various forms of state violence all represented on a continuum. The threat of rape by the state's agent is also linked to the very same regime that sends young adolescent boys to war, and that tortures its opponents. Both chapters, "The Shabbat" and "The Dowry" assign responsibility for the death of two revolutionary republics—the Iraqi and the Iranian.

They precede the Satrapi family's crucial decision that their daughter must leave Iran at once. Together these two chapters prepare the reader for the inevitable departure, forming a vital crossroad at the beginning of the protagonist's exilic Odyssey.

The Iran-Iraq War provokes a remarkable *Prise de conscience* in the memoirs. Roya Hakakian's *Journey from the Land of No*, for example, performs the bifurcated history of Iran visually through two maps that frame her book: one at the very beginning of the memoir, visualizing Tehran of 1978, and the other at the end of the memoir, of 1984 Tehran. Hakakian compares the names of places on both maps, lamenting the disappearance of her intimately familiar urban environment. She writes:

> Yearning for the memories of the old, familiar places, I kept buying maps of the city. One in particular, Map # 255, touted itself "The Most Complete Atlas of the New Tehran: Planned, Produced, and Lithographed by the Geographical and Cartographic Society." On its upper right corner, a zip code, telephone, fax number, appeared—anything to impress an unknowing customer. Though I knew nothing about cartography, I went about examining this map. I knew Tehran; why be intimidated? Under a magnifying glass, I looked and looked for Saba Street or Alley of the Distinguished, but on the map of the New Tehran, there was no sign of my old neighborhood. The schools where I had studied, the places I had known, everything was either renamed or dropped. Instead of a magnifying glass, I thought, I ought to hold a pen. Instead of maps, I ought to buy notebooks. For those cartographers, geographers, and their fancy societies could not be trusted. And I had to record, commit every detail to memory, in words, what the cartographers had not done in their maps, a testament to the existence of a time and alley and its children whose traces were on the verge of vanishing.[4]

Hakakian is underlining the renaming of familiar streets after a *shahid* (martyr), many of whom were children from her own age group, sent to the war with plastic keys to heaven. Their carved names highlight the futile death while also evoking a forever-transformed urban topography. The question of trauma cathected with a place, then, even in the context of war, is seen through the visual cartography of an intimately familiar and yet thoroughly alien Tehran. Although hardly incorporating

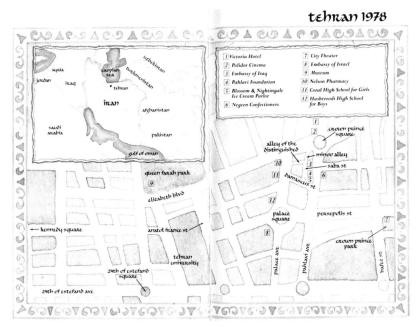

Figure 2.2. Teheran's Old Map, *Journey from the Land of No*

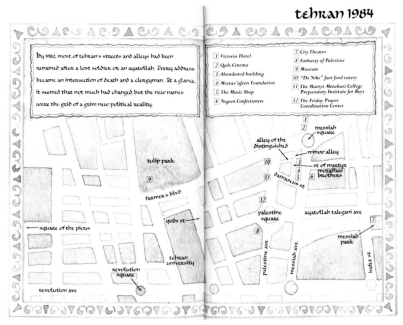

Figure 2.3. Teheran's New Map, *Journey from the Land of No*

visual materials, Hakakian's memoir does include visual evidence for the erased world. "Number 3: Abandoned Building" on the map is actually the Iraqi embassy, and "Number 8: Embassy of Palestine" indicates the former site of the Israeli Embassy, evidencing two places where deletion and renaming are enacted. Within this context, *Journey from the Land of No* zooms in, as it were, on the question of Iranian Jews. Hakakian offers a kind of comparison between the position of Jews under the Shah and under Ayatollah regimes. Rather than explicitly criticize these particular re-namings, the text highlights the way lives and dreams have been kidnapped by the war. Ironically, however, all these transformations and comparisons mandate another turn of the translational screw, the act of renaming and translation into English.

In the *Journey from the Land of No* as well as in *Persepolis*, one finds a certain nostalgia for the revolutionary moment when social utopia could still be imagined and dreamt about, before the leftist vision was taken away by the Islamic state. Both memoirs reflect the dead end for Iranian leftists persecuted first by the Shah and then by the Ayatollah. In contrast to contemporary Middle Eastern Jewish memoirs that portray a negative image of Islam, Hakakian depicts Tehran as the site of cross-ethnic and cross-religious solidarity for those struggling for democracy and freedom. Like the Iraq in the novels by Shimon Ballas and Sami Michael that I will discuss subsequently, the Iran of Hakakian's memoir is a space where people of diverse ethnic and religious backgrounds share a utopian desire for an equal multi-faith society. Ballas and Michael's Hebrew novels about Iraq also similarly manifest a "revolutionary nostalgia" for the era when communism was a thriving ideology, before the party was crushed by successive regimes, culminating with the persecution by the Ba'ath Party and Saddam Hussein. Although in Ballas's novel *Outcast*, Qassem, the communist, is not the protagonist, he nonetheless carries the "norms of the text" through which the various ideological points of view are being evaluated. *Outcast* thus celebrates the ways in which revolutionaries from different religious backgrounds marched together and fought for democracy, even though the leftists (especially but not exclusively) were tortured by all regimes. Qassem, for example, tried to escape to the Soviet Union because he was about to be executed; but he was then caught by the Shah's regime, tortured, and handed over to Saddam Hussein and the Ba'ath Party. Iranian memoirs such as *Persepolis* and *Journey from the Land of No* stage the same dead-end situation. In *Persepolis*, Satrapi's uncle Anoush is the victim of the same historical double whammy of being tortured first by the Shah and then by the Islamicist regime. These texts portray a world of no exit for those utopianists who fought for equality and democracy, when both Iraq and Iran were crushing movements for social transformations. Iraqi and Iranian exilic literature demonstrates that exile actually begins *before* the physical dislocation. Prior to their displacement from Iran or Iraq, the leftist characters are depicted as already suffering a kind of internal exile in their own respective countries.

The exilic language simultaneously inscribes the exilic condition while also intimating its possible transcendence. Hakakian, it is worth noting, aspired to write in Farsi rather than in English, and she continues to write poetry in Farsi in the United States. That the memoir is written in English is itself a testament to the fact that the act of narrating Iran, which first takes place in the context of kidnapped leftist dreams in Iran, now takes place in the context of dislocation to the United States, with the narration of Iran now displaced into the English language. Marjane Satrapi, meanwhile, although she grew up in Tehran and spoke Farsi as a first language even while receiving a French education, writes her memoir in French, the language of her new cultural geography. In other words, Satrapi writes about her experience not in the dominant language of her home country—Farsi—but in a European language—French—which in a sense stands in for Farsi, much as English stands in for Farsi in Roya Hakakian's memoir, or for Arabic in Nissim Rejwan's memoir, while Hebrew stands in for Arabic in Shimon Ballas's and Sami Michael's novels. In these narratives, where the actual exile is narrated in English, French, or Hebrew, the writing itself forms an exilic mode of denial of the possibility of writing in the language of the geographies in which the authors were raised. The linguistic mediation of belonging to a place and the question of homeland entail a move from one linguistic geography to another, yet within this new linguistic zone, the author articulates the dissonance of identities and their palimpsestic emotional geographies. This embedded bifurcation is not, however, simply a loyalty test, as is implied by the axioms of persistent nation-state patriotism. Through the literary act of representing Farsi or Arabic through the medium of another language, these memoirs and novels open up spaces of imaginary belonging that complicate any simplistic equation between a single language and a single identity. At times the memoir's language is doubly removed, as in the case Rejwan's *The Last Jews in Baghdad*, since it is written in Israel about Iraq, but in the English language.

While war generates massive dislocations, ironically, it sometimes indirectly facilitates the reuniting of old friends. One consequence of the Iran-Iraq War, for example, was an opening that enabled members of various exilic groups to reconnect. Even when they ended up in "enemy" countries, feelings of affection, friendship, and love nonetheless persisted on both sides of the war zone. Initially, for example in the case of Iraqi Jews in Israel and their friends in Iraq, even the most rudimentary forms of communication were virtually impossible. Paradoxically, it was a number of negative developments—the repressive measures of the Ba'athist regime, a series of wars, and especially the Iran-Iraq War—that made it possible for the burgeoning Iraqi diaspora in the West to renew relationships with their Jewish Iraqi friends, including even with those in Israel. Nissim Rejwan's memoir, *The Last Jews in Baghdad: Remembering a Lost Homeland*, recounts the close friendships among diverse Iraqis that were disrupted when most Jews had to leave Baghdad in the wake of the partition of Palestine and the establishment of the state of Israel. While the memoir focuses largely on Rejwan's coming of age in Baghdad, it concludes with the attempts, several decades later, to reconnect with his friends, those whom he has neither seen nor heard from for three or four decades. Toward the end of the memoir, in the chapter titled, "Disposing of a Library," Rejwan recounts how he discovered the whereabouts of one of his closest Baghdadi friends, Najib El-Mani', who formed part of Rejwan's intellectual literary circle that frequented Al-Rabita Bookshop. When finally Rejwan hears about Najib's whereabouts, Najib has died of heart failure in London:

> After nearly ten more years during which I heard nothing either from
> or about Najib, a friend sent me photocopies of parts of *Al-Ightirab al-*
> *Adabi*, a literary quarterly published in London and devoted to the work
> of writers and poets living in exile, mainly Iraqis who found they couldn't
> do their work in the suffocating atmosphere of Ba'ath-dominated Iraq.
> To my shock and grief, the first several articles were tributes by friends

and fellow émigré writers and intellectuals to the work and the personality of Najib al-Mani', who had died suddenly of heart failure one night in
his flat in London, alone amongst his thousands of books and records of
classical music. . . . Feeling the urge to know more about my unfortunate
friend and seeing that Najib's sister Samira was *Al-Ightirab's* assistant editor, I wrote her a long letter of condolences and asked her to give me
additional information about her brother's years in exile. Did he die a
happy man? Was he married? Lived with someone? Any children? And
so on. All I learned from the tributes was that his room was scattered
with books and records and papers. Damn the books, I murmured to
myself, being then in the midst of a colossal operation aimed at getting
rid of some two-thirds of my private library.[5]

In a pre-digital era, when communication only took place through
"snail-mail" letters and phone calls, communicating across enemy borders was virtually impossible. Memoirs written about dislocations in the
wake of war therefore tend to delve into the details of the "how" one
learns about the whereabouts of old friends. Rejwan learns that Najib
remained in Iraq throughout the 1950s and '60s while occupying fairly
high official positions, and only came to London in 1979. Najib left Iraq
hoping "for some fresh air" away from the Ba'athist regime, but with
the outbreak of the Iran-Iraq War, his wife, three sons, and daughter
could not join him. Two of his sons were sent to the front, which also
prevented Najib's wife from joining him. In his London exile Najib was
unable to attend the wedding of his daughter, whose husband left for
Holland shortly after their marriage in order to avoid being drafted to
serve in the Iran-Iraq War. Najib's son-in-law, it was discovered later,
had married another woman in Holland. The Iran-Iraq War thus sometimes devastated the lives even of those who survived the bombs and
destruction. Whereas the 1948 establishment of Israel caused Rejwan's
dislocation from Iraq, it was the Ba'athist repression and the Iran-Iraq
War that dislocated Najib al-Mani' from Iraq. By the time Rejwan hears
about his old friend, it is too late. But he does manage to hear from
Najib's sister, who writes Rejwan about Najib's last years in London: "He
lived alone with his lame cat in a flat in London . . . He died in the company of someone he loved, his open book was on Najib's chest. Is there
anyone better than Proust in situations like these!"[6] The Iran-Iraq War

turned Najib into a lonely man, shorn of his wife and children, as he was unable to see them. Yet the same Iran-Iraq War that forced him to remain in exile also allowed Iraqis in the UK to communicate directly with old friends in Israel, facilitating Rejwan's learning of Najib's unfolding story in exile. The communication between Rejwan and Najib's sister, Samira, subsequently generates several other enthusiastic reconnections and sometimes actual meetings, between Iraqi Jews from Israel and their exiled Iraqi friends who had moved to Limassol, Cyprus, London, Montreal, or California.

Over Iraq's tumultuous decades, the diverse waves of departures—whether ethnic, religious, or political in nature—ironically allowed for a re-encounter of the diverse groups of exilic Iraqis. Rejwan's grief over the death of an old friend is also exacerbated by the exilic melancholia in the wake of the loss of a bygone time and place. The death of his dear friend comes to allegorize Rejwan's own anxieties about loss and death, triggered by previous multiple losses: the earlier symbolic loss of that friend, even prior to his death, due to Rejwan's earlier exile from Baghdad; the mediated loss of Iraq through Najib's exile in the wake of the Iran-Iraq War; the multiple waves of dislocations that led to the dissolution of a religiously and ethnically mixed intellectual circle of friends; and the erasure of the Jewish chapter of Iraqi history as aptly encapsulated by the title of the book, *The Last Jews in Baghdad: Remembering a Lost Homeland* (emphasis mine). The memoir is written under the sign of loss and dispersal, i.e., the scattering of the Jewish community of Mesopotamia, and ironically the diasporization of "the Babylonian Diaspora." The Iraqi homeland, no longer available to Iraqi Jews, is also lost for the majority of Iraqi people. Rejwan's memoir offers an elegy for multiple worlds lost, largely in the wake of the Israel-Arab War but also in the wake of the relatively distant Iran-Iraq War.

The eulogy for the life of Middle Eastern Jews in the context of Islam, explicitly narrated in appendix A of that work, titled, "The Jews of Iraq: A Brief Historical Sketch," is not merely a coda for Rejwan's book but also a final "chapter" for Babylonian Iraqi Jewish history. In this sense, the losses turn individual death into an allegory of communal disappearance, which necessitates the writing of its history, a kind of firm grounding of the past in the text. Yet books themselves are haunted by the possibility of their own disappearance, by the liquidation of an archive. The death of his friend Najib among books is paralleled by Rejwan's own forced disposal of most of his library, a kind of a metaphorical death for an aging writer forced to part with his beloved lifelong book companions. Books may recover communal past but not offer a remedy for loss. The eulogy/elegy is expressed in Rejwan's words:

> So it was Proust that he was reading in his last night—Proust to whose work we had all been introduced as early as the late 1940s and whose *Remembrance of Things Past* in its English rendering was made available for the first time in Iraq by Al-Rabita Bookshop. Truth to tell, I found myself regretting the scant part I myself had played in Najib's incessant preoccupation with works of literature—apparently to the exclusion of much else by way of real life.[7]

The memoir reflexively evokes Proust's novel to address "things past" where their "remembrance" (as well their forgetting) takes place not merely within individual-subjective memory but also within communal recollection. To the extent to which Rejwan's memoir touches on his experiences in Israel, it relates those experiences to those of the Iraqi diaspora displaced elsewhere. In the excerpts of his memoirs published in a London quarterly describing the life of Iraqis in exile in this fashion, Rejwan articulates his displacement experience largely in relation to other displaced Iraqis in the wake of wars not directly linked to Iraqi-Israeli life, i.e., the Iran-Iraq War. Like the evocation of the Iran-Iraq War in Shimon Ballas's and Sami Michael's novels, Rejwan's memoir also goes against the grain of the Zionist metanarrative of *aliya* to Israel as *telos*, a narrative that ideologically detaches Iraqi Israelis from their Iraqi emotional geography. Rather than endorse the celebratory trope of the "ingathering of the exiles," Rejwan firmly places his dislocation within the larger context of the multiple Iraqi dislocations of a broader assembly of oppressed minorities and political groups, whether religious minorities such as Jews, Christians, and Shi'a Muslims, or political opponents such as communists, liberals, and other anti-regime dissidents. His eulogy is dedicated to a lost world that is not simply and reductively Jewish but rather richly multi-faithed, thus subverting not merely the biblical tale but also the Zionist metanarrative of exile and return to the Promised Land. In this sense, the reference to the Iran-Iraq

War is not merely to a coincidental factor in the life of his old friend, Najib, but rather to a major event that also affects the friend's friend, i.e., Rejwan himself. The Jewish Iranian and Jewish Iraqi novels and memoirs, in sum, highlight Jewish affinities with Iran and Iraq, even in a context where Israel's unofficial stance toward the Iran-Iraq War (like that of the United States) was ultimately a preference for the war to persist.

Writing an Absence

Shimon Ballas's Hebrew novel *Outcast* (*Ve-Hu Akher*, in Hebrew "*And He is an Other*," 1991), written by an Iraqi Jew in Israel, offers a vital sampling of the kinds of tensions and paradoxes arising from war, dislocation, and multiple belongings. *Outcast* is based on the historical case of an Iraqi Jewish intellectual—Dr. Nissim / Naseem / Ahmed Sousa—who converted to Islam and who remained in Iraq even after the departure of most Iraqi Jews in 1950–51. The novel, set during the Iran-Iraq War, is reflexively written as a posthumously published memoir of the protagonist, Haroun / Ahmad Sousan. While narrated in the first person, the novel "stages" a polyphony of Iraqi voices. The Iran-Iraq War serves as a pretext to discuss the history of Iraq through multiple perspectives, including those of its minorities. The novel is premised on a refusal, in this case the refusal to conform to the Zionist idea or expectation that Iraqi Jews after leaving Iraq would sever themselves politically, intellectually, and emotionally from Iraq as a magnet for identification. The Iraqi Jewish protagonist, an intellectual writing in Arabic—even though the novel itself is written in Hebrew—has studied the history of Iraq and Islam and converted to Islam, viewing his adopted religion as representing universalism in contrast to his birth religion's penchant for separatism and particularism. The text thus orchestrates an ongoing debate about the place of Jews within Islam and, specifically, within Iraq. Ballas's novel, in this sense, clearly goes against the grain of the Zionist master narrative that assumes that arrival in Israel naturally brings with it an end of affective ties to one's former homeland, especially in the case of an "enemy" homeland.

In the novel, the protagonist's books, *My Path to Islam* and *The Jews in History*, are used by the president—alluding to Saddam Hussein—in order to attack both Israel and Jews, as well as to attack Iran.[8] One is reminded of the pamphlet, not referenced in the text but reportedly distributed by Saddam Hussein's government, titled, "Three Whom God Should Not Have Created: Persians, Jews, and Flies."[9] Within this view, Jews were traitors, allied from antiquity with the Persians. Seeing himself as the modern heir of King Nebuchadnezzar II, Saddam had bricks inscribed with his name inserted into the ancient remnants of Babylon's walls.[10] If Nebuchadnezzar destroyed the first temple and exiled the Jews to Babylon, the King of Persia, Cyrus the Great, conquered Babylon, and assumed the title of "King of Babylon," ending the Babylonian captivity and allowing Jews to return to Jerusalem and rebuild the temple. The Iran-Iraq War, in this sense, became discursively grafted onto the memory of ancient Babylonian /Persian wars, now projected onto the contemporary Arab / Iranian conflict into which modern Jews are interpellated as well. In *Outcast*, the protagonist Haroun / Ahmad Sousan gets caught up in a political maelstrom where his own words are used in a way that he neither predicted nor approved. He sought a version of Islam that was neither fanatic nor extremist, thus in a sense defending the Shi'a of Iraq against massacres and oppression by the Sunni elite. At the same time, however, the protagonist did not foresee that what was emerging from Iran was also not the philosophical version of Islam that he was seeking. The two opposing sides in the Iran-Iraq conflict represent two versions of state-controlled intolerance, whether in the hegemonic Sunni modernist secular version of the Iraqi Ba'ath party, or in the hegemonic Shi'a religious version of the Iranian state. Neither represents the pluralistic, universalistic Islam of the protagonist's cosmopolitan vision. In this sense, the novel rejects the sectarian tendencies of two nation-state regimes, within both of which critical intellectuals are "in excess" of their totalitarianism.

Outcast also sheds a skeptical light on the Zionist nation-state version of Jewish religion, not merely in the novel's content, where Jewish nationalism is debated, but also through the very act of writing about Iraq while in Israel, thus challenging the metanarrative of an Arab "enemy country" by imagining Iraq as a geography of identification for the Hebrew reader. During the Iran-Iraq War, the protagonist Haroun Sousan begins to reflect on the 1941 attacks on the Jews (the *farhoud*) in conjunction with the present attacks on the Shi'as. Linking past and present, the memories allow for a multiple cross-religious identification through the hybrid Jew/Sunni protagonist. In other moments in *Outcast*, the place of the Shiʿa in the Iran-Iraq War comes to allegorize the place of the Iraqi Jew during the Israeli Arab conflict.[11] Both religious communities are implicitly "on trial" for loyalty and patriotism, even though the war is against an outside force. The conflation of Iraqi Jews with the Zionist enterprise and the Jewish state, and later the conflation of Iraqi Shiʿa with the Shiʿa-dominated Iranian state, place first the Jews and then the Shiʿites under suspicion, leading to a life of fear and anxiety of being perceived as traitors by the Iraqi state. In *Outcast*, the protagonist Haroun is not depicted as a heroic figure, a portrayal largely incarnated by the relatively marginal character and friend of the protagonist, the communist Qassem. In one heated moment in the text, taking place in the 1940s but recalled by Haroun during the Iran-Iraq War, Qassem criticizes the protagonist's critical remarks about his fellow Jews. Evoking his books about Jews in Islam, Haroun Sousan defends his thesis: "I wrote of what I know from the inside."[12] Sousan alludes to his experiential knowledge as an Iraqi Jew (prior to his conversion) but Qassem refuses Haroun's "insider discourse," stating: "I know Jews from the inside, too. I lived with them. They are great patriots."[13] Haroun replies: "Precisely what I had wished for, that they be patriots." Qassem however insists: "Don't try to wiggle out of it . . . You couldn't find a good word to write about them. And it's time you replied to the fascist provocateurs. Tell them that Jews have withstood the toughest of trials and proven their loyalty to their homeland."[14] "[T]he real test," Haroun responds, "is Palestine." To which Qassem responds: "Palestine? . . . You want them to go to Palestine to fight? Who sold Palestine to the Zionists? They're fighting for Iraq. We're all fighting for Iraq!"[15]

Significantly, in this dialogue it is not the "real" and originary Jew who defends Iraqi Jews, but rather the Muslim leftist. Qassem asks Haroun to admit that his writing presented a biased picture of the Jewish community.[16] The words of the leftist Qassem, as suggested earlier, function as the "norms of the text," the novel's ideological voice of reason. In a temporal palimpsest, the protagonist's recollections during the Iran-Iraq War become a mode of exposing discrimination against all minorities and censuring the way dictatorial regimes oppress, repress, and suffocate the spirit of freedom. The time of the Jewish departure from Iraq comes to be viewed retroactively through the prism of massive Shi'a deportations during the Iran-Iraq War. The novel constructs the issue of homeland and belonging *through* an implicit analogy. The recollection of the debate about the patriotism of Iraqi Jews takes place exactly at the moment the Iran-Iraq War is unfolding. Thus the question of the loyalty of the Jews in the 1940s evokes the 1980s accusation of Shi'a's lack of patriotism especially during the Iran-Iraq War. While the Iraqi Shi'as were the primary targets during the Iran-Iraq War, they continued to be deported, imprisoned, and killed even after the war ended. Their fate came in the wake of the similar experiences of other ethnic and religious minorities, all accused by the state of treason. Shi'as, as a community, have been massively dislocated within an Iraqi history that displaced Assyrians, Jews, and Kurds as well, along with diverse political opponents, including communists—all suffering dislocation, imprisonment, and massacre.

Outcast reveals the uneasy closeness of the protagonist to the regime, implicitly undermining the ethno-nationalism of the Ba'ath regime. The novel deploys the fictional last name of the protagonist "Sousan," a name that maintains an intimate proximity with the actual family name of the historical figure "Sousa," a proximity that, I would argue, casts an ironic light on anti-Persian Arab nationalism. Both names originate from the Persian "Susa" (Sousa) or "Shoush" (Shush), an ancient city of the Elamite, Persian, and Parthian empires of Iran, in the Zagros Mountains and east of the Tigris River. "Shushan," Shushan (or Shoushan) is mainly mentioned in the biblical book of Esther but also in the books of Nehemiah and Daniel, both of whom lived in Sousa / Shousha during the Babylonian captivity of sixteenth century BCE, where a presumed tomb of Daniel is located in Shoush area.[17] Ballas adds to the family name of the historical figure "Sousa" the letter "n," turning it into "Sousan," accentuating the link to the Hebrew biblical pronunciation of the city "Shushan."[18] The name of the protagonist is thus a mixture of the Persian element in the name of the historical figure, the Iraqi Sousa with the Hebrew reference Shoushan, thus emphasizing in Hebrew the allusion to ancient Persia and Babylonia. The mixture of letters in the protagonist's name blurs the boundary not only between ancient Babylonia and Persia but also between contemporary Iraq and Iran. This palimpsestic blurriness goes against the grain of the purism typical of Iran-Iraq

War official propagandas. Indeed, the memoir-within-the-novel of *Outcast* alludes to the complexity of religious and ethnic identities within Iraq. The protagonist writes: "Our family is one of the oldest in town, and according to one theory its origins lay in Persia, its lineage going back to the celebrated city of Shushan, the very Shushan that figures so prominently in the *Book of Esther*."[19]

The town that the protagonist refers to is Al Hillah, which is adjacent to the ancient city of Babylon and its ruins. It is also near Al Kifl, the site of the tomb of Ezekiel, where Iraqi Jews would go on their annual pilgrimage (*'id al-ziyara*), and later had been protected as a holy site by Saddam Hussein. Al Hillah was largely a Shi'a city and the site of Saddam's acts of executions and massive graves. *Outcast*, in this sense, highlights the multilayered history of Iraq, that includes Bablyonians, Persians, Jews, as well as Shi'a and Sunni, in such a way as to undo any narrow definition of Mesopotamia/Iraq and indirectly of Persia/Iran. Ironically, that ancient history, encoded, as it were, in the name of the Jewish/Muslim protagonist, challenges the Iran/Iraq nation-state borders that have led to the senseless Iran-Iraq War. The modern Iranian town of Shush is actually located at the site of the ancient city Shushan/Shoushan, in Khuzestan Province, which Saddam Hussein attempted to control during the Iran-Iraq War, claiming that it belonged to Iraq because of its large number of Arabic speakers. Located on the border with Iraq, Khuzestan suffered the heaviest damage of all Iranian provinces during the war, forcing thousands of Iranians to flee. Ballas's *Outcast*, which begins with the Iran-Iraq War, thus also undermines the modern ideology of Sunni/ Shi'a nation-state conflict by alluding to a region that could be seen as simultaneously Persian and Arab, and which includes indigenous Jews and Christians. Millennia of mixing and intermingling from antiquity to the modern era offer evidence of cultural syncretism across the region and beyond. Indeed, this deeper *longue durée* of Shimon Ballas's text also reverberates with the historical overtones of Marjane Satrapi's very title "Persepolis"—Greek for "city of Persians" known in antiquity as Parsa, invaded and destroyed by Alexander the Great, and thus functions as the memoir's subliminal reminder of the ancient Greek-Persian wars. In 1971, Shah Mohammad Reza Shah Pahlavi organized festivities for the 2,500-year celebration of the Persian Empire that began with Cyrus the Great. Rather than offering a modern monumental version of antiquity in the style of modern nationalist discourses, Ballas and Satrapi subtly invoke antiquity in order to undermine purist narratives of contemporary identity, including between "East" and "West." In this sense, the Persians are not only partly Arabs, and vice versa, but they are also partly Greeks.

Published at the time of the 1991 Gulf War between the Allies and Iraq, Ballas's novel must be read against the backdrop of the Iran-Iraq War, during the period within which it was written and also represents. Within its historical span, moving from the 1930s to the 1990s, the novel also deals with the antecedents to the Iran-Iraq War and the ongoing political debates in Iraq about Iraqi Shi'a supporting Khomeini during the period of the Shah. For example, one of the characters, Mostafa, is concerned with the Iranian problem and "the subversive activities of Iranian exiles that were constantly in the headlines."[20] Another character, Khalid, meanwhile argues that: "[t]he matter was not as simple as it appeared, because Iraq had not provided a refuge to Khomeini and company out of pure hospitality, but also because we supported his struggle against the Shah."[21] Mostafa, in response, argues: "Struggling against the Shah wasn't the same as working to establish a Shi'ite Party in Iraq." And another character, Jawad, concurs and says: "Khomeini was meddling into Iraq's internal affairs and inciting a war between religious factions."[22] Although *Outcast* begins with a speech by the protagonist who is honored by the president during the Iran-Iraq War, it relays the history of animosity that paved the way for the Iran-Iraq War, as reported in the memoir-within-the-novel:

> Events in Iran and reactions in our country have disrupted my writing routine. A fortnight hasn't gone by since the outbreak of the revolution and already demonstrations against the Iraqi embassy have resumed, as well as allegations that Iraq persecuted Khomeini and was hostile to the revolution. Radio Tehran has launched a series of venomous tirades against Iraq as a collaborator with Israel and the United States, as wanting to reinstate the Shah and drown the Islamic revolution in torrents of blood. One cannot believe one's ears. Such hatred after fourteen years of living among us? Jawad al-Alawi is not surprised. Khomeini's expulsion is not the cause of this hate, but the deeply rooted hatred of the Shi'a. Indeed, that's how it is, this hostility never died down, but even so

one cannot ignore the progressive nature of a revolution that managed to overthrow a rotten monarchy and proclaim a republic. "That is the positive aspect," agrees Jawad.[23]

In the novel, the Sunnis largely view the Shi'ite as a "fifth column"[24] although some Shi'a characters are described as loyal and principled and free of Shi'ite tribalism.[25] However, Ballas is careful to represent multiple Iraqi perspectives on the Iran-Iraq War. The novel stages an ideological, political, and historical debate among diverse Iraqi characters, each one of them representing a different take on post-revolutionary Iran and its impact on the definition of Iraqi identity. Interestingly, one of the sharpest criticisms of the government is voiced by the protagonist, Haroun Sousan, who is on one level a regime loyalist but who on another level is a critic who wonders if a pro-government supporter had "forgotten the blood bath, two years ago, when the army attacked a procession of pilgrims coming out of Najaf with live ammunition? Has he forgotten the hundreds of detainees and those executed without trial, or tried in absentia because they're already six feet under? If one cannot condemn the government, why must one praise it? And all the recent arrests, should these, too, be justified?"[26] Ballas here has his Jewish convert to Islam express sympathy with the Shi'ites under the Ba'ath regime. In another moment, the protagonist writes: "I had some sympathy for the Shi'ites to begin with, as the disenfranchised, not to mention that I grew up among them and naturally felt part of the Ja'afri school of thought, adhered to by my townsmen. The same Shi'ite group that was one day to become the party established a non-ethnic image by taking Sunnis and even Christians into its ranks."[27]

At another point, Ballas moves immediately from the description of the 1941 *farhoud* attack on Iraqi Jews to the persecution of the Shi'ites during the Ba'athist era, thus generating a critical sequencing of the historically disparate moments of the vulnerability of Jews and Shi'a in Iraq.[28] At the same time, Haroun Sousan does not represent the novel's ideological center or the "norms of the text," since Ballas is careful to show that the Iran-Iraq War was used by both regimes as a pretext to repress the left, whether in Iran or in Iraq.[29] Within the framework of the novel, the persecution of the Communists seems to traverse the Iran/

Iraq battle lines. The novel actually shows that leftists in both countries were vulnerable during the monarchy as well as during the Ba'athist Republic regime, just as they were vulnerable during the Shah and during the Ayatollah Republic regime.[30] This history of the persecution of the communists under the diverse regimes of Iraq and Iran is largely relayed through the character of Qassem, who escapes the Ba'athist Iraq and, while on his way to the Soviet Union is caught by the Iranian SAVAK, which brutally tortures him, pulling out his fingernails, breaking his ribs and limbs, "before hanging him upside down and scalding his afflicted body with red hot stakes."[31] Then they send him back to Iraq "in accordance with a pact initiating neighborly friendship between the two countries."[32] Ballas continues: "He limped along on one leg following the unsuccessful treatment he had gotten for his other broken limb . . . from the SAVAK [who] tortured him because he was a communist who expressed animosity towards the Shah and the *mukhabarat* because he was a communist who opposed Ba'athist ideology."[33]

The neighborly relations between the Ba'athist and the Shah regimes, between the *mukhabarat* and the SAVAK, were later deployed for propaganda purposes by Khomeini, which itself continued the persecution of leftists as emphasized both in *Persepolis* and in *Journey from the Land of No*. The fate of communists in both countries is also narrated through a positive grid in *Outcast* through its emphasis on the network of camaraderie linking Iranian and Iraqi communists.[34] The idea of ethnic and religious solidarity between Jews and Muslims of Sunni and Shi'a backgrounds goes against the Ba'athist discourse of unending hate and resentment toward Jews and Persians. Saddam himself, as we have seen, deployed an animalizing trope to yoke the two groups as despicable "flies." While the novels suggest that the protagonist Sousan remains a kind of loyalist to the Ba'athist regime, stating that Iraq needs to be defended,[35] the novel itself takes a distant view toward this Ba'athist rhetoric, instead highlighting the multiple historical violences and dislocations that came long before the Iran-Iraq War.[36] Exilic leftist Iraqi literature, in other words, tends to highlight the multiplicity that constitutes Iraqi history and culture, staging a polyphony of Iraqi voices, just as exilic leftist Iranian literature tends to register the close network of relationships among Muslims, Jews, and diverse other Iranians.

Forging Imagined Memories

Like Ballas's *Outcast,* Sami Michael's novel *Aida* is also concerned with the powerlessness of the majority of Iraqi people. At the same time, it is also concerned with cross-ethnic and cross-religious solidarities that partially counteract that powerlessness. In *Aida,* the Jewish protagonist, Zaki Dali, a host of a popular TV documentary show, harbors a Kurdish woman who has been kidnapped, tortured, and raped by agents of the Saddam Hussein regime. As they embark on a romantic relationship, the novel generates a symbolic alliance between an ethnic minority, the Kurds, and a religious minority, the Jews, while also conjuring up a utopian space of interreligious and interethnic romance. Such a romance is especially meaningful in a novel by a former Jewish Iraqi communist, Sami Michael, for whom communism represents more than a political party fighting for sociopolitical and economic equality; it signifies a universalist humanist refuge that transcends ethnic, religious, and nationalist particularities.[37] The interreligious romance also goes against the grain of the social conventions of the Middle East that decree that marriage takes place within the religious identities into which one is born. While religious communities normally intersected in their commercial, social, and neighborly interminglings, they also carefully monitored interreligious romantic entanglements. Through the mixed romance, *Aida* offers a "revolutionary nostalgia" toward Iraq's social-political potentialities. Although written in Hebrew, the language of an enemy country, the novel can be seen as mourning Iraq's melancholy descent into chaos and civil war. Witnessing dictatorship and even genocide, the Jewish protagonist, Zaki, transports the Hebrew reader into the largely unfamiliar terrain of Iraq of the 1980s and 1990s. "The last Jew," as the novel often describes the protagonist, mediates between Iraq as remembered by the dislocated Jews and Iraq as experienced over the past three decades. Events in the present evoke incidents in the past, generating a sense of historical repetition, while also re-familiarizing Iraq for its displaced absentees.

Set in the Iraq of the post–Iran-Iraq War, during the 1991 Gulf War that ended with the suppression of the Kurdish and Shi'a uprisings, and during the sanctions period of the following decade, Sami Michael's novel *Aida* represents Iraq as a multiethnic and multireligious space.

Apart from the Jewish protagonist Zaki, and the title character, the Kurdish Aida, the novel depicts a close relationship between Zaki and Samia, his Shi'a neighbor and childhood friend. Samia too suffers from the regime's violence in the wake of the Iran-Iraq War. Her husband, her son, and her pregnant daughter were executed while her remaining two sons have disappeared, listed by the regime as "missing" although the novel reveals that Samia is actually hiding her two sons in the basement, where they live in darkness, cared for by their mother for twenty years. Every now and then Samia bursts into the offices of the *mukhabarat* to demand information about the whereabouts of her "missing" sons, a clever ruse to make the police believe in their disappearance and prevent them from searching her house. Secretly Samia marries off one of her sons to a young Shi'a woman, Siham, who descends into the dark basement and eventually becomes pregnant. Thus, even after the Iran-Iraq War is over, the Shi'ites continue to suffer at the hand of the regime. And yet, despite loss and death, the passion for life continues and new life is born. Samia asks her neighbor/friend Zaki to marry Siham in order to protect them by offering a cover for her hidden son and her impregnated daughter-in-law. She tells Zaki he can officially convert to Islam and then divorce Siham, this time using the fact that she is Shi'a to their advantage, since during the Iran-Iraq War, Sunni husbands were encouraged to abandon their Shi'a wives, and some did so for crass material interest and the financial benefits offered by the state. Zaki agrees to help Samia for the sake of old neighborly friendship, and also in order to help protect the Kurdish Aida, whom he hides in his house. The war thus ended up creating spatially bifurcated lives—one lived above ground and the other lived below. Invisibility-as-survival impacts the lives of even the most visible—Zaki's popularity on television is possible precisely because he is not recognized as a Jew.

Portraying a multi-voiced Iraq of diverse minorities, the novel includes Christian Iraqis as well as diverse Sunni characters. The Christian Rim is an Iran-Iraq War widow who, like most Iraqis, ends up sacrificing for Saddam Hussein's grandiose war policies. She is portrayed as a sensitive person who would cry at the sight of a cat that had been run over. She sympathizes with the tragedy of her Shi'a neighbor Samia, but at the same time, Rim regards Samia as the widow of a Shi'a traitor and the mother of sons and daughters who collaborated with the Ayatollahs of Iran, a situation reminiscent, to her mind, of the descendents of the Persians from centuries before, who fought every Arab regime. The point of view of the Sunni regime is relayed through the eyes of the young Renin, whose mind has been shaped by the Ba'ath regime since kindergarten. She believed in the mythology of Saddam Hussein as a lion who came to the rescue of humiliated Iraqis under the domination of foreign empires and corrupt rulers but does not question his acts of atrocities. For her, Saddam was only cleansing Iraq's rotten innards, represented not only by enemies from the outside but also from the inside. She identifies with the Iraqi leader who forcefully rejected "the influence of the Persians, who connivingly brought destruction and devastation on the empire of Haroun Al-Rashid."[38] For Renin, Saddam defends Sunni against the Shi'a, excelling "in crushing the poisonous snakehead of their agents."[39] The Caliph Haroun Al-Rashid and his descendents were "innocent rulers," while Iraq's present-day leader "is made of armored steel."[40] Through the eyes of young Renin, Sami Michael registers the power of Ba'athist propaganda to instill hatred toward the persecuted Shi'a majority during the Iran-Iraq War. The multiethnic and multireligious space of the novel *Aida*, in such instances, relays a dystopic Iraq deeply haunted by the Iran-Iraq War, which despite its official end continues in the attacks endured by the Shi'a characters.

To counter this propaganda, Michael portrays the devastation brought upon the Shi'a character Samia, while also invoking other historical moments and figures. In her sorrow, Samia whispers in Zaki's ear to note the resemblance between Saddam Hussein and the mass murderer of twelve hundred years ago, Al Hajjaj bin Yusef al-Taqafi, who was appointed as the ruler of Najaf, then the most important city in Iraq, and which throughout the years became a holy Shi'a city. The elders of the city came to greet Al Hajjaj bin Yusef al-Taqafi, but the ruler surveyed them with an expression of scorn and gave an unusual speech that became deeply inscribed in Arabic cultural memory. Full of cruelty, violence, and brutality, al-Taqafi announces his decision regarding who will be killed, and also explains that he will be the person to carry out the mission. The novel presents Samia's personal and communal pain, like that of Aida, as a kind of a historical recurrence. The very title of the novel, "'aida," signifies in Arabic ('aida) the feminine form of "returnee."[41] The Sunni/Shi'a past haunts the present, and the oppressed cannot escape the tragedy that the Iran-Iraq War brought on them and their family. Yet, recent modern history also seems to repeat itself. The novel narrates Samia's story in conjunction with that of the Jewish protagonist Zaki. In a kind of return of the repressed, the recent tragedies echo a millennial memory. The deep sorrow and devastation experienced by the Shi'a are largely mediated through the Jewish protagonist Zaki. Samia and Zaki both lack the comfort of being surrounded by their families, due to different wars and tensions—Zaki, because of the exodus of the majority of Jews, and Samia because of the violent conflict between the Sunni and the Shi'a. The novel encodes analogical oppressions by shaping a certain parallelism between the devastation wrought on the Jewish community and that wrought on other minorities—the Shi'a through Samia's story and the Kurds through Aida's story. The deep historical connection is allegorized through the novel's description of the Jewish (Zaki's) and the Shi'a (Samia's) neighboring houses:

> The two houses were built by their parents decades ago, attached to each other, and only a low brick fence separated the two roofs, and another fence divided the two gardens. The hopes that were cemented in the foundations and in the walls of the houses faded away in the bitter and violent reality that tormented the country year after year, since then and until now.[42]

Zaki's family was "forced to run for its life" in the beginning of the 1950s with its children dispersed, some to Israel, and some to England and to the United States, while Samia's family paid dearly for the Shi'a / Sunni conflict during and in the aftermath of the Iran-Iraq War. The novel describes Zaki and Samia as aging in the absence of their large, close-knit families, living as remnants of a disappearing past. Here too the novel connects the dots between the uprooting ('aqira) of Jews during the monarchy and the deportation (gerush) of the Shi'as during the Ba'athist Republic era.[43]

Zaki's life is simultaneously caught up in the Israeli-Arab conflict and in the Iran-Iraq War, as well as with the Allied war on Iraq. He stayed in Iraq in the name of his first love, his blood-relative Nur, even after his family departed to Israel. Although his love for Nur never reached fruition, he remained in Baghdad because she was buried there, ending up without blood relatives. In the meantime, Nur's brother Shlomo converts to Islam, now adopting the name Jalil. In contrast to the intellectual protagonist of Ballas's *Outcast*, Haroun / Ahmad, who converted to Islam for theological-philosophical reasons, the character of Shlomo / Jalil is portrayed as an addicted gambler who seems to have converted to Islam purely for convenience. Ballas's convert character Haroun does come under suspicion as an opportunist, when some insinuate: "A Jew doesn't convert to Islam because the light of truth has penetrated his heart. Don't tell me such tales!"[44] But *Outcast* ultimately absolves the protagonist of such accusations as a sincere intellectual in search of religious philosophy. The convert in Michael's *Aida*, in contrast, is an opportunistic character, even praised by the Ba'ath leadership. His first wife and young children had to escape to Israel after he left them living in debt. After converting to Islam, Shlomo / Jalil married four war widows in succession during the Iran-Iraq War. Thanks to these marriages, he managed to collect government grants given to married couples in order to encourage men to marry war widows, whose numbers were increasing during the protracted war. He divorced each after obtaining their money, leaving behind him both legitimate and illegitimate children. In contrast to Zaki, who rescues his Shi'a neighbors by faking marriage to Samia's daughter-in-law, Shlomo / Jalil represents the corruption of power.

True to its universalist vision, *Aida* does not idealize any community. Apart from Shlomo's opportunism, the protagonist Zaki is hardly a heroic idealist figure in the sense of resisting the regime. His patriotic TV program *Landscapes and Sites* offers homage to a country that witnessed many massacres, and his noble act of saving his Shi'a neighbor is meaningful, but also forms part of a longer neighborly history of mutual sacrifice. Samia's father protected Zaki's family during the *farhoud*. The novel portrays the complexity of the diverse communities. The Shi'a Siham, Samia's daughter-in-law, does not hide her perception of "the Jew" as polluted (*nijes*), while the Sunni agent of the genocidal regime, the high-ranking *mukhabarat* officer, Nizar, saves the life of the Jewish protagonist. Such complexities also apply to the war zone between Israel and its neighbors. In a subplot, Michael is careful to portray Iraq and Israel, at the time of the Iran-Iraq War and the Allies' Gulf War, as places of familial and cultural continuities. The dislocation of Shlomo's

Figure 2.4. *Aida*'s Book Cover—Reading Iraq in Hebrew

family to Israel is represented in the novel as a matter neither of love for Zion nor of persecution by the Iraqi regime, but merely the consequence of a shaky domestic situation where Israel becomes an alternative for Shlomo's wife escaping an irresponsible husband. Yet, in an ironic twist of history, the children of Jalil / Shlomo in Israel have kinship relations with the widows of the Iran-Iraq War. As in Ballas's *Outcast*, and in

Rejwan's memoir, Michael's draws a map of biological and emotional continuity of a kind that does not usually register in portrayals of either Israel or Iraq. Zaki's family experiences the wars within different zones, even enemy geographies. While Zaki remains in Baghdad, his sister lives in Oxford, and his mother lives in Israel, at a time of careening bombs, when the British and Americans are dropping smart bombs on Iraq, and Iraq is sending scuds to Israel. Thus Zaki, in Iraq, while coping with a harsh reality of war, is also concerned about his mother and blood relatives in Israel. In this way, the novel highlights the ironic absurdities inherent in the simplistic notions of "Arab-versus-Jew" and of "enemy countries," reminding the readers of the dense familial and human connections across borders. Most importantly, the text carries the Hebrew reader into the Iraqi reality-on-the-ground, which during the '91 Gulf War was largely televised through the aerial point of view of the smart bombs.

The Sunni-Iraqis in the novel, meanwhile, are largely represented through the characters of Maher and Nizar, both of whom are friends of the protagonist, Zaki. But while Nizar has a high position in the *mukhabarat*, Maher resists affiliation with the regime. Throughout the eight years of the Iran-Iraq War, and despite state pressure to abandon Shi'a wives, he refuses to divorce his wife. He tells Zaki that he would not have replaced his Shi'a wife with any other family, and certainly not after all the tragedy and killing that they had to face. "The last Jew" of Iraq thus becomes inadvertently embroiled in the ongoing Sunni-Shi'a conflict. When Nizar visits Zaki's house, the protagonist feels compelled to warn his neighbor / friend Samia of this visit, in order to protect her. The novel contrasts the happy party atmosphere in Zaki's house during Nizar's visit with the deep sorrow and mourning in the neighboring house of Samia. Here, the novel links the histories of fear and disappearances; the Jews first disappeared from Iraq's landscape and now, the Shi'a are in hiding, deported, and "being disappeared." The Jewish Zaki, meanwhile, can befriend a prominent Sunni *mukhabarat* person Nizar who insists to Zaki that the Shi'a "will not rest until the entire Arab world begins to speak Persian."[45] A sense of irony reigns when "the last Jew of Iraq"—a kind of a last of the Mohicans—becomes an unofficial mediator between the Sunni and the Shi'a. The end of the Iran-Iraq War does not bring relief to the vulnerable Shi'as. The authorities burn Samia's house, leading to the deaths of Samia and her family. Zaki's adjacent house is also destroyed in the process, obliterating a history of neighborly respect and co-existence.

While the Iran-Iraq War haunts all characters in the novel, *Aida* largely takes place during the sanctions era, beginning with the invasion of Kuwait, the Gulf War, which resulted in the suppression of the Shi'a and Kurdish rebellions. The novel describes air raids on Baghdad by the United States and British during the early days of the war, with moving descriptions of the consequences of the war "on the ground," where innocent civilians face hunger, power cuts, intense cold, and the stench of rotting meat in the refrigerator. The novel also inventories the effects of sanctions and the inability to secure needed medicines. The Sunni Nizar becomes ill and Zaki's heart weakens and sickens as well. Zaki's revelation to Aida at the beginning of the novel that "in fact, all I want is to be the last Jew in this place, which they say used to be paradise"[46] does not materialize. Zaki begins to realize that the true motherland is not just a piece of earth but also the woman he loves, and as long as he loved the Jewish Nur, his first love, who was buried in Iraq, he was inextricably bound to Iraq. But after losing Nur, who was tortured in a desert prison and eventually died in Zaki's arms, he then shelters the Kurdish woman Aida, who was also tortured by the regime yet somehow survived, and finds love with her. The various regimes' utilization of rape as a weapon, evoked so vividly in *Persepolis*, is also depicted in *Aida*, conveyed through the fright of the about-to-be-imprisoned Jewish communist Nur, who, it is suggested, endured multiple rapes, as well as through the present-day repetition of this terrorizing tactic toward the Kurdish Aida. Yet, Nur symbolically returns to Zaki's life via the Kurdish woman, allowing for Eros to somewhat transcend Thanatos, and the possibility of returning to life. At the end of the novel, Aida, the Kurd, and Zaki, the Jew, fly out of Iraq— though their destination remains unknown—much as Qassem, the communist in Ballas's *Outcast*, ends up in exile, having found refuge in Czechoslovakia.[47] In *Aida*, the departure of "the last Jew" at the end of the novel is interwoven with his flashbacks about his departing family members during the mass exodus of the early 1950s. The present-day dislocations are viewed retroactively as anticipated by past displacements.

The diverse wars—the partition of Palestine in the '48 war, and the '67 war, which made the place of Jews impossible in Iraq; the Iran-Iraq War, which made Shiʻa life in Iraq impossible; the ongoing war on the Kurds; along with the U.S. and British war on Iraq—turned Iraq, for its people, into a hellish place from which exile becomes the only possible salvation. *Aida* however does not end with a separatist view of Iraq, but rather with an allegorical utopia of cross-ethnic and cross-religious solidarity. Like Ballas's *Outcast*, Michael's *Aida* concludes with the expression of a longing to transcend ethnic religious conflict through humanist universalism. In these novels, both Ballas and Michael, who left Iraq during the mass Jewish exodus of 1950–1951, are not writing about an Iraq of autobiographical memory but rather about the could-have-beens of history, i.e., what might have happened had they stayed in Iraq. In this sense, the authors convey allegories of belonging, where writing about an Iraq of a time in which they never lived becomes a way of expressing a desire to belong to the place they were forced to leave. The title of *Aida* also refers to Verdi's opera, which revolves around the kidnapping of an Ethiopian princess by the ancient Egyptians, an allusion made by the Jewish protagonist in relation to the Kurdish refugee who found shelter in his house. The theme of kidnapping that runs through these texts comes to allegorize the kidnapping of a country in its entirety. For the exilic writer, the depiction of the regime robbing people of their lives forms a mode of solidarity with the unattainable homeland.[48] And in their relative safe haven, these authors produce a literature that conveys their own sense of having been kidnapped from Iraq.

In one of many paradoxical and anomalous situations, both authors who were non-Zionist communists nonetheless ended up in Israel. Yet, through narratives that do not revolve around Iraqis in Israel, or around the Iraq of the 1930s or 1940s, but rather around post–Jewish-exodus Iraq, this exilic literature creates a narrative space through which they come to belong—almost prosthetically, as it were—to an Iraq that was no longer accessible to them. The novels allow for an imaginary affiliation with the revolutionary and anti-dictatorial forces of contemporary Iraq. They vicariously join the anti-totalitarian efforts to overthrow the dictatorial regimes as though continuing their youthful communist *thawra* (revolution) of their time directed against monarchy, but transposed in the novels into solidarity with the revolutionary opponents of the dictatorship of Saddam's Ba'ath party. Setting *Outcast* during the Iran-Iraq War and setting *Aida* between the 1991 and 2003 Gulf wars, Ballas and Michael demonstrate clear empathy for the Iraqi people suffering not only from the atrocities committed by the Saddam Hussein regime but also from the Allied war against Iraq. At the same time, both the Iran-Iraq War and later the two Gulf wars come to provide sites whereby the authors can allegorically continue to exist as Iraqis even if *in absentia*. In sum, these novels and memoirs, all written under the sign and impact of war, orchestrate multiple religious and ethnic voices as a way out of ethnic and religious monologism, as well as out of nationalist xenophobia.

Between Elegy and Eulogy

Through novels set in Iraq, Iraqi-Israeli authors are staking a claim in the debate over the Middle East, and not simply as Israelis. It is as if they were refusing the notion that their departure from Iraq and their move to Israel disqualifies them as legitimate participants in the Iraqi debates about freedom and democracy. From the Iraqi nationalist standpoint, the Jews who left Iraq, even those who did not want to depart, were seen as traitors, and therefore no longer possessing any right or presumably any stake in Iraq. This implicit desire to intervene in Iraq's debates, even after the massive departure of the Jews, is therefore a mode of reclaiming Iraqi-ness for Arab Jews in exile. The work of Iraqi Israeli writers is thus partially motivated by a desire to assuage a double feeling of rejection; first, from the very place from which they have been physically dislocated—Iraq, and second, from the place to which they were virtually forced to go—Israel. In Iraq, their departure meant a disappearance from Iraqi political affairs and debates, and while in Israel, any pronouncement on Iraq was subject to an alignment with the Israeli "structure of feeling" to an enemy country. Novels such as *Aida* and *Outcast* offer an imaginary space for inserting the departed Iraqi Jews back into Iraqi history. They "re-enter" Iraqi geography at a time when Iraq has been rendered unavailable. During the horrifying Iran-Iraq War, their respective novels enact an imaginary return to Baghdad during a tumultuous time of war that scarcely scanned in dominant

Israel, unless as a case of two enemy countries (Iran and Iraq) fighting each other in a not entirely unwelcome fratricide, or in the context of the Iran-Contra affair. Indeed, in *Outcast*, Ballas offers a critique of the Israeli stance toward the Iran-Iraq War, voiced through his Jewish-turned-Muslim protagonist: "A war of Muslims against Muslims, Sunnis against Shi'ites, could Israel have hoped for anything better?"[49] For the Hebrew reader, these words produce an "alienation effect," defamiliarizing Israel through Jewish Muslim eyes.

The paradoxes and contradictions of Iraqi, Iranian, and generally Middle Eastern Jews in Israel are inadvertently captured in an American film set during the Iran-Iraq War, but which does not concern Israel and Iranian Jews. The 1991 film *Not Without My Daughter*, adapted from Betty Mahmoody's memoir, revolves around the experience of an American woman married to an Iranian, who, in 1984, travels with his wife and daughter to visit his family in Tehran, a holiday that turns into a virtual captivity. The memoir/film is set against the backdrop of the Iran-Iraq War, but Brian Gilbert's film was released during the buildup to the 1991 Gulf War. As Iraqi missiles are falling over Tehran, the mother desperately looks for ways to flee. Finally, she escapes with the assistance of Iranians opposed to the regime, and later with Kurdish smugglers who help her cross the border to Turkey where, in the final scene, Betty and her daughter happily walk to the American embassy and to freedom. While the film does not address the question of Israel, it indirectly embeds the history of dislocation of Jews from Arab and Muslim countries to Israel. Shot in Turkey and in Israel, which stand in for Iran, the film was made with the help of Golan-Globus Studios in Israel. Many of the Iranian and Kurdish characters are actually played by Israeli actors and actresses. This casting practice in fact has a long Hollywood history for its numerous films set in the Arab and Muslim world, for example, *Rambo III* (1988) and *True Lies* (1994). In *Not Without my Daughter,* the cast includes: Sasson Gabay as Hamid; Yacov Banai as Aga Hakim; Gili Ben-Ozilio as Fereshte; Racheli Chaimian as Zoreh; Yosef Shiloach as Mohsen's companion; and Daphna Armoni as the Quran teacher. Along with the roles of Iranians, the Israeli actors also play the roles of Kurds, speaking in all these roles in a heavy English accent with a Hebrew accent occasionally heard "through" the English-speaking Iranian or Kurdish characters. In one sequence, one of the Kurdish smugglers actually uses a Hebrew phrase, "tov, yallah" (meaning ok, let's go)—the last word is Hebrew slang borrowed from the Arabic "yallah." Here, Hebrew, including in its syncretic absorption of colloquial Arabic, stands in for Kurdish.

It would be misleading, however, to discuss the actors as simply "Israelis," since many were selected precisely for their "Middle Eastern physiognomies," and indeed many of them come from Arab and Muslim countries. Sasson Gabay, of Iraqi origin, speaks heavily accented English, which stands in for Farsi and is inflected by an Iraqi-Arabic musicality. Meanwhile, Yosef Shiloach, an actor of Kurdish Iraqi origins, plays a Kurdish smuggler, and ironically is well-known for his impeccable imitation of the Farsi accent in Hebrew, performed in the ethnic-based *bourekas* film genre. In other words, while *Not Without My Daughter* does not directly concern Israel, a Middle Eastern Jewish presence is submerged and inferential, a result of Hollywood's production practices with regard to the Middle East as linked to Israeli cinema's ethnic politics of casting.[50] While seemingly irrelevant to the Iran-Iraq War, Middle Eastern Jews are present in *Not Without My Daughter* through their physical presence via casting, thus implicitly invoking the previous wars and violent events that forced the dislocation of the Jews of Iraq and later of Iran, especially after the 1979 revolution. In this sense the dislocation of Middle Eastern Jews is allegorized in films that do not explicitly thematize the question of Arab Jews/Middle Eastern Jews.

The subject of the Iran-Iraq War has become a trigger for remembering lost homelands. Literary and cinematic representations, in this sense, involve an act of imaginary return to the places that shaped the authors' childhood landscape, a landscape to which he or she can no longer return. Even when actual return does occur, as in Sinan Antoon's film, *About Baghdad*, which focuses on an Iraqi novelist returning home in 2003 to witness the effects of war, sanctions, and occupation, return is far from an act of gratifying repetition. Having left a Baghdad that was still under the regime of Saddam Hussein, and having lived through the years of the Iran-Iraq War, Sinan returns from the United States to a post-2003 Iraq, registering the multiple transformations in his devastated city. In one scene, Sinan visits the memorial site for the Iraqi soldiers built by Saddam Hussein's regime for the martyrs of the Iran-Iraq War. The names of numerous *shahids* (the martyrs) are inscribed on the walls in Arabic; but now the walls also display, in English, an American military parking sign, in complete disregard for the significance of the memorial. The oblivious U.S. soldiers have little in the way of a good explanation for the Iraqi American returnee, who is visibly upset by the sacrilege of this military action. In this way, the Iran-Iraq War memorial, a reminder of the many young Iraqis killed in a senseless war, is now an occupied American site that in itself becomes a reminder of the many afflictions Iraqis have had to endure after the Iran-Iraq War, i.e., the Gulf War, sanctions, the 2003 war—all of which resulted in countless killed, maimed, and wounded as well as the death of the elderly, babies, and the sick due to malnutrition, lack of medicine, and environmental disasters. Such superimposed devastations have continued to haunt Iraqi people long after the Iran-Iraq War. In *About Baghdad*, the post-2003 encounter with the Iran-Iraq War memorial site triggers the memory of a fresh war whose reality "on the ground" is documented in every scene.

Official monuments for a past war—Iran-Iraq—sometimes themselves become the casualties of another war—the 2003 Gulf War. But more than a memory of the people killed, of millions of casualties and billions of dollars in damages, the monuments make sense only within a governmental grammar of demonization of "us and them," "the Persian enemy," or "the Arab enemy." When, as in the case of Iraq, the regime itself disappears, the war monument remains as a concrete token of grandiose desires and the senseless sacrifice of Iraqis of all backgrounds. In the case of Iran, the regime continues to commemorate victims as part of a celebration of national strength. Past steadfastness comes to allegorize contemporary resilience. Recently, commemorations in Iran under the Rouhani presidency have unveiled a new monument, one specifically dedicated to the Jewish soldiers killed in the Iran-Iraq War. The monument has the engraved Hebrew calligraphy *"Shalom le'Olam"* ("peace forever") along with the design of a menorah.[51] Iranian news agencies IRNA and Tasnim published photographs of the ceremony, which included Jewish community leaders and a number of Iranian religious officials, displaying banners showing the images of the fallen soldiers, hailed as *shahids* in both Farsi and Hebrew inscriptions. The monument reflects President Hassan Rouhani's moderate stance, expressed in the words of the vice-speaker of the Iranian parliament, Mohammad

Figure 2.5. Iran's monument for the Jewish Shahids of the Iran-Iraq War. Source: *Washington Post*, December 18, 2014; www.washingtonpost.com. See also "Iran unveils monument to Jewish soldiers killed in war with Iraq," Haaretz and the Associated Press, December 18, 2014, www.haaretz.com.

Hassan Aboutorabi-Fard, who praised the Jewish community and its support for the Islamic Republic, emphasizing "their obedience to the Supreme Leader of the Revolution," which demonstrates "the bonds originating from the teachings of the divine religions." Aboutorabi-Fard also used the occasion to denounce the "violent and inhumane" behavior of Israeli Prime Minister Benjamin Netanyahu.[52] The *Times of Israel*, meanwhile, accused Iran of sheer manipulation, arguing that the "Jewish war monument is yet more shameful propaganda from the Iranian regime."[53] Following the departure of about 100,000–150,000 Jews from Iran since 1979, about 20,000–25,000 Jews remain in the country. At the same time, the leader of the Tehran Jewish Association, Homayoun Samiah, saw the event and generally the current regime's willingness to listen to the community's grievance as an improvement over the attitude of the former President Mahmoud Ahmadinejad.

The ceremony for the Jewish dead of the Iran-Iraq War, while acknowledging Iranian Jews, also indirectly highlighted the vacuum left in the wake of the many who departed. As the recent monument reveals, the Iran-Iraq War has come to allegorize the contemporary battles about the place of religious minorities within the Muslim world, on the one hand, and about the place of a Jewish state in the Middle East, on the other. For the Iraqi and Iranian Jews, the desire to return remains largely a fantastic tale articulated within textual spaces. While for Roya Hakakian, Sami Michael, Shimon Ballas, and Nissim Rejwan return is impossible, even for the younger generation of Iraqis and Iranians, if not impossible, return is nonetheless nightmarish, especially when the landscape of one's city has been totally transformed in one's absence. The fact that many Iraqis of very diverse backgrounds have left the country over the past few decades seems to echo the departure of earlier generations of minorities and of the regime's opponents; or perhaps they did so simply because the Mesopotamia Paradise has become a hellish un-ending war zone. The departure of Iraqi Jews in the late 1940s and 1950s became a harbinger for later departures. For many of the Iranian Jews displaced in the wake of the 1979 Islamicist revolution, that departure took place within a context of multiple Iranian dislocations that cover the wide spectrum of the ethnic, religious ad ideological spectrum. Tropes of return can be seen as symbolic and vicarious imaginings of the return of many previous generations of Iraqis and Iranians forced into exile. Such imaginary returns compose an elegy for a lost homeland, combined with a eulogy of its culture, but with a deep investment in writing as a site to articulate the utopianist desire for political transformation.

NOTES

1 Marjane Satrapi, *The Complete Persepolis* (New York: Pantheon Books, 2007), 142.

2 Roland Barthes, "The Rhetoric of the Image," in *Image/Music/Text* (New York: Hill and Wang, 1977), 32–51.

3 Satrapi, *The Complete Persepolis*, 145.

4 Roya Hakakian, *Journey from the Land of No: A Girlhood Caught in Revolutionary Iran* (New York: Three Rivers Press, 2004), 201.

5 Nissim Rejwan, *The Last Jews in Baghdad: Remembering a Lost Homeland* (Austin: University of Texas Press, 2004), 184.

6 Ibid., 185.

7 Ibid.

8 Indeed, among the books authored by the historian Dr. Ahmed Sousa are *Fi Tariqi ila al-Islam* (*In My Way to Islam*, 1936); *Al-'Arab wal-Yahud fi al-Ta'rikh* (*The Arabs*

and the Jews in History, 1972); and *Malameh min al-Tarikh al-Qadeem li-Yahud al-'Iraq (Aspects of the Ancient History of the Jews of Iraq*, 1978).

9 "Thalatha kan 'ala Allah an la yakhluqahum: al-Fars, al-Yahud, wa al-dhabib."

10 On Saddam Hussein's usage of Mesopotamian archeology, see Michael L. Galaty and Charles Watkinson, eds., *Archeology Under Dictatorship* (New York: Kluwer Academic/Plenum Publishers, 2004).

11 Shimon Ballas, *Outcast* (English), Ammiel Alcalay and Oz Shelach, trans. (San Francisco: City Lights Publishers, 2007), 182–183.

12 Ibid., 183.

13 Ibid., 182.

14 Ibid.

15 Ibid., 183.

16 Ibid.

17 Other traditions regard the tomb of Daniel as located in Iraq, including in Babylon, Kirkuk, and Mosul, which was detonated by the Islamic State of Iraq and the Levant in July 2014.

18 In order to highlight the Persian reference in the protagonist's name, I transliterated it from the Hebrew to the English as "Sousan" with one "s," although in the English translation of *Outcast* it is transliterated as "Soussan" (Shimon Ballas, *Ve-Hu Akher*. Tel Aviv: Zmora-Bitan Publishers, 1991).

19 Ballas, *Outcast*, 59.

20 Ibid., 71.

21 Ibid.

22 Ibid.

23 Ibid., 108–109.

24 Ibid., 148.

25 Ibid., 109.

26 Ibid., 111.

27 Ibid., 161.

28 Ibid., 167.

29 Ibid., 113.

30 Ibid., 174.

31 Ibid., 174–175.

32 Ibid., 175.

33 Ibid.

34 Ibid., 114.

35 Ibid., 209.

36 Tragically, Dr. Aliya Sousa, the daughter of the historical figure Dr. Ahmad Sousa, was killed in the August 19, 2003 explosion of the UN Headquarters in Baghdad.

37 Indeed, the title to another novel by Michael is *Refuge*, focusing on communists in Israel, including Palestinians and Arab Jews.

38 Sami Michael, *Aida* (Kinneret, Zmora-Bitan: Dvir-Publishing House, 2008), 30. Translation from the Hebrew by Ella Shohat.

39 Sami Michael, *Aida*, p. 30.

40 Ibid.

41 One is reminded here of Emile Habiby's novel, *The Secret Life of Saeed: The Pessoptimist*, which attributes to one of the female characters, a representative of the Palestinians in the diaspora, the symbolic name "Yu'ad," or "the one to be returned." (*Al-Waqā'i' al-gharībah fī 'khtifā' Sa'īd Abī 'l-Naḥsh al-Mutashā'il*), 1974.

42 Michael, *Aida*, 13.

43 *Aida* often deploys the Hebrew words "'aqira and "gerush."

44 Ballas, *Outcast*, 116.

45 *Aida*, 258.

46 Ibid., 68.

47 Ibid., 187.

48 Sami Michael was among the founders of the Society for Solidarity between the People of Israel and the People of Iraq, which also included Shimon Ballas. Despite the emphasis on "the people of Israel" rather than "Iraqi Jews," the Interior Ministry refused to register the society as a non-profit organization, arguing that Israeli Law forbids "contact with enemy states."

49 Ballas, *Outcast*, 198.

50 See Ella Shohat, *Israeli Cinema: East/West and the Politics of Representation* (Austin: University of Texas Press, 1989). See especially the postscript in the New Edition, 2010.

51 Ishaan Tharoor, "Iran unveils a memorial honoring Jewish heroes," *Washington Post*, December 18, 2014; www.washingtonpost.com. See also "Iran unveils monument to Jewish soldiers killed in war with Iraq," *Haaretz* and *Associated Press*, December 18, 2014, www.haaretz.com.

52 Tharoor, "Iran unveils a memorial honoring Jewish heroes."

53 Karmel Melamed, "Jewish war monument is yet more shameful propaganda from the Iranian regime," *Times of Israel*, December 26, 2014.

PART II

Theorizing Cultural Expressions of War

3

Treacherous Memory

Bashu the Little Stranger and the Sacred Defense

KAMRAN RASTEGAR

Questions of ideological dedication are perhaps most fraught within the context of war. Memory discourse, in particular on the memory of war and its traumas, is often a legitimating instrument in the contest to elaborate who serves as hero and who as traitor during the war and afterward. In post-revolutionary Iran, the onset of the Iran-Iraq War allowed for the articulation of new if shifting parameters for ideological commitment and heroism, as well as treachery or cowardice. The evolution of the "sacred defense" concept allowed for the most articulate elaboration of these binaries, and wartime and postwar cultural producers, bureaucrats, and theorists have all contributed to the definition of their boundaries.

This chapter examines the shifting discourse on sacred defense cinema, and on filmmaking that lies outside of its legitimizing mantle. After articulating the parameters of sacred defense culture with one or two examples drawn from cinema, I will turn my attention to incipient memory discourses on the war in cinematic works on the Iran-Iraq War that produce a counter-discourse to sacred defense. I will present a reading of *Bashu, the Little Stranger* (Bahram Beyza'i 1987), comparing the film to other wartime "naive dramas" of Lebanese civil war films such as Joseph Fares's film *Zozo* (2005) so as to explore the limits of the sacred defense discourse, by proposing that the film be viewed as a product of the sustained crisis that characterizes memory practices around the Iran-Iraq War. This discussion also outlines attempts to address memory practices concerning the war outside of the realm of the state-sponsored narrative(s) on the war, the potential use or abuse of the war for state ideological ends.

In fact, every war produces a crisis of memory, yet each context is unique in how institutional and social reactions to this crisis come to define communal memory of the war. Memory practices outside of the sacred defense field were, from the beginning of the war, coded as potentially treacherous, themselves subject to accusations of the abuse of memory.[1] As Paul Ricoeur has eloquently suggested, such shifting articulations of memory discourse are most acute in the moment when "ideologizing of memory" occurs.

> In fact, before the abuse, there was the use, that is the unavoidably selective nature of narrative. [. . .] the ideologizing of memory is made possible by the resources of variation offered by the work of narrative configuration. The strategies of forgetting are directly grafted upon this work of configuration: one can always recount differently, by eliminating, by shifting the emphasis, by recasting the protagonists of the action in a different light along with the outlines of the action.[2]

Ricoeur here suggests that the use and abuse of memory, what we may term the ideologizing of what is heroic and treacherous through memory, is due to narrative exigencies in the structuring of memory discourse. Sacred defense cinema is a form of memory discourse that through narrative techniques—"shifting the emphasis" of particular memories and narratives, "recasting the protagonists of the action" that surrounds the war to promote specific communal memories—pursues the constitution of a particular discursive limit to how the war is remembered. Cinema of the sacred defense, which here may be seen as a reassigning of Freud's conception of "screen-memories" to the social register, aimed to utilize memory and visuality for a coherent project whose aim was projecting the officially sanctioned interpretations of the past, that is, of the war. The formation of screen-memories is key to the now widely accepted lay idea that, in the aftermath of traumatic experience, the psyche covers the painful memory of trauma with a repressive alternative. Screen-memories are memories that displace the true memory, produced by the mind in order to give stability to a psyche threatened through trauma with instability or neurosis.[3] By allegorizing sacred defense cinema as screen-memories, it is not the case that a counter-cinema may provide a window upon real memory. Socially constituted memory practices are inherent in cinematic technique, production, and consumption, so that cinema offers a unique crucible for determining the parameters of social contestation over forms of memories. Some memory practices reaffirm (as screen-memories do) a sense of coherence for the prevailing order, while others aim to undermine or challenge this very same putative coherence, in favor of what may be counter-memories, or most radically, of aporetic memory discourses that do not offer foreclosure upon interpretations of the past. These relate to what I term here treacherous memories, which work to counteract the stated national agenda of constituting war memory within a particular and delimited framework.

The Sacred Defense Field: Boundaries, Studies

As suggested above, all Iranian war and postwar cultural enunciations must be viewed as being fundamentally defined by the discourse of sacred defense. These enunciations are either envisioned by and legitimated within this project, or are set outside of it and are thus coded as treacherous. Defining the term sacred defense is a fraught endeavor, even for those who work within the field. Generically, the term has come to be applied by many as pertaining to any war cultural works concerning the Iran-Iraq War and its aftermath (usually in the form of films about former veterans of the war). However, many who play roles within sacred defense institutions insist upon a more ideologically refined definition, distinguishing between "war cinema" and "sacred defense cinema," for example.

Here I will first focus upon the constitution of the *sacred defense field*, applying a Pierre Bourdieu–inspired framing to the term innovated by the Islamic Republic to describe the ideological ethos that surrounded the war. In this sense, the sacred defense field is the dominant expression of social trauma, and specifically of trauma production, in the postwar Iranian context. The field is subject to ongoing contestation, not only from without but also from within, which means that the field has shown a surprising dynamism and a capacity for transformation. However, despite this, it is also true that for many years after the end of the war this project has remained remarkably coherent in its core ideological orientations. The sacred defense field thus serves as a singular, dominating, field of representational and memorializing activity regarding the war, although it is not the only one. And again, the sacred defense field is not static, but rather is marked by intense conflict and redefinition within itself.[4]

In postwar Iran, state intervention into both the representation of the war and its aftermath has led cultural producers to adopt very different strategies, largely relating to their own political commitments and subjective identification within the parameters of post-revolutionary ideology. State sponsorship of film production about the war, led by the *Anjoman-e Sinama-ye Defa'-e Moghaddas* (the Council of Sacred Defense Cinema), has promoted work that followed state imperatives for interpretations of the war.[5] This council has carried out a myriad of activities since the war's end, including organizing film festivals of sacred defense cinema, providing production support to selected film projects, training filmmakers and screenwriters, among other activities. Perhaps the greatest impact of sacred defense cinema institutions was felt in the early and mid-1990s, when the genre produced many of the most popular films in Iran, and attracted a wide range of talented filmmakers to contribute to the sacred defense project. For example, in 1993, *From the Karkheh to the Rhine* was the highest-grossing Iranian domestic film, and its director Ebrahim Hatamikia produced a string of highly popular and critically acclaimed films on sacred defense themes throughout the 1990s and early 2000s.

When Iranian filmmakers elected to document the war with a measure of poetic distance or ambivalence, as, for example, in Amir Naderi's two documentary films titled, *The Search I and II* (*Jostejoo 1*, 1981 and *Jostejoo 2*, 1982), the films were repressed or censored.[6] Both parts of *The Search* were commissioned by state television in the early years of the war, but were not shown and then were embargoed, ostensibly for focusing on the question of losses brought about by the war rather than promoting sacred defense themes. In this way the various cultural agencies of the Iranian state apparati, including film and television censors, film production funds, training facilities, festival curators, and many others, have contributed to the formation of the sacred defense field. To be a cultural producer during and in the years just after the war was to be surrounded by the relative prestige and favor afforded to sacred defense themes, which was joined with a strong project of denying or delegitimizing engagements with war that were outside of these authorized themes. For stepping outside of the sacred defense field, a high price could be paid in the form of pre-production obstacles such as denial of funding or script censorship, or in terms of barriers raised after the film's completion, from complete banning to simply a lack of distribution or broadcasting opportunities being made available to it. Thus it is not surprising that very few films have been made that address the war in a way that does not participate in reproducing sacred defense themes, tropes, and forms of legitimation. However, alternative interpretations to the war experience have circulated in Iranian cultural productions, and cinema works have reflected, often in oblique fashion, these countervailing approaches. While ideologically committed filmmakers began to explore the war largely through narrative, fictional, means, quickly developing a language and repertoire for sacred defense cinema that became enclosed, self-referential, and self-reifying, those for whom participation in sacred defense culture was socially impossible or politically unacceptable were driven to find other outlets for expressing the social trauma to which the war gave rise.

To better illuminate the contours of this paradigm, we may compare the Iranian context to another setting where war and postwar cultural productions have played a significant social role, that of Lebanon. Set against the Iranian, state-sponsored project of predetermining the interpretive parameters for war traumas, the Lebanese civil war discourse offers what may be a nearly diametrically opposing context, wherein official discourse on the war is limited only to what Sune Haugbolle calls "state-sponsored amnesia," against which a preponderance of memorial projects may be viewed as potentially threatening to the political status quo and national unity.[7] Narratives on the Lebanese civil war range broadly, but as in Iran find themselves delimited by certain discursive and institutional boundaries. In Lebanon these boundaries are set not only by a disinclination and inability for a weak state to tackle difficult war questions, but also by the demands and interests of the funders of these films, most often European national funds, legitimating memory discourse that occasion non-sectarian views of the war, but which are also open to complaints of a fetishization of the spectacle and trauma of war.[8] What a comparison of these two contexts illuminates are the congruences and distinctions they share in how traumatic memory may be harnessed for productive social ends. In Lebanon, the state has relinquished the grounds of trauma production, which in turn have been occupied by cultural productions that use memory discourses to animate critical questions about postwar Lebanon's failures, and to militate against the terms of official amnesia. In Iran, the state's aim to monopolize the terms of trauma production has led some filmmakers to cede the grounds of representing war memory to the sacred defense project, while others have entered the state delimited grounds, but have had to stake out dissenting views largely through works that emerge from the discursive grounds of sacred defense discourse, and which made use of its claims to legitimacy in articulating the social traumas of the war.

A few words regarding the term *social trauma* are necessary here. Social trauma is always communally and institutionally constructed, its discursive limits articulated and reiterated by institutions and collectivities whose aim is the reproduction of this trauma discourse. In the Iranian context, social trauma was a project to which nearly every organ of the government contributed, with a more or less cohesive set of interpretive parameters for the project of constructing sacred defense culture. Social trauma is never innocent, it is never disinterested. The constellation of social values that come to define particular interpretations of specific historical experiences as traumatic may be termed *trauma production*. Trauma production, put briefly, is here meant as shorthand for the institutional and social processes involved in articulating and codifying the interpretive parameters of (and values accorded to) collective trauma, an operation quite often carried out at the level of the nation. Dominick LaCapra's conception of "founding traumas," which he defines as "traumas that paradoxically become the valorized or intensely cathected basis of identity for an individual or a group rather than events that pose the problematic question of identity," resonate with the concept of trauma production.[9] We are here more concerned with his application of the term for collectivities than for individuals, but in either case it would seem that the articulation of a particular trauma as "foundational" for identity is a significant moment in the process of trauma production. In this sense trauma production does not generally refer to any and all commemorative practices relating to traumatic histories, but instead the term is limited to those efforts that "valorize" and thus perpetuate the narratives of trauma for use in the formation of national or other communal identities. Put otherwise, trauma production is not primarily concerned with the *resolution* of social trauma (although it is often accompanied by the discourse of "healing" and "overcoming" trauma as a mechanism for self-legitimation), but is rather more broadly linked to the circulation of founding traumas that play a productive role in ideological and political contestations. In the Iranian case, there is little doubt that the sacred defense project plays just such a role.

To better understand the sacred defense field, we must begin by addressing how its institutions have collaborated in articulating a discourse of social trauma that is productive to the state's ideological aims. Historically, the sacred defense field had roots in the war effort itself. Initially, for a period after the beginning of hostilities, the cultural response to the war was poorly defined and lacked direction. Nonetheless, within months of the initial Iraqi invasion in September 1980, the revolutionary state had begun to develop key elements of what would become the sacred defense project. This distinction may be noted quite clearly in comparing the earliest cinematic responses to the war, such as the 1984 film *Eagles* (*'Uqabha,* director Samuel Khachikian), to later, more developed sacred defense works. Although it was made to support the war effort, *Eagles* is fundamentally a conventional war film with Iranian soldiers set as national heroes in the fight against the Iraqi enemy, and it lacks any use of the conventions and tropes that would later define sacred defense productions. In order to improve upon the ideologically insufficient if patriotic responses of filmmakers such as Khachikian, the state began to develop institutions to formulate more ideologically sound means by which to represent the war and to formulate memory discourse around it. One Iranian critic, a supporter and theorist of sacred defense cinema, describes the qualities that characterize this earlier form of war film, which "generate sympathy based on Western forms of fantastical and exaggerated heroism on one side, and place on the other side a group that is stupid, cowardly, criminal, and doomed to defeat [. . .] The works of those years [i.e., the first years of the war] were also characterized by use of exaggerated film techniques. Disconcerting zooms, unnecessary camera movements in various directions, overwrought music, long close-ups for effect on the faces of famous actors, chase scenes and drawn-out and bloody fighting that result in victory for the heroes of the film."[10]

* * *

Sacred defense filmmaking is based on a rejection of these aesthetic formulae and a reappropriation of cinematic technique to more exalted ends. The aesthetics of sacred defense move away from military heroism and flag-waving, to emphasize what are seen as the transcendental aims of the war, both personal and communal. In this conception, the sacred defense encompasses human activities of a wide variety beyond their battlefield conduct, and the front lines of the war only provide what may be seen as the most opportune and distilled manifestations of a struggle that precedes the conflict with Iraq, and which will no doubt only find its resolution at the end of time. As Pedram Partovi suggests, what distinguishes the ideological subtext of sacred defense cinema from that of more common national war cinemas is that, "It is not out of legal obligation or national pride or family honor but rather out of love for God that one goes to the front. The ultimate victory is not the vanquishing of the enemy but the spiritual fulfillment and eternal life gained through freedom from the bonds of flesh."[11] Roxanne Varzi echoes some of the same themes in her discussion of sacred defense cinema, saying that "the film images of the sacred defense were also used as metaphors or examples for how a young man might commence on the path to God."[12] These aims cast the Iranian articulation of a war culture in terms that are rather distinct from those of many other modern international wars, which have tended to rely upon nationalist conceptions of the homeland and sacrifice for the national body to legitimize the losses brought about in war. So it is perhaps to be expected that practitioners of sacred defense culture, and cinema in particular, conceived of their work as at odds with predominant, often Western, narrative or aesthetic conventions. And yet, despite these aims, most Iranian sacred defense films adopt a decidedly traditional narrative structure, that of the melodrama, with the sacrifice of the protagonist as an emotively cathartic point within a "family" drama involving either biological families or those involving the "brotherhood" of soldiers. Yet, in distinction to the secular sublimity of a patriot's death in defense of his nation, the sacred defense martyr is celebrated for his achievement of a transcendental status in defense of religion, of the oppressed, and of humanity.

Working from the materiel of this ideological framework, a new genre developed. The elaboration of its aesthetic and formal conventions was significantly complemented by the emergence of a wide variety of institutions supporting such filmmaking. During the war, training programs were instituted by the state television broadcasting service through its office TelFilm, so as to bring to the fore a new generation of filmmakers and documentarians to provide wartime materials for both television and cinema.[13] Other filmmakers were given support and training opportunities through the *Hozeh-ye Honari-Islami* (Islamic Cultural Center), a quasi-independent, ideologically committed Islamic cultural organization that began to offer funding for sacred defense films during the war.[14] Some of these filmmakers, who initially began as volunteers, came to establish successful careers for themselves over the course of the war and the first postwar years, deriving support from the state as well as gaining large audiences for their works. A number of Iran's most commercially successful post-revolutionary filmmakers rose through these ranks: Ebrahim Hatamikia, Jafar Panahi, Mohsen Makhmalbaf, Kamal Tabrizi, to name a few. The emergence of the national Farabi Film Foundation in 1983 provided another institutional basis for the development of the sacred defense field, with its War Films Bureau which was established to promulgate the ideological aims of sacred defense. This project was further developed in the postwar period during the the Rafsanjani presidency of 1990–1997, through further institutionalization. Most of these projects found affiliation with, or support from, the cultural organs of the state, and in particular the Ministry of Culture and Guidance, with the collaboration of other ministries.[15]

However, despite the rigid terms and ideological focus adopted by the founding institutions of the sacred defense field, contestation even within the field has consistently demanded rearticulations of these terms. This phenomenon may be traced not only in the shift in tone visible in the works of sacred defense filmmakers such as Ebrahim Hatamikia—whose 1997 hit *The Glass Agency* may be viewed as a melancholic challenge to the pieties of the sacred defense field (although hints of such a move may be traced as far back as 1993's *From the Karkheh to the Rhine*), these are echoed in administrative arenas as well.

This is no better illuminated than in the attempted impeachment of Ataollah Mohajerani, the minister of culture under Mohammad Khatami, by principlist and ultra-conservative parliamentarians in 1999. The articles of his impeachment give evidence to the fact that the parliamentary committee viewed the perpetuation of the sacred defense field to be a key imperative of the minister of culture, one alleged to have been abrogated by Mohajerani. During Mohajerani's administration, the privileged position of sacred defense cinema had begun to erode. This is noted in plain language in the following points in the articles of impeachment: "Lack of attention to Sacred Defense filmmakers, which has resulted in the drastic decrease in the number of the[se] films. Stopping the subsidies for this sort of cinema (which is one of the main incentives for the spread and propagation of the values of the eight years of Sacred Defense and its transfer to the next generation)."[16]

In the case of the Mohajerani impeachment, which is a reflection of broader internal conflicts within the sacred defense field, we clearly see the conflicts that lie at the heart of state projects of trauma production. The legitimating terms of the trauma are here harnessed by the state, but this control is fragile and subject to threat. The sacred defense field, overlaid by the traumatic discourse of loss and mourning, comes to seek a new elaboration in the changes that actors in the field begin to demand of it. Since the early years of the millennium, a number of events have signaled a profound crisis in sacred defense cinema, as former practitioners such as Ebrahim Hatamikia have abandoned the genre, and as new films in the genre have enjoyed smaller and smaller audiences; we may even posit an impending collapse of the sacred defense field. During the Khatami administration, there was already official acknowledgment of a crisis for this genre, as a Ministry of Culture-funded study found that only "3.6% of the general public liked Sacred Defense films."[17] One sacred defense filmmaker, Abu al-Qasim Talebani, sees the genre as having become marked by opportunism, saying, "sacred defense cinema today has taken on the appearance of commerce and trade. Now those who want to make films just grow beards [i.e., affect religiosity] and then enter the profession. This person makes his first film on the war and the sacred defense. No one remembers it, but after making this first film he enters the Iranian commercial cinema and pursues other topics."[18] Despite the fact that institutional support has invited opportunism among neophytes, many of whom are too young to have participated or possibly even remember the war, the foundations of sacred defense have been seen to be shaky, and even the annual sacred defense film festival has been cancelled several times in the 2000s. As a solution to this crisis, the sacred defense film festival of 2010 incorporated a wide range of international films under the heading of "resistance, revolution and sacred defense." This seems to have been a formula to rejuvenate sacred defense as participating in broader international currents. However, this decision was not uncontroversial, as some filmmakers protested the internationalization of the festival, saying that it deviated from the core concerns of the sacred defense.[19] And yet, despite gloomy predictions for its future, the field may well be rejuvenated with new ideological and institutional investments in the sacred defense narrative, should Iran again be placed on a war footing.

Bashu, the Little Stranger

Comparative Perspectives

Although from an institutional perspective the Iranian war film is rightly identified with the emergence of the sacred defense field, questions of postwar trauma may well be read through films that were produced outside of the sacred defense context as well. In fact, a focus on these works provides perspectives that are often lost or sublimated within the sacred defense framework. This division of wartime and postwar trauma cinema is also a reflection of generational as well as ideological divides in Iran: the sacred defense field became an outlet for younger, ideologically committed revolutionary artists to train and gain skills, and in a sense served as an institutional base for a generational conflict between more ideologically committed revolutionary filmmakers and the prior generation of the largely secular-leftist cultural and cinema elite. While this prior generation retained significant cultural capital both for their resistance activity before and during the revolution, and for the prestige they had gained for their work nationally and internationally, they were seen by the ascendant post-revolutionary political establishment as ideologically problematic and suspect. In most cases, members of this generation either elected to work in explicitly non-ideological and even non-socially engaged topics, or they faced significant barriers in production and distribution of their films. While it would have been impossible for a filmmaker within Iran to have directly challenged the pieties of the developing sacred defense cultural field, nonetheless some were compelled to seek ways to elaborate alternative memory discourses on the experiences of war.

Moves to forge a counter-narrative to that which was advanced by the sacred defense field cinema can be traced in a variety of forms and settings both during and after the war. Here I will present a reading of Bahram Beyzai's *Bashu, the Little Stranger* (*Bashu, Gharibeh-ye Kuchak*), shot in 1985 and released in 1987), arguing that this film participates in an indirect contestation of the grounds of traumatic memory as defined by the sacred defense field.[20] *Bashu* is a work that cannot but respond to the traumas of the war, even while it searches for a language and context outside the hermetic sphere of sacred defense culture. Works such as this were also a result of the crisis for the prior generation of film elites and their uncertainty with how to engage with the experience of the war with Iraq. Responding to this crisis, these works have tended to resonate with the significant Iranian film audiences who were also ambivalent about the dominance of sacred defense discourse.

This potentially treacherous ambivalence marks the works of several filmmakers drawn from this milieu in the earlier years of the war. Before making *Bashu*, Bahram Beyzai edited another iconic film made during the war period, Amir Naderi's *The Runner* (*Davandeh*, made in 1982, released in 1986). While *The Runner* makes no direct allusion to the war, there are many reasons to consider it within the current discussion. *The Runner* is set somewhere in Iran's southwestern coast and appears to be at least partially autobiographical, as the young protagonist of the film shares Amir Naderi's first name. Naderi is from Abadan, a city that by 1982, the year of *The Runner's* production, was nearly completely destroyed. So while the film does not overtly reference the war, one may perceive the traces of the war on the filmmaker and the film itself. If *The Runner* represents a sublimated engagement with the effects of the war, *Bashu* may be rather understood as an attempt, coming several years later, to engage more directly with the subject of the war, although in a manner that would also similarly refuse co-optation to the sacred defense project. . Both Bashu and Amiro are sons of Iran's south, both are orphans, and both narratives are structured around the struggle of each protagonist to overcome difficult circumstances in what may be termed a quest for subjectivity—these are tales of *becoming*. While it is not difficult to conclude that the inspiration for *Bashu* may have originated in part in Beyzai's experience of working on *The Runner*, further links between these films must be examined elsewhere.

Bashu begins on the front lines of the war. In the introductory scenes of the film, a young boy, Bashu, is transported to a tranquil northern Iranian village after escaping the war by hiding in the back of a truck, when his parents are killed after a shell hits their simple home. After riding for hours he leaves the truck and finds himself in an unfamiliar landscape, surrounded by people who speak Gilaki rather than the Arabic dialect that is his mother tongue. The mutually incomprehensible nature of the languages forms the central problematic of the film and leaves Bashu an outsider in his new setting, despite being taken in by a single mother, Na'i, who has two small children of her own. Over the course of the film, Na'i adopts Bashu, as he takes on more and more responsibility as the man of the household. Overcoming many cultural and social obstacles, Bashu eventually finds a settled place in the family and village, but this arrangement is challenged at the end of the film with the return of Na'i's husband to the village. Bashu's position is threatened by this turn of events, but then it is disclosed that Na'i's husband has lost his arm, and Bashu communes with him in their shared loss.[21] In the last scene of the film, Bashu and Na'i's husband join together in the defense of the farm from an unseen predatory animal that has terrorized the household for some time.

As a film driven by the narrative of an orphaned child, living through the war, *Bashu* falls into a subgenre of war cinema that explores the experiences of child characters in war settings. Within Lebanese cinema, for example, the genre has several entries, including *West Beirut* (1996), *In the Battlefields* (2004), and in particular *Zozo* (2005). Each of these films fundamentally depends upon the naiveté of its protagonist for the developments within its narrative, for it is only his or her inability to comprehend the ideological rationales of the ongoing war that allows for the story's development.

While by no means as aesthetically innovative as *Bashu* in terms of cinema language, Joseph Fares's film *Zozo* shares broadly with Beyzai's film its interest in challenging war pieties through its employment of the traumatic narrative of a young boy looking for protection and community after the death of his family. In *Zozo*, the narrative strategy of examining the war through the eyes of an orphaned boy allows two simultaneous threads to emerge. The first is that of a naive perspective, one that is presented as pre-ideological and even pre-identitarian in constitution.[22] The second is the opening of the film to vistas of fantasy as a form of traumatic recuperation of meaning in the face of incomprehensible loss. In this setting, *Zozo* shares with *Bashu* a concern with the manner by which traumatic experience may be articulated by survivors, and the extent to which it is possible for those in their new social setting to acknowledge their experiences.

Zozo is the youngest child in a middle-class family comprised of his parents and a brother and sister. In an early scene, the family gathers around a cassette tape player to listen to a recording mailed to them by Zozo's grandparents, who have fairly recently sought refuge in Sweden to escape the war. The family is also planning to join the grandparents, as soon as arrangements are in place to do so. At this point, the diaspora is represented purely as a refuge and escape from the violence of the civil war. The question of trauma is generally absent from the early scenes of the film, as in these sequences Zozo plays with his friends, attends school, and enjoys a pleasant and relatively comfortable home life. The war is only an intrusion at one point when he and his family rush to a shelter with other residents of his building when shelling occurs close by.

However, this sense of relative calm, even while the war grinds on, is eventually broken. Just days before the family is to leave, Zozo walks down his street to go to school, and a mortar shell explodes above him, hitting his family's apartment. He and his older brother converge in the doorway to find their parents and sister dead. They flee together and find themselves pursued by gunmen. Eventually his brother hides Zozo in a dumpster and leaves with a promise to return shortly, but never does. Here, Zozo is beset by traumatic reactions, as represented in a dream sequence where he is visited by a bright light. He shouts at the light, "Who are you? What do you want with me?" but receives no reply. Other aspects of fantasy also begin to intrude upon the harsh reality of living alone in a war-torn city. He finds and picks up a small chick, and finds that the bird speaks to him in the voice of a man. He carries out conversations with the animal, while sitting in the rubble of destroyed buildings. Eventually, Zozo is able to reach the airport and with the assistance of a sympathetic soldier, he makes use of the tickets his parents had purchased before their death to fly to Sweden.

The second half of the film depicts Zozo's experiences in Sweden, following fairly conventional diaspora themes relating to the difficulties with assimilation and the experience of social alienation. Zozo lives with his grandparents and attends a local school, but is unhappy there and unable to make friends. The trauma of having lost his family, marked by the recurring dream of the bright light, hangs over him as he attempts to learn Swedish. In one scene, after his grandfather is hospitalized for a heart attack, Zozo collapses in their apartment and breaks down emotionally, fearful of losing yet another family member. In these scenes the trauma of the war haunts him and intrudes upon and intensifies the alienating experiences of having to adapt to a new society.

Eventually, Zozo befriends a quiet outcast in his class and finds in his new friend's eccentricities a sense of freedom and individuality. However, this does little to improve his social standing in the school, and the two of them are bullied and harassed. Eventually, in the film's climactic scene, Zozo confronts the bullies, and as they begin to beat him, mortar charges begin to explode around the school grounds. In this fantasy sequence, the trauma of diaspora is overlaid by the prior trauma of war. Yet, the melodramatic structure of the film aims to find a definitive resolution to this trauma. In this sequence, Zozo's dead mother appears, pulling him to safety as the mortars explode around them. Zozo asks to

Figure 3.1

Figure 3.2

go with her, but with her encouragement he finally finds a resolution to the trauma of her death, and at that moment the explosions cease. The scene restarts, revealing the prior scene to have been only a traumatic fantasy, and rather than fighting the bullies, Zozo and his friend ignore their taunts and walk away. In the next and final scene, Zozo and his new friend stand fishing and joking in Swedish in a lakeside park with his grandparents sitting behind him—the traumas of both war and diaspora now apparently resolved.

Zozo uses the youthful naiveté of its young protagonist to probe the artifices of sectarian identity, and to deliver a broadly antiwar message, idealizing his European refuge even while acknowledging the struggle that Zozo undergoes to find acceptance there. Yet *Bashu* goes further in using its protagonist to mark out a world outside of the ideological impositions of wartime Iran, for in choosing a remote northern Iranian village setting, the action of the film occurs in a social context that appears to be completely ignorant of the war being waged on the country's border. This allows for the villagers to displace a degree of ethno-racial prejudice toward the darker-skinned Bashu, but frees their relationship of the problematic dialectic of Persian and Arab that underscored the war's divisions. Bashu, as an Arab Iranian, falls on the fault line of war discourse, which occasionally did make use of anti-Arab Persianist chauvinism.[23] This dislocative strategy in *Bashu* (removing the young war victim from the front lines and placing him in a setting where the war has little if any social imprint) is one significant way by which sacred defense discourse is denied any place within the film.

Rather than imagining the home front as a site of committed support for soldiers sent to the battlefield, the village here is a location free of the marks of war. This allows Beyzai to set the conflict of the film in terms that exceed or at very least escape the defining terms of sacred defense. Bashu's journey does not bring him to a better understanding of his role within the cosmological battle that sacred defense imagines—rather, his story is one of finding radical reconfigurations of family and belonging despite the trauma of wartime losses. Bashu is fundamentally alienated not only by his ethno-linguistic difference, but also by the fact that the villagers have no way to comprehend (and he has no way to narrate) his experience of trauma. These alienating factors only stoke Bashu's traumatic memory and prevent him from what otherwise may be a full integration into the village society. As in *Zozo*, traumatic memory is woven through the fabric of the quotidian, as Bashu frequently experiences hallucinations of his dead parents and flashbacks to the experience of war.

In representing Bashu's traumatic memory, Beyzai layers two or more temporalities within a single cinematic space. This layering produces

Figure 3.3

Figure 3.4

open-ended interpretive possibilities, a strategy that threatens the putative coherence of sacred defense discourse by illuminating the limits
and impossibilities of commensurability between traumatic experience
and its representation. In one scene, Bashu is working with Na'i, having
achieved a degree of integration in the family. However, within the village he is still subject to harassment and ostracization by other children.
The young boys of the village have gathered at the gates of Na'i's property and laugh as Bashu begins to experience what seems to be the effect
of a flashback, triggered by the fire of a tannour clay oven.

While he shouts at the family to seek cover, the boys first mock
and mimic Bashu, before storming into the yard to fight him. Bashu
attempts to fight back, but the scrum is only ended when Na'i throws a
pail of water over the group, pulling Bashu aside. Thrown to the ground,
Bashu first reaches for a rock, as if to use it as a weapon, but then moves
over to pick up a textbook that has fallen on the soil. As Na'i scolds the
boys, Bashu begins to read the stock text of the textbook, in Persian:
"Iran is our country, we come from one soil, one spring. We are the
children of Iran." The boys circle him and begin to ask him questions,

Figure 3.5

Figure 3.6

among them, "Where are your mother and father?" and finally, "What happened to your school?" As if in response, Bashu picks up the rock and throws it, hitting a small wood structure and knocking it apart. The collapse of the structure is filmed from three angles, and replayed three times. Then the children look back at Bashu, and he looks away.

While in *Zozo* the traumatic response to the protagonist's confrontation with a group of peer tormentors is that of a violent fantasy sequence, in *Bashu* this response is one in which the worlds of symbolic and linguistic meaning collide. Bashu is able to mount the linguistic barrier between himself and the boys in the village by displaying a knowledge of formal Persian, which is taught to both ethnic groups as part of the national curriculum mandated within their schools. However, when the boys press him to explain his personal history, Bashu reverts back to the symbolical communication which he had been compelled to employ previously, telling his story through an abstracted gesture. Throwing the rock and shattering the small wood structure, Bashu has expressed his memory of loss in the only way available to him—nonverbally. This sub-linguistic form of communication is charged with primal knowledge and ritual, and emphasized through Beyzai's staging and framing of the action.[24] Beyzai intimates that Bashu's path through trauma is one that cannot be resolved through language.

While this scene is often cited in discussions of the film for its overt insertion of the nationalist recuperative statement, "We are all Iran's children," there is much more to the scene when viewed as a whole.[25] On first glance, the scene seems to intimate a resolution to Bashu's crisis, by his recourse to the use of the national language, Persian, and the nationalist discourse found in the textbook. However, a more complex viewing of the entire scene, from the traumatic flashback that is its beginning, to Bashu looking away in the final shot, requires a reconsideration of this reading. The scene begins with the most explicit depiction of traumatic symptoms in the character of Bashu, who is portrayed as suffering a psychotic hallucination triggered by the sight of the fire of the clay oven. His traumatic reaction is, however, a trigger for his harassment by the village children, whose giggling overlays his cries for them to take cover from what he believes is an imminent attack. While his recitation of the communal discourse of the textbook in the common national language of formal Persian promises to end his alienation from the village children, the end of the scene seems to set limits on this hopeful outcome. When asked to learn about his reasons for being in their village, Bashu is still unable to communicate linguistically. His experience is incommensurable to the nationalist discourse he has just recited, and is still beyond linguistic representability. There exists a gap between the precomposed text found in the schoolbook and his ability to communicate, and he resorts instead to an act that is semiotically open, lacking the ideological closure that linguistic iteration would produce. Bashu's traumatic experience has resulted in an aporia caused by the ideological fixity of the formal language taught in the schools, a crisis of meaning that cannot be resolved easily. The gaze of the children, which moves from the structure back to Bashu, is not met by his eyes. His turning away restates the line of incommensurability that exists between the official nationalist discursive realm—the only realm where he and the boys have a common language—and that of his traumatic experience. This moment fundamentally undermines attempts to create a foreclosed-upon state discourse on the war, what would become sacred defense discourse, and charts personal traumatic memory as marked by a crisis of representability.

However, Bashu's trauma later eventually proves a cause for his integration into the family. In the final sequence of the film, Na'i's husband returns to the village, potentially threatening Bashu's position in the family. Na'i and her husband argue over Bashu, with her husband critical of her decision to adopt him into the family. It is unclear if Bashu understands the discussion, but he rushes to confront Na'i's husband with a stick, shouting twice, "who is this man?" Na'i's husband finally replies, "father," omitting any possessive pronoun to indicate whose father he believes himself to be. Bashu then extends a hand in greeting, to which Na'i's husband is unable to reciprocate, given that he has lost his arm. Bashu, recognizing this, suddenly rushes to embrace "father" and bursts into tears. Na'i's husband communes with Bashu in their shared loss; it is as if they immediately perceive their commonality in trauma. Constituting a family now, in the very last scene of the film the three of them set out to chase away the wild animals that have been terrorizing the farm.

The ending of *Bashu* is nonetheless more open-ended than that of *Zozo*, which seems to idealize an eventual "integrative" solution to the

Figure 3.7

Figure 3.8

traumas of its young protagonist. In *Bashu*, the family is still threatened and must come together to defend their home. Bashu's complementary role in replacing the lost appendage of the father, thus completing the incomplete family, is in essence a different one from that of *Zozo's* final scene, set at a peaceful lakeside, where Zozo finally has found a place in his new home, Sweden, mastering his new language, making friends while in view of his approving grandparents. The integrationist message here accords directly with European official discourse on immigration. Given the film's funding by Swedish and EU agencies, it may not be surprising that this end hardly constitutes a counter-narrative to Swedish self-projections of its role as a benevolent and tolerant refuge. One may go so far as to say that *Zozo* uses the traumas of the Lebanese civil war to actively promote a view of European multiculturalism that is at odds with the rising right-wing populism of the People's Party in Sweden and of other ultra-nationalist parties in other parts of Europe.

While *Bashu* may be seen to mirror sacred defense narratives that focus upon the sacrifices of the family in pursuit of the war's aims, it does so in a way that ultimately is subversive to the sacred defense. The cathartic resolution of sacred defense narratives, often coded in the sacrificial death of the father/husband, aims to expunge traumatic irresolution through a sacred valorization of his death, and the redemption of the family through this loss. In *Bashu* this redemption instead comes from a reconstitution of the family in terms that radically rethink the boundaries of this institution. A young Arab Iranian boy has arrived within this Persian Gilaki milieu in order to compensate for the functional loss of the father's arm, but both retain traces of their traumatic exclusions. The lack of a referent to the sacred defense themes, and indeed the visible nature of the continued traumas of both Bashu and Na'i's family, are deeply unsettling to the sacred defense discourse, constituting a treacherous questioning of the coherence of this discourse.

* * *

Bashu adopts the narrative strategies of other home front war films, presenting a family compelled to seek reconstitution after its losses, and resolves it through the overcoming of ethnic particularism in this quest. A comparison to *Zozo* shows both a shared use of the formal device of a child protagonist to question and challenge predominant interpretations of the war and the use of memory discourse to frame the war in ideologically limiting ways. *Bashu* may be seen as participating in some of the conventional techniques that are at the heart of sacred defense narratives, particularly in its melodramatic structure and through the resolution of the narrative in terms of the re-constitution of a heteronormative family. Yet, in nearly every other possible manner, *Bashu* refuses to participate in the fundamental tropes of sacred defense treacherously, rejecting the ideologizing of memory that sacred defense themes demand. Beyzai's film sets the question of loss within the framework of ethnic and regional difference in Iran, and the need for a reformulation of national identity so as to overcome the traumas of the war. What motivates the form of radical community imagined in *Bashu*—radical in the sense of its challenge to ethno-linguistic particularism—is the shared experience of loss. Bashu's adoptive family is one that has "lost" a father, and this absence is shown to be essential to the boy's acceptance. This becomes most radical when the film is able to suggest the little boy as a (temporary) replacement for the missing father. In this way, the film achieves what so many war films set within domestic spaces attempt to do—that is, to imagine a reconstitution of the family, usually through the return of the father. In *Bashu*, the father does return, but he bears the indelible marks, the wounds, of the family as well as of the nation at war. He has lost an arm, and it is only through the inclusion of Bashu into their family that a sort of compensation for his lost limb is imagined. By taking on the role as compensatory object for the trauma-scarred body of the father, Bashu is again fully constituted within the national family. However, the way this occurs allows for no valorization of sacrifice, no brotherhood of fighters, no cathartic death to pay blood to the war ideals. The traumas of the war are instead displaced within the fantasies of reconstituting the self, reconstituting the family, in ways that are fundamentally at odds with the ideologized memory discourses produced and promoted in support of the sacred defense.

NOTES

This article draws from material published in the monograph *Surviving Images: War, Cinema and Cultural Memory in the Middle East* (New York and Oxford: Oxford University Press, 2015).

1 I explore sacred defense cinema and the shifting parameters for heroism and treason in more detail in *"The Glass Agency:* Iranian War Veterans as Heroes or Traitors?" in *Traitors: Suspicion, Intimacy and the Ethics of State-Building,* S. Thiranagama and T. Kelly, eds., Philadelphia: University of Pennsylvania University Press, 2010. 188–200.

2 Paul Ricoeur, *History, Memory, Forgetting,* 448.

3 Freud, "Screen Memories," 1899.

4 Bourdieu's field of cultural production provides an understanding of the state-led definitions of the culture of sacred defense in a way that is more useful than comparable theoretical models, by viewing culture as a series of interrelating "fields" that may be subject to legitimation either by the state or by other actors, but which are also subject to forms of contestation and resistance in struggles that involve accumulation of cultural capital by the competing actors.

5 This council was later renamed Anjoman-e Sinama-ye Enqelab va Defa'-e Moqaddas (The Council on Revolutionary and Sacred Defense Cinema). Alireza Sajadpour, "Sepah ulgu-ye sarmaye gozari-ye salem dar sinama," Chehrehha-ye Aftab. Mehr 1382 (2003): 52.

6 The work of Seyyed Morteza Avini remains the paradigmatic example of the marriage of documentary technique and ideological aims in line with state policy, and is definitive of sacred defense culture in its first, highly committed, phase. Avini's documentaries—collectively called "Revayate Fath" (Tales of Victory)—present witnessing-discourse through footage of front-line sacrifices set against commentary by Avini, framing the quotidian struggles of the soldiers within a discourse of metaphysical collisions between good and evil, and the search for martyrdom as a path toward God. Avini's films rarely speak of the enemy in terms of national identity, but rather posit the battle as a transcendental field of conflict where the lessons of past Shi'i martyrs are put into practice by young Iranian soldiers in an abstracted, and cosmologically dense, battlefield which operates both as a literal front line and as an allegorical stage for performing the codes of commitment to revolutionary ideals. For more on Revayat-e Fath, see chapter 3 of Roxanne Varzi's book, *Warring Souls.*

7 Sune Haugbolle, "Public and Private Memory of the Lebanese Civil War," 193.

8 As Mark Westmoreland comments, "Some Lebanese filmmakers also critique the predominance of Western funding for feature films, believing that this dependence negatively dictates what gets made and how it gets made [. . .] Some also critique the West's fascination with watching the Arab world at war, saying funding for films that probe into the 'civil' war is easier to come by than other themes." Westmoreland, "Cinematic Dreaming," 47–48.

9 Dominic LaCapra, *Writing History, Writing Trauma,* 23.

10 Sa'id Mosteghasi, "Janr-e sinama-ye defa'-e moghaddas dar Iran," 147.

11 Pedram Partovi, "Martyrdom and the 'Good Life' in the Iranian Cinema," 519.

12 Varzi, *Warring Souls,* 79.

13 Partovi, "Martyrdom and the 'Good Life' in the Iranian Cinema," 516.

14 Zeydabadi-Nejad, *The Politics of Iranian Cinema*, 38.

15 Varzi, *Warring Souls*, 98.

16 Zeydabadi-Nejad, *The Politics of Iranian Cinema*, 52.

17 Ibid., 50.

18 Zabihollah Rahmani, "Filmsazi baraye defa'-e moghaddas tofigh ast: Goft o gou ba Abolqasem Talebi, filmsaz va rooznameh negar," 45.

19 Mohammad Khazaei, "58 Film az 36 keshvar jahan dar jashnvareh film defa'-e moghaddas," Bani Film, 26 Tir, 1389 (2010). Accessed online, November 26, 2011, www.bfilmnews.com.

20 It is worth noting that scholars differ on the dating of *Bashu*, primarily because the film was not released for some two or so years after its completion: Zeydabadi-Nejad cites 1985 (109), Dabashi, 1986 (91), and Mottahedeh 1987 (20). The problem leads to different dates being cited in the same edited volume. In Tapper's *New Iranian Cinema*, Tapper himself suggests 1988 in the introduction of the book, but then in her chapter in the volume Azadeh Farahmand cites date of 1986 for the film (105), while in her contribution to the same work, Nasrin Rahimieh cites 1985 (238). As both Rahimieh and Mottahedeh confirm, the film was in fact completed in 1985 but was withheld from release until later due to political problems faced by Beyza'i in those years. Mottahedeh cites the date of 1987 for its release, while Rahimieh cites 1988 (a distinction perhaps presented by the ambiguity that accompanies converting Hijri Shamsi dates to Gregorian ones). After reviewing a wide range of materials on the film, I have found 1987 to be the most likely date for its release.

21 It is unclear if this is due to the war, or to some workplace injury; the only hint comes when Na'i asks him, "Couldn't you find any other kind of work?" This statement seems to indicate the injury was not war-related. However, for an Iranian audience in that period, the image of a man who has lost an arm cannot but conjure associations with war injuries.

22 I discuss the use of a naive perspective in trauma literature in "Trauma and Maturation in Women's War Narratives: The Eye of the Mirror and Cracking India," *Journal of Middle East Women's Studies* 2, no. 2 (Fall 2006): 23–47.

23 Rahimieh's analysis of the film focuses on this question. Nasrin Rahimieh, "Marking Gender and Difference in the Myth of the Nation," 238–253. Anecdotally, as a child growing up in Shiraz during the war, I observed fairly widespread anti-Arab racism toward internally displaced war refugees in my school and elsewhere, often paradoxically on the presumption that they shared an ethnic link with the "enemy." However, sacred defense rhetoric rarely made use of such prejudice, given that it made use of transcendental religious claims and not claims based upon national or ethnic difference.

24 Dabashi's discussions of the film emphasize the ritual and mythical elements present in the work. Hamid Dabashi, *Close Up Iranian Cinema*.

25 Both Rahimieh and Mottahedeh discuss the scene at length, using rather different but not incongruent approaches. Mottahedeh's reading focuses on semiological

dimensions of the work, arguing that the film must be read against "ta'ziyeh's spatial tropes." Rahimieh, "Marking Gender and Difference in the Myth of the Nation," and Negar Mottahedeh, *Displaced Allegories, Post-Revolutionary Iranian Cinema* (Raleigh: Duke University Press, 2008), 20–48.

WORKS CITED

Dabashi, Hamid. *Masters and Masterpieces of Iranian Cinema*. Los Angeles: Mage Publishers, 2007.

Dabashi, Hamid. *Close Up Iranian Cinema*. New York: Verso, 2001.

Freud, Sigmund. "Screen Memories," 1899.

Haugbolle, Sune. "Public and Private Memory of the Lebanese Civil War." *Comparative Studies of South Asia, Africa and the Middle East* 25, no. 1 (2005): 191–203.

LaCapra, Dominic. *Writing History, Writing Trauma*. Baltimore: Johns Hopkins University Press, 2001.

Mosteghasi, Sa'id. "Janr-e sinama-ye defa'-e moghaddas dar Iran." *Farabi* 11, no. 2 and 3, 147–155.

Mo'azzi-Nia, Hossein. "Chand nokte dar morede hamzisti-ye sinama-ye Iran va sinama-ye defa'-e moghaddas." *Mahname-ye naghd-e film*, no. 7, 27–29.

Partovi, Pedram. "Martyrdom and the 'Good Life' in the Iranian Cinema of Sacred Defense." *Comparative Studies of South Asia, Africa and the Middle East* 28, no 3. (2008): 513–532.

Rahimieh, Nasrin. "Marking Gender and Difference in the Myth of the Nation: A Post-revolutionary Iranian Film." In Richard Tapper, ed., *The New Iranian Cinema: Politics, Representation and Identity*. New York: IB Tauris, 2002. 238–253.

Rahmani, Zabihollah. "Filmsazi baraye defa'-e moghaddas tofigh ast: Goft o gou ba Abolqasem Talebi, filmsaz va rooznameh negar." *Soureh* no. 40, Azar 1387 (2008): 42–51.

Ricouer, Paul. *History, Memory, Forgetting*. Chicago: University of Chicago Press, 2004.

Varzi, Roxanne. *Warring Souls: Youth, Media, and Martyrdom in Post-Revolutionary Iran*. Raleigh: Duke University Press, 2006.

Westmoreland, Mark. "Cinematic Dreaming: Phantom Poetics and the Longing for a Lebanese National Cinema." *Text, Practice, Performance* 4 (2002): 33–50.

Zeydabadi-Nejad, *The Politics of Iranian Cinema: Film and Society in the Islamic Republic*. London: Routledge, 2009.

4

War Veterans Turned Writers of War Narratives

M. R. GHANOONPARVAR

Writers of fiction often rely on their imagination in their work, and professional writers are able to recreate scenes, events, and incidents of actual or imagined wars by imagining them. In contrast, some of those who experience war first hand, especially as combat soldiers, write about those experiences using the format of memoirs, and on occasion in the form of novels and short stories. The creative process for these veterans who have become writers of fiction is the reverse to that of what I have called professional writers. They fictionalize the actual traumatic events they have experienced.

Although two world wars, the Korean War, as well as many other conflicts occurred in the past century, the Iran-Iraq War turned out to be the longest war in the twentieth century, lasting eight years. During that war, both countries were trying to cope with the losses of human life and the destruction caused by the war. As in all wars, each side was convinced that it was right and that it had God on its side. Each side believed itself to be fighting for Islam and Muslims and regarded its adversaries as infidels and inhumane. Iranians termed the conflict "The Sacred Defense" (defa'-e moqaddas) and "The Battle of Truth against Falsehood" (jang-e haqq alayh-e batel), while the Iraqi government at the time, terming the war "The Second Qadessiyyeh," tried to appeal to the sentiments of pan-Arabism in Iraq as well as other neighboring countries and justified its aggression as a campaign to liberate the minority Arabic-speaking population in Khuzestan and the region, which it called "Arabistan." The propaganda machines of both sides were also at work. Such efforts in Iran included a relatively large number of books of poetry and fiction in addition to movies produced mainly for television, all of which were sponsored by government-affiliated organizations and naturally advanced the official view. Thematically, these poems, stories, and films emphasize such notions as martyrdom, heroism, camaraderie among Islamic combatants, and self-sacrifice. The Islamic soldier, these works maintain, unlike the mercenaries who fought on the Iraqi side or in other wars throughout the world, fought for Islam and God and not, like others, for material and worldly gain. While the Iranian soldiers are portrayed as compassionate, faithful, and devout Muslims, the Iraqi enemies are generally presented as either bloodthirsty fiends or misguided victims of the machinations of Saddam Hussein and his Western supporters.

Examples of the poetry published in the early years of the war are found in a volume called *She'r-e Shahadat* (*Poetry of Martyrdom*), published in 1988 on the recommendation of Ayatollah Khameneh'i.[1] Among the important works of fiction, *Esma'il Esma'il* (1981) by the well-known writer Mahmud Golabdarreh'i, is about the sense of duty an old shoemaker and his son feel when their country is occupied by the enemy.[2] Even stories written for children and young adults were viewed by many writers as a vehicle for propaganda. In a recent book entitled *Adabiyyat-e Kudakan va Nowjavanan-e Iran va Dastan-e Jang* (*The Literature of Children and Young Adults and the Story of the War*), writer and critic Mohammad Reza Sarshar writes that a group of "committed writers" during the war made a patriotic effort to write stories for children in which, wittingly or unwittingly, they pursued one or several of the following objectives:

> At that astonishing predicament and turning point in history when every honorable Iranian would find it mandatory on the basis of his religious, national, or human duty, as his or her contribution, to take some steps in this connection, they [the writers] wanted to play their proper role. In other words, with their fictional work, they wanted to support their people's struggle and resistance until the ejection of the enemy and to make the enemy regret his aggression.[3]

Further stating that these writers wanted to bring the voice of the victimized people to the ears of the free people of the world and show the savagery of the aggressive enemy and his supporters, Sarshar adds that "by recording the self-sacrifice and bravery of the committed people of their country, they wanted to bear witness to all this greatness and in this way to pass it on to the future generations."⁴ Moreover, according to this critic, their purpose was to commiserate with the children and young adults harmed by the war and help them cope with the new and difficult conditions and in this way provide them with an essential and gradual solution to the problems. In the same vein, Sarshar believes that such authors intended to show the children and young adults the special predicament in which the country had been placed, and to reveal to them their place under such conditions and help them to assume their proper historical role by fully understanding those conditions. By taking advantage of the completely "special and divine feelings" created on the front and in the war, Sarshar observes, these writers wanted to spread this "rare and special culture" among the children and young adults and help to "spiritually uplift" their readers. He then continues:

> Benefiting from the adventurous and heroic spirit of the children and young adults, while making use of the endless sea of stirring events and incidents of the war, they wanted to prepare appealing stories coupled with valuable models and themes for them, since the extraordinary novelty of the subject matter and the climate, the greatness and severity of the events, the high dramatic weight, and the great excitement hidden in the events—regardless of the content and the value of the task—would bestow on the subject matter of the Sacred Defense such high fictional value that neglecting it by any writer of fiction would be a clear disregard for his or her own professional fortune and the loss of an absolutely rare and exceptional opportunity.⁵

Sarshar's language and tone alone are indicative of the zeal and passion expected and found in this type of fiction advocated by the state and advanced by its propaganda machine. An example of the type of stories for children and young adults that Sarshar advocates is "Naqqashiha-ye Abud" ("Abud's Drawings") by Qodsi Qazinur.⁶ A group of young children, mostly boys, are playing in an alley in a relatively poor working-class neighborhood. With the war going on and the fact that many young men from the neighborhood are serving on the front or have been "martyred" by the Iraqi forces, the war has also become a part of the children's daily life and they decide to play a war game. They determine that they need to form two teams, the Iranian and Iraqi "soldiers," but no one wants to play an Iraqi. The narrator's younger brother also wants to play, and he is only allowed to join the game if he plays an Iraqi soldier. The problem is the game becomes divisive and even members of the same family begin to consider the members of the opposite team as real enemies. A new boy then appears on the scene. Abud is a refugee from the war-stricken southern region who does not want to play the war game. "War is not a game," he says to the others, who initially think that there is something odd about him. Abud's experience of the war is first hand. The next morning, he brings some drawings he has made about the war and explains how members of his own family and his friend were killed by the Iraqis. When asked if one of the drawings shows the picture of his school that was destroyed, Abud says, "Yes, but it is now occupied by the Iraqi soldiers." He then adds:

> I wish that was all they had done. They are going to destroy everything. When my younger sister heard on the radio that her school was taken over, she cried in her sleep all night . . . My father was baking bread for soldiers on the front when a bomb killed him. My brother's head was smashed by a piece of grenade, while fighting. Now my mother talks with them in her sleep every night.[7]

Even though a writer of children's stories such as Qodsi Qazinur intends to educate her young readers about the horrors of war through this and her other stories, she inadvertently also serves the purpose and the goals advocated by Sarshar. The narrator's older brother is going to be deployed to the war front. When their mother begins to cry because she realizes that her son is going to leave the next day, the older brother consoles her by saying, "You know, Mom, that most of the boys in the neighborhood are at the front now! You're not alone, thank God!" The mother's unfinished response, "I wasn't complaining, son . . . ," indicates that her devotion to the Sacred Defense is greater than the possibility of losing her son, thus advancing the ideas promoted by the government.[8]

The government-sponsored Sureh-ye Mehr Publishers, which is affiliated with the Islamic Arts Center usually referred to as Howzeh-ye Honari, has regularly published books as well as other publications about the Iran-Iraq War, including novels, short story collections, and memoirs. The Office of the Literature and Arts of the Resistance

(Daftar-e Adabiyyat va Honar-e Moqavemat) in this publishing house lists a large number of titles in this series under various headings, such as "Qesseh-ye Farmandehan" ("The Stories of Commanders"), "Majmu'eh-ye Qessehha-ye Shahr-e Jangi" ("The Stories of the War-Stricken City"), "Zanan va Jang: Majmu'eh-ye Ketabha-ye Khaterat-e Zanan dar Jang" ("Women and War: Memoirs of Women in the War"), and "Khaterat-e Azadegan" ("Memoirs of Freed Prisoners of War").[9] Even though two decades have passed since the Iran-Iraq War ended, the continuous publication of these books is an effort not only to keep the memory of the "martyrs" (*shohada*) and "self-sacrificers" (*janbazan*, i.e., disabled veterans) alive, but also to make certain that the history of that war is written by those who advance the official view of the government.

Habib Ahmadzadeh's collection of short stories, *Dastanha-ye Shahr-e Jangi* (*A City under Siege*), chronicles first-hand experiences of the war by young patriotic soldiers.[10] "Oqab" ("Eagle") is a dramatic monologue of a member of a small resistance team who through binoculars is watching an Iraqi soldier on the road to the city of Khorramshahr during the Iraqi occupation of that city. Having done this routinely for some time, the narrator knows that it will only take twenty minutes for the Iraqi soldier to be within range of fire, whereby the narrator can inform his teammates via wireless radio to launch a mortar. Addressing the Iraqi soldier, who cannot hear him since there is a distance of several kilometers between them, the narrator describes the scene and his own thoughts and emotions as well as what he imagines to be those of his adversary, minute-by-minute and toward the end second-by-second, as the Iraqi soldier progresses toward his fate. In a way, his narrative is a justification of why he must kill his enemy, whom he imagines to be someone like himself but devoid of his "principles." Remembering that his own aunt is married to an Iraqi and lives in Basra, the narrator imagines that the soldier might be his own cousin, but still he says: "You might ask what if you are the son of my aunt, would I still press the button on the wireless? The answer is, Yes, I will."[11]

"Havapeyma" ("Airplane") is about a soldier who arrives in Halab-cheh after the chemical bombing by Saddam's forces.[12] The narrator remembers that as a child he had seen a toy airplane in a store that he wanted to have but that the shopkeeper would not sell to him. At that time, in his childish imagination, he had wished that he had the power to make people freeze in a state of suspended animation for a few moments so he could take the toy airplane. In Halabcheh, he can now see what he had imagined, people frozen motionless, but dead.

Habib Ahmadzadeh was a navy commander during the Iran-Iraq War and his perspective in *The War-Involved City Stories* is that of a biased soldier. This bias is also evident in the other stories of the collection, including "Si-o-noh va Yek Asir" ("Thirty-Nine and One Prisoners"), in which a young soldier is assigned to transport a group of blindfolded Iraqi prisoners of war to a prison camp, fearing that they might discover that he is the only one watching them. In another story, "Nameh'i beh Khanevadeh-ye Sa'd" ("A Letter to Sa'd's Family") the narrator tells the Iraqi soldier's family that the Iraqi military had actually executed their son for desertion several years earlier and left him at the side of the road tied to a post as a warning to others who might refuse to fight, and that is where the narrator had found him and buried him.[13] Interestingly, this volume of short stories also includes a letter the author wrote and sent to Captain Will Rogers, the former captain of the USS *Vincennes*, who was allegedly responsible for ordering the Iranian airbus shot down on July 3, 1988.[14] In this letter, as well, Ahmadzadeh's main purpose is to convince the American officer and others that while the Iranian side was defending the country and fighting on the right side and for sacred principles, the adversary, in this case the Americans, similar to the Iraqis, was fighting for material and worldly gains. These views are shared even by a critic, the prominent poet Manuchehr Ateshi, who in a review states that, unlike the war literature of other nations, "Our war stories are stories of resistance and of the truly Sacred Defense."[15]

Mohammad Reza Bayrami's novel, *Pol-e Mo'allaq* (*The Suspension Bridge*), is also based on his own experiences as a soldier during the Iran-Iraq War.[16] Nader is an anti-aircraft artillery air force officer who blames himself for having failed to shoot down the airplane that bombed his family's home, killing all of them. Depressed and alienated from society, he has volunteered to serve in a remote area in the mountains of Lorestan, where a vital railroad bridge has been destroyed recently by Iraqi bombs. The temporary suspension bridge, which is erected over the roaring river and is still the target of enemy bombers, represents Nader's state of mind; he describes himself as a "sleepwalker" and a person who has reached "the end of the line." Remembering his fatalist father who would refuse to go to a shelter during air raids, Nader has also become a fatalist and believes that he has no control over his destiny. In contrast to Ahmadzadeh's stories in which the protagonists and narrators are conscious of the enemy as individuals with families, lives, and aspirations similar to themselves, albeit fighting on the "wrong" side, Bayrami's story describes a dehumanized war. The two sides of the conflict are represented by the airplanes that drop the bombs and the anti-aircraft guns that try to shoot them down. To Bayrami, man in this war is abandoned by God. Nader has even lost the ability to weep:

> Once again he found himself by the river, all alone, looking at a demolished bridge. Why was he incapable of crying so that perhaps he could calm down a little? Why had God even taken this gift from him? He could not endure it any longer. He realized that he was about to collapse. He sat down on the ground. He said: "Oh God! I am neither Christ nor is this Golgotha. By Your glory, either take my life or give me respite!"[17]

The aforementioned objectives outlined by Sarshar are also pursued in other media, particularly cinema. Despite the traditional objections of the religious establishment and devout Iranians to cinema, which they regarded as a place of debauchery, sin, and Western cultural influence, with the change in the political system and the start of the Iran-Iraq War, the Islamic regime found the cinema to be a useful tool in the propagation of its ideology, particularly in rallying support and recruiting soldiers for its war with Iraq. A slogan that is often repeated and appears at the beginning of some movies and in movie theaters quotes Ayatollah Khomeyni: "We do not oppose the cinema; we oppose debauchery (*fahsha*)." Hence, various government organizations began to produce feature films about the war, mainly for propaganda purposes, which were shown on television.[18] Depicting battles very realistically in terms of cinematic technique, the story plots of these films are generally simple, straightforward, and formulaic. Unlike the "new wave" Iranian films, which were at times rather abstract and therefore often inaccessible to ordinary audiences, following established narrative conventions and appealing to the emotions of the audience, these films are entertaining and can sustain the viewer's interest to the end, since, in Hollywood terms, they are generally action-packed and suspenseful. An example of a film that can be entertaining and at the same time serve a propagandist and ideological purpose is *Balami Besu-ye Sahel* (*Sailing toward the Shore*; 1984). Written and directed by Rasul Mollaqolipur, the film focuses on the fall of the city of Khorramshahr to the Iraqi forces. It begins with the "heroic" resistance of the Revolutionary Guards in the city in their confrontation with the much larger and better equipped Iraqi forces. They await the arrival of a regiment from Ahvaz, which is delayed because the regular army, instructed by President Bani-Sadr, does not provide the Guards with helicopters for transportation. Nevertheless, despite the overwhelming odds, the Guards reach Abadan in small boats and start their operation to liberate Khorramshahr. The Iraqis are depicted as a cowardly group of infidels who kill innocent people, even a man who is standing at prayer. They loot people's homes and businesses, which, the film conveys to the audience, is in effect the only incentive they have as soldiers. On the other hand, the Iranian Revolutionary Guards are all devout Muslims who display great heroism and camaraderie and are always ready to sacrifice their lives and become martyrs for their cause. The film is dedicated to several "martyrs of the battle of Khorramshahr," who are mentioned by name. Even some of the actors, who may actually be Revolutionary Guards, are listed as martyrs.

In the wake of the war, however, while the government and many of its supporters still held firmly to their previous view of the war, other views began to emerge in the arts in general, particularly in fiction and film, that challenged the official discourse. Films such as Bahram Beyza'i's *Bashu, Gharibeh-ye Kuchak* (*Bashu, the Little Stranger*) and novels such as Davud Ghaffarzadegan's *Fal-e Khun* (*Fortune Told in Blood*) and Ahmad Dehqan's *Safar beh Gara-ye 270 Darajeh* (*Journey to Heading 270 Degrees*) are notable examples in which the artists present a humanistic account of the war and the experiences of war, rather than a sectarian and nationalistic one.[19] Such stories and films, in fact, challenge the previously dominant government discourse regarding the war. In other words, two contending histories of the Iran-Iraq War are being written, each claiming to tell the true story of that war.

The expression of the view in fiction that challenges the government discourse is by no means exclusive to the postwar period. Anti-war fiction written and published during the war includes Qazi Rabihavi's

Vaqti Dud-e Jang dar Asman Dideh Shod (*When the Smoke of War Was Seen in the Sky*; 1981), Nasim Khaksar's *Man Solhra Dust Daram* (I Love Peace; 1981), Qodsi Qazinur's *Vietnam Gavahi Ast* (*Vietnam Is Proof*; 1980), Ahmad Mahmud's *Zamin-e Sukhteh* (*Burned Land*; 1981), and Esma'il Fasih's *Zemestan-e '62* (*Winter of '83*; 1987), which expressed the sense of frustration, helplessness, and desperation of Iranians suffering the death and destruction caused by the extended outreach of modern warfare to their cities and villages. With regard to feature films, however, there were obviously more restrictions, and it was at the end of the war and when the ceasefire was agreed on by the two governments that anti-war films were allowed to be shown. An important feature film that deals with the effects of the war on the soldiers who fought it is Mohsen Makhmalbaf's *Arusi-ye Khuban* (*The Marriage of the Blessed*), which appeared in 1988. Equally significant in terms of its anti-war theme but more important in artistic terms is *Bashu, the Little Stranger*, by the renowned film director Bahram Beyza'i, which was made in the same year, although its distribution was not allowed until the early 1990s.

In fiction, Ahmad Dehqan's 1996 novel *Journey to Heading 270 Degrees* is among the most important postwar novels, in which its author, a veteran of the war with first-hand experience of the battlefield, takes a step back, as it were, and casts a sober and sobering look at the war in a tangible form, and also at its effects on and consequences for those who fought in it.[20] The story chronicles in a journal format the day-to-day experiences of Naser, a teenage soldier, who has already experienced several battles in the Iran-Iraq War. Having served his tour of duty, he returns home, but soon realizes that his friends and comrades have returned to the front and he feels left out. Hence, persuaded by a former comrade, he returns to the front and, given his record of service and previous experience in the war, he is eventually put in charge of an anti-tank squad with the assignment of helping to break through the Iraqi forces, which have superior weapons and equipment. The battle is one of the most devastating and many of Naser's fellow combatants lose their lives. Although lucky to have survived with only a shrapnel injury, Naser is not certain whether his dead comrades are not better off, since they do not have to return home where ordinary people go on with their lives as if nothing has happened and seem oblivious to the terrible experiences of young veterans such as Naser, who have encountered the horrors of war first hand.

Similar to Dehqan's *Journey to Heading 270 Degrees* and Makhmal-baf's *The Marriage of the Blessed* is Davud Ghaffarzadegan's novel *Shab-e Ayyub* (*Ayyub's Night*), which deals with the physical and psychological consequences of the war for those who fought in it.[21] *Ayyub's Night* is a nightmarish account of a young veteran's recollections of when, at the age of fourteen or fifteen, bored with school and envious of his friends who had volunteered for the Basij Resistance Force (Niru-ye Moqavemat-e Basij), he enlisted and, after completing a short period of training, was deployed along with his classmates to help with the war effort. Like his friends, Ayyub has also concealed his decision from his family. He recalls:

> When the bus began to take off, we already knew that we had left behind one period of our lives. Everything had gone well and we four guys, who had lived near the river, were going to war. We felt a sense of pride we had never experienced before and we already felt as if we were holding our guns in our hands.[22]

Ayyub had been trained as a rescue worker and soon, amid the sound of artillery and the smoke of war, he realizes that war is not a game: "We did not have any idea about our distance from the front line, but we could hear the sound of artillery; and now for the first time we could see death flying and circling above our heads, and we were completely in a new situation."[23]

Before long, one of his friends is killed and the narrator, who is wounded, returns home for treatment. He goes back to school; but guilt, depression, alienation, and a sense of not belonging eventually make him realize that he can no longer live as if nothing has happened:

> I was restless at the exam session and did not know how I should write down the answers. I had studied well, but I was shaky because others were on the front and I was sitting at a school desk. I did not know why. Once a person has experienced the front line, staying at home is hard for him, and now that my wounds had healed and I had completed training

for helping chemical weapons victims, I was in a hurry to get the last exam over and return to the front.[24]

Although *Ayyub's Night*, similar to Dehqan's *Journey to Heading 270 Degrees*, depicts gruesome scenes of battle, its central focus is on the physical and psychological effects of war on individuals who experience it. Ayyub eventually loses his eyes, perhaps, the reader is led to assume, as a result of exposure to chemical warfare agents; but more devastating are his recollections of the war and his nightmares, with which he is forced to live in darkness.

* * *

In a volume of short stories entitled *Jazireh'i Baray-e Tab'id-e Kaghazparehha* (*An Island for the Exile of Paper Scraps*) by another war veteran, Majid Teymuri, which are reminiscent of the ramblings of a patient in an insane asylum, the final paragraph of the last story presents the nightmarish thought processes of one of the patients, who suffers from the psychological effects of the war. His hallucinations provide the reader with perhaps a more telling account and history of that war:

I killed them. They themselves wanted to die; I am not a murderer. They themselves said, even when you see a camel, you pretend that you didn't. And I agreed. I'm not a pigeon fancier, I haven't been a reader, I've never ridden a camel, I have not committed a murder, I have not asked for a prayer writer, I haven't had a mother, I have had nightmares, I haven't figured out the past, I'm a *warrior*, a model soldier. I have not received service discharge papers, I've been wounded, I've put on my wedding suit, I've gone on a trip, I'm on leave, look at the sky!—suddenly several birds appear circling above my head—enemy airplanes! It's a red alert. On the ground everyone! Start shooting the antiaircraft guns! Come here, little bird . . . come . . . coo . . . coo . . . catch that cross-eyed one. Give it seeds. Turn off the lavenders! Remove the radioactive barrels from the area! Pit the nightmares of those who suck blood against those who drop bombs on each other in a war! Make holes in all the boats! Give spoiled yogurt to those who are in love! Cancel all leaves! Disrupt the wedding celebrations! Make faces at those who are making memories for themselves! Shoot at those who do not bend down to ride a camel!—several of those in white gowns are coming and pulling me off the platform—we have proven that when there is a war, the camel does not see anything in his dreams.[25]

Another remarkable story also published in 1996, but this time from a different perspective, is Davud Ghaffarzadegan's *Fortune Told in Blood*.[26] In 1995, when Ghaffarzadegan finished writing this story, perhaps enough time had passed for the extremely hostile emotions to subside to some degree and for both nations, or at least many people in both countries, to begin to view certain human attributes in their adversary, in a sense to humanize the enemy. As mentioned, much of what had been produced and sanctioned by the government in Iran in the form of poems, stories, and films during the war had directly or indirectly served as war propaganda to demonize the enemy, dealing with themes such as self-sacrifice and martyrdom, and while depicting Iranians as embodiments of these virtues, they present a dehumanized picture of the enemy. But following the tradition of the antiwar literature and film mentioned earlier, Ghaffarzadegan's *Fortune Told in Blood* goes one step further. It humanizes the Iraqi enemy. This aspect of his work can be regarded as a positive development, especially in the context of the animosity that was ignited particularly by the anti-Iranian rhetoric of Saddam Hussein and his regime, which advertised the war as "the second Qadesiyyeh," with reference to what is known as the Battle of Qadesiyyeh in the seventh century, when the Islamic Arab army invaded the Persian Empire.

Fortune Told in Blood is an internal novel for the most part, but it is also a story of interaction primarily between two individuals from different classes: an ordinary conscript from a lower, working-class Iraqi family and an educated officer, also a draftee. But they also have much in common. They look to the future with both hope and uncertainty, and in the course of their close association on the top of a mountain, where they have been assigned as lookouts for enemy troop movements, they begin to know each other, as well as themselves. They learn about loyalty to their country and government, but also, more importantly, about loyalty to each other as human beings. They have been cast in an extraordinary situation in which their courage is tested, but they also face and are tested in terms of what they come to realize is the meaning of life, their own individual but also collective human existence. The intimate glance, as it were, that Ghaffarzadegan allows his readers at the two fictional characters, individuals who happen to be Iraqis, encourages a sense of empathy. To the reader, it is no longer the Iraqi soldiers who are the object of disdain but the war itself. *Fortune Told in Blood* is a story of death and destruction, but as the characters confront death, we also find a confrontation with life and an understanding of the value of life.

The humanization of the enemy can of course be seen in Ghaffarzadegan's choice of characters and the story he tells. But it is also addressed by the character of the young soldier who, from a distance and through binoculars, can empathize and even identify with people he is supposed to regard as enemies.

Ghaffarzadegan's novel was published in Iran at a time when many veterans of the war were gradually looking back and trying to reassess the war and their own role and place in the society. With the experiences of thousands of young people, many of whom were trying to cope with their disabilities, with their experiences as prisoners of war, and with other consequences of the war, a new discourse began among the veterans that divided them into two camps, a division that has continued to the present. One camp consists of those who still adhere to the political and ideological rhetoric of war time, e.g., referring to the conflict as the "Sacred Defense" and the "Imposed War" (*jang-e tahmili*) and considering it a sacrilege to question the reasons for it. The other group is comprised of those who are trying to view the war and their experiences with a more sober outlook. To the first group, the members of the second are regarded as traitors to the idea that the Iran-Iraq War was the "war between good and evil," the Islamic Republic and Saddam's regime. One critic from the first camp, for example, even reprimanded the translator of Ahmad Dehqan's *Journey to Heading 270 Degrees* for translating this novel into English, which was published in the same year as *Fortune Told in Blood*. With regard to Ghaffarzadegan's novel, which was published in the same climate of conflict, however, given that Ghaffarzadegan was not a veteran of the Iran-Iraq War, to some extent his book was disregarded by the first group of critics while praised by readers in the second camp, and it went through a second printing in less than a year.

In light of the popularity and increasing interest in the works of writers such as Ahmad Dehqan and Davud Ghaffarzadegan and filmmakers such as Bahram Beyza'i and Mohsen Makhmalbaf, among others, and also considering the prominence of these artists in Iran, one might predict that, despite the attempt by supporters of the official discourse who, with government backing, try to silence proponents of the opposing view, future generations may find the true story and eventually accept it as the true history of the Iran-Iraq War in novels such as *Journey to Heading 270 Degrees* and *Fortune Told in Blood* and in films such as *The Marriage of the Blessed* and *Bashu, the Little Stranger*.

NOTES

1 *She'r-e Shahadat*, compiled by the Public Relations and International Unit of the Foundation for the Martyrs of the Islamic Revolution (Tehran: Edareh-ye Koll-e Entesharat va Tablighat-e Vezarat-e Farhang va Ershad-e Eslami, 1367 [1988]).

2 Mahmud Golabdarreh'i, *Esma'il, Esma'il*, 3rd printing (Tehran: Kanun-e Parvaresh-e Fekri-ye Kudakan va Nowjavanan, 1363 [1985]).

3 Mohammad Reza Sarshar, *Adabiyyat-e Kudakan va Nowjavanan va Dastan-e Jang* (Tehran: Entesharat-e Sureh-e Mehr, n.d.), p. 3.

4 Ibid.

5 Ibid., pp. 3–4.

6 Qodsi Qazinur, "Naqqashiha-ye Abud," first appeared in the journal *Bidaran* in 1981. An English translation of this story called "Aboud's Drawings" by Soraya Sullivan is available in *Stories by Iranian Women Since the Revolution* (Austin: Center for Middle Eastern Studies, University of Texas at Austin, 1991), pp. 88–99.

7 Ibid., p. 99.

8 Ibid., p. 96.

9 A recent list of these books is found in Seyyed Qasem Yahoseyni, editor and interviewer, *Zeytun-e Sorkh: Khaterat-e Nahid Yusefian* (Tehran: Entesharat-e Sureh-ye Mehr, 1387 [2008]).

10 Habib Ahmadzadeh, *Dastanha-ye Shahr-e Jangi*, 8th printing (Tehran: Entesharat-e Sureh-ye Mehr, 2007).

11 Ibid., "Oqab," p. 24.

12 Ibid., "Havapeyma," pp. 29–42.

13 Ibid., "Si-o Noh va Yek Asir," pp. 57–74; "Nameh'i beh Khanevadeh-ye Sa'd," pp. 93–103.

14 This 12-page letter along with email correspondences of several U.S. Navy officers as well as a number of news reports about the incident are included in both Persian and English in this edition of *Dastanha-ye Shahr-e Jangi*, pp. 3–46 and 146–203.

15 Manuchehr Ateshi's review, which was first published in *Majalleh-ye Kaman* 3, no. 41, p. 14, is included in *Dastanha-ye Shahr-e Jangi*, p. 115.

16 Mohammad Reza Bayrami, *Pol-e Mo'allaq*, 5th printing (Tehran: Nashr-e Ofoq, 1382 [2003]).

17 Ibid., p. 102.

18 For a more detailed discussion of these films, see M. R. Ghanoonparvar, "Iranian War Films: Entertainment and Propaganda," *Iranian War Cinema*, edited by Pedram Khosronejad (forthcoming, 2008), and also "Moruri bar Chand Film-e Sinema'i-ye Tablighi dar Dowreh-ye Jang-e Iran va Eraq," *Mehregan* 2, no. 3 (Fall 1993): 93–99.

19 Davud Ghaffarzadegan, *Fal-e Khun*, 2nd printing (Tehran: Mo'asseseh-ye Entesharat-e Qadyani, 1376 [1997]); Ahmad Dehqan, *Safar beh Gara-ye 270 Darajeh* (Tehran: Nashr-e Negah-e Emruz, 1380 [2001].

20 This novel has been translated by Paul Sprachman as *Journey to Heading 270 Degrees* (Costa Mesa, CA: Mazda Publishers, 2006).

21 Davud Ghaffarzadegan, *Shab-e Ayyub* (Tehran: Entesharat-e Sureh-ye Mehr, 1386 [2007]).

22 Ibid., p. 35.

23 Ibid., p. 56.

24 Ibid., pp. 129–130.

25 Majid Teymuri, *Jazireh'i Baray-e Tab'id-e Kaghazparehha*, 2nd printing (Tehran: Nashr-e Cheshmeh, 1382 [2003]), p. 72.

26 For an English translation of this novel, see Davud Ghaffarzadegan, *Fortune Told in Blood*, trans. M. R. Ghanoonparvar (Austin: University of Texas Press, 2008).

5

Between Betrayal and Steadfastness

Iraqi Prisoners of War Narrate Their Lives

DINA RIZK KHOURY

Two iconic photographs symbolize the distinct meanings that Iranian and Iraqi governments ascribed to the figure of the prisoner of war. The first is of thousands of Iraqi prisoners of war taken in April 1982 in the wake of the beginning of retreat of Iraq from Iranian cities. Iraqi soldiers sit facing the camera, unshackled and holding large pictures of Khomeini and the executed Iraqi Shi'i cleric Muhammad Baqir al-Sadr. The other is of an Iranian prisoner that graced the cover the Iraqi weekly *Alef Ba* on March 5, 1986, a few weeks after the Iranians conquered Faw. The Iranian soldier's face is buried in his chest, his hands tied behind his back and his eyes covered with a green bandana emblazoned with the name of Imam Husayn that he had bound, before his capture, around his head. For the Iraqi government, the figure of a single Iranian prisoner is meant to highlight the subjugation of the Iranian soldier to the will of the Iraqi soldier, a metaphor for the eventual military defeat of the Iranian enemy. The Iranian prisoner was not a soldier of Imam Husayn, rather he was a blind follower of a regime that manipulated religion for its own ends. In contrast, the Iraqi soldiers are portrayed as a disciplined mass, organized in rows of converts to Khomeini's Islamic Republic and recruits for the Da'wa Party whose spiritual leader was the executed Sadr. They were to become enlightened believers in the message of the Islamic Republic and enlisted as foot soldiers for the overthrow of the "atheistic" Ba'thist regime.

More than 100,000 soldiers were captured by Iran and Iraq during the war years. Of these some 70,000 were Iraqis. The capture, treatment, and exchange of these prisoners became part and parcel of the wrangling, often mediated by the International Committee of the Red

Cross, between the Iraqi and Iranian governments until the fall of the Ba'th regime.[1] But such wrangling did not confine itself to the realm of high politics. For most of the Iran-Iraq War, prisoners of war were hostages in an intense ideological battle between Iran and Iraq, a battle at which the Iranian government and its Iraqi allies in Tehran were much more successful than their Iraqi counterparts. While the Iraqi government subjected the Iranian prisoners of war to re-education sessions, sometimes run by their Iranian allies among the Mujahidin al-Khalq, their main purpose was to extract information, often through torture, from their prisoners.[2] By contrast the Iranian government and its Iraqi allies wanted to convert their prisoners, asking them to publicly recant their allegiance to the Ba'thist state by declaring their support "*bay'a*" to Khomeini.

In all sixteen prison camps, Iraqi prisoners were subjected, often by their own compatriots, to a systematic and relentless policy of "conversion" aimed at destroying their former selves and creating new ones. The purpose of the policy was twofold: to transform the prisoners into believers (*mu'minun*) by forcing them to repent their beliefs in Ba'thism, and to rehabilitate them by recruiting them into the military wing of the Iraqi Islamist parties fighting alongside Iran.[3] The religious and transformative terminology that infused the process and gave it cover was the same as that applied to imprisoned Iranian political opponents of the Islamic Republic.[4] However, Iranian political prisoners were tortured to recant their former political allegiances and not their national allegiances. Iraqi prisoners of war were forced to suspend their national identity since that was tantamount to an allegiance to the Ba'th. In addition, they were systematically recruited to preach, pressure, and sometimes torture other prisoners to survive. The result was to create a prison culture in which an elaborate hierarchy of degrees of collaboration and resistance existed among the prisoners.

The experiences of Iraqi prisoners of war do not easily fit into narratives of victimhood, collaboration, or resistance, in which narrators presuppose the existence of an "authentic" self that tells the "truth" against the hegemonic narratives of the state. Nor do they easily fit into nationalist myths of a heroic Iraqi soldier and prisoner steadfast in his loyalty to comrades and nation. Iraqi prisoners switched allegiances, reported on their comrades, held steadfast, and rebelled against their prison conditions. Often the same Iraqi prisoner was both resister and collaborator, torturer and savior. I use three sets of narratives produced by Iraqi prisoners of war under radically different contexts to illustrate that personal narratives, whether produced to bear witness or as state documents, are artifacts. As anthropologist Allen Feldman reminds us, they are produced in conversation with legal, institutional, and other constraints that make it difficult to posit an authentic self, separate from the context and idioms within which it was produced.[5] The question that emerges from these narratives is not what is authentic and what is true, but how, under what circumstances, and for what purposes is truthfulness produced. I use depositions taken by Ba'th party interrogators of returnees, testimonies written by prisoners of war during the 1990s, and an oral interview I conducted with a former Iraqi prisoner of war in the summer of 2007.

During the Iran-Iraq War, institutions of public culture and party propaganda were invested in creating the mythology of an Iraqi soldier heroically battling the enemy. Insofar as the prisoner of war appeared in the press or in the literature on war, he was a heroic victim of Iran's flouting of international laws on humanitarian treatment of prisoners. In 1982, the government designated the first day of December as Martyr's Day in commemoration of the execution of Iraqi prisoners of war by Iranian soldiers in the battle of Bostan a year earlier. The choice of the date was deliberate. It highlighted the inhumanity of the Iranian government's actions, and it absolved the Iraqi government from its responsibility for the death of its soldiers. They did not die in the heat of battle, but as victims of Iranian atrocity. Although the press covered the mistreatment of Iraqi prisoners of war, there was complete silence in the press about the scale of imprisonment and the divisions within the Iraqi prison population.

The figure of the Iraqi prisoner of war took center stage in Iraqi public culture in the 1990s. The repatriation of close to 57,000 over the course of the 1990s, their deposition by the Ba'th party and security service, and their re-integration and rehabilitation became a burden on a financially strapped state during the embargo years.[6] At the same time the government was concerned with the return of Iraqis who had a history of collaborating with Iran and who had connections with opposition parties active in Kurdistan and Iran and now were supported by the

United States. Finally, the borders with Iran were so porous, and Iraqi sovereignty in the south so tenuous, that returning prisoners were often able to go back and forth between the two countries. Many had families in both countries as well. Thus, the issue of repatriation and the control of movement of Iraqi prisoners became a bone of contention between Iraq and Iran during this period. The Iraqi government pushed for their repatriation, insisted that it obtain the names of prisoners who refused repatriation, and organized days of solidarity with Iraqi prisoners of war whenever it determined it politically expedient to do so. The propaganda war, however, intensified around times of negotiation between the two countries over the return of prisoners. There was an intense propaganda campaign in 1991–92 and again in 1997–98. [7]

It is within the context of the politics of the 1990s that prisoners of war wrote their depositions and Ba'th party cadres produced their reports assessing the possibilities for their rehabilitation. Ba'th party commissars in Iranian prison camps and their counterparts at home kept close track of the prisoners of war and their families. Party commissars who had been prisoners themselves devised a system of classification that assigned guilt to collaborating prisoners of war according to a hierarchy used by the regime in the 1990s to reward and punish returning prisoners. Soon after the largest repatriation prisoners took place in the summer and fall of 1990, the regime designated the prisoners who had "converted" as "apostates" (*murtadun*) using a religious language that echoed that of the Iranian regime. [8]

The reports collected by the local branches of the Ba'th party were taken from several categories of prisoners: Ba'thist commissars who were repatriated at different times in the 1990s, the bulk of them coming in 1990; prisoners who had been "converted" and been repatriated or had infiltrated back to Iraq through the porous borders in the Kurdish north or the south in the 1990s; and prisoners who had been recruited into the Badr brigade, the military wing of the Supreme Assembly of the Islamic Revolution in Iraq. [9]

The reports were written to produce a certain kind of knowledge about prisoners of war that allowed the state to group them and their families in a hierarchy of rewards and punishment dependent on their level of resistance and collaboration. They were written with four purposes in mind. Of utmost important was the information that returnees provided on prisoners who had collaborated or resisted within the prison camps. Every deposition by a prisoner, whether a "heroic" Ba'thist commissar or a "convert," included a list of names with information about the level of collaboration of the prisoner. Thus, prisoners who were guards, preachers, or defectors to the Badr brigade were deemed more difficult to rehabilitate into the nation than those who had simply manned the prison system's facilities. The reports were also written with a view to compensation or punishment. Those written by Ba'thist commissars were geared to elicit rewards for heroism. Those who resisted were grouped, as were those who were steadfast (*samidun*) and those who were exceptional (*mutamayizun*). The latter consisted of those who led resistance cells or rebellions and were punished by the Iranians.[10] Other reports were written by friends or relatives of those who had been killed by the prison authorities for their refusal to "convert." The purpose was to list these as martyrs and allow their families entitlements due to martyrs of the war. Finally, there are reports by conscripts who appear to have been converts but had not actively collaborated with the enemy. These listed the various methods of torture the conscripts had to endure and listed the names of collaborators. The prisoners emphasized their need to survive as the justification of their conversion and requested that they not be included in the category of active collaborators. The third purpose of these reports pertained to security. Returning prisoners of war had to be monitored at all times because they might establish links with opposition parties in Iran or Iraqi Kurdistan. Finally, these reports had much to do with the problem of rehabilitating prisoners. The state and the Ba'th party attempted to re-integrate prisoners, even those who had converted out of "weakness" and psychological breakdown back into society. Reeducation, visits to families, and active attempts to recruit them into the Ba'th party were some of the ways proposed by the Ba'thist authors of these reports.

Although these reports were produced under the auspices of Ba'th party organization and were meant to be formulaic in their depiction of resisters and collaborators, as texts they exhibit some noticeable variations that complicate our understanding of the narrator as a truth teller. The deposed prisoner was asked by his own compatriot to inform on his comrades. Only then would he be rehabilitated, forgiven as an "apostate," and accepted into his nation. As in the prison camp, he had to tell a certain kind of truth to survive. This included his place in the prison system and the names of collaborators and their function in the prison camps. Yet, within the narratives provided by returnees, there is a hidden text that provides a challenge to the officially accepted narrative. Reports written by Ba'th party prisoners list the names of collaborators, their place of origin, and their addresses. Reports written by conscripts, some of them converts, list only the names of collaborators and their place of origin. In other words, although they inform on others, they do so with some elisions. One has to remember that in Iraq there is no use of family names and there must be a great number of people in Shamiyya or Nasiriyya, Shi'i dominated cities from which a large number of converts were drawn, with such names as Hamza Hasan. They were hard to track down by the state.

The second aspect of these reports is the marked difference in prose. Ba'thist prisoners of war wrote texts replete with Ba'thist language that described their sponsorship within the prison camps of celebrations of the founding of the Ba'th on April 7, the birthday of the great leader on April 28, and Army Day on January 6. The language of the reports is political, speaking of the sectarianism of the collaborators and the Iranians, of the heroism of the Ba'thist commissars who resisted the prison system. The language of the reports by the rank and file is much sparer, often closer to colloquial, and some of it written in rough script. They emphasize their physical pain, their hunger, their torture, and their conversion as a means of survival.[11] Again, the idiom here, as it was in the prison camps, is to survive, to ask for the mercy. While in the prison camps that mercy allowed prisoners access to necessities of biological survival; for the returnees, mercy meant that they would once again be included into the nation even as they continued to be branded as apostates.

The story of an apostate, a *murtad*, who fought in the Badr brigade, that appears in the Ba'th party records in 1999, illustrates the difficulties of drawing a distinct line between official and "authentic" narratives of imprisonment. As an Iraqi, the prisoner's designation of apostate defined his relationship with the state and the party and determined his and his family's access to entitlements. Within local Ba'th party offices, there was a special committee that oversaw the affairs of returning prisoners of war. They reported on the apostates regularly. This particular repatriated prisoner of war had changed his place of residence from Madinat Saddam in the eastern section of Baghdad, in part to avoid the close monitoring of the party and security service. We know the details of his life mainly because they were collected by different party organizations that were investigating his disappearance.[12]

The prisoner hailed from the city of Amara in the southern border province of Maysan, one of the main centers for the movement of troops and home to a strong opposition movement to the Ba'th led by the Da'wa party. He and sixty others were taken prisoner in March 1982, in the battle of Dezful. He was released in 1998 through an International Committee of the Red Cross prisoner exchange. He had been married with children when he was conscripted into the army. As he was never registered with the International Committee of the Red Cross, his wife had thought he was dead and had married someone else. When he returned she divorced her second husband and remarried her first.

In Iran, he was imprisoned with 1,500 other Iraqi soldiers. While there, he was contacted by an Iraqi who sought to convert him and threatened him with torture. He agreed to join the converts and was subjected to political and religious indoctrination. The Iraqi who was the leader (his exact position is not clear in the text), had a list of soldiers he wanted to recruit to the Badr brigade. Worried about his fate if he joined the Badr brigade in the event that the war ended with an Iraqi victory, he was told that he would be given the option to settle in Iran. Reassured, he agreed to join to get out of the prison camps. The Iranian Hezbollah then took him to a camp for two months of military training. The first month was devoted to ideological indoctrination and the second to military training. He then joined the Badr brigade in Khorramshahr where he stayed until the "events of Kuwait," the officially sanctioned euphemism used by the Iraqi state to talk about the first Gulf War. He appears to have supported the rebels in the Intifada of 1991 by taking food to the border town of Tannuma, outside the city of Basra. When Saddam Husayn issued a general amnesty for the apostates in 1993, he decided to go back to Iraq through the Kurdish north, where the Kurdish nationalist parties were in control. He was betrayed by his handlers and imprisoned by the Iranians. After his repatriation in 1998, he was processed at the Prisoners of War processing center in Jalawla in Diyali province and he provided the requisite set of apostates to his handlers.

There are two striking features of the handwritten text provided by the apostate from Madinat Saddam. First was the use of the non-Ba'thist sanctioned term to talk about collaborators. Reports written by returnees who were Ba'thist commissars employed the terminology used by prison camps to designate the hierarchical system set up by prison authorities to differentiate between the prisoners' degree of collaboration from converts, preachers, torturers, and military recruiters. They often alluded to the collaborators as agents—weak, unmanly, and easily manipulated. They were never referred to as Iraqis, their behavior rendering the use of the term untenable for the Ba'thist commissar and difficult to explain to his superiors, who insisted against all evidence to the contrary that no "true" Iraqi could become a convert. By contrast, our apostate insisted on using the term Iraqi to designate converts. They were not outside the fold of the nation, they were Iraqis and their behavior in the prison camps in no way deprived them from that identity.

The other feature of the report is the elision of certain events, the blurring of time lines, a feature absent from all the reports of high-ranking Ba'thist commissars. The prisoner was captured in 1982 but only joined the Badr brigade in 1984. His narrative does not explain his role in the prison camp in the intervening years. Nor does he make clear his level of participation in the 1991 uprising. Neither victim nor hero, he fashioned for himself a space as a reluctant collaborator. He was, according to his report, one of many Iraqis who played that role.

The figure of the prisoner of war took on multiple meanings in the public culture of Iraq during the 1990s. Not all were consistent with the narrative of a nation that had fought a heroic battle against Iran. On the one hand, the various institutions of state, particularly that of the Ministry of Culture and Information and the Ba'th party apparatus, sought to portray and publicize the stories of returning prisoners who had persevered despite their deprivation and isolation. On the other, the institutions of public culture had to account for the fact that many of these prisoners had not always been steadfast, that they had collaborated with an enemy that continued to support Shi'i Islamist parties seeking to overthrow the regime.

A wide range of stories about and by prisoners, both heroes and apostates, appeared in the press and in media outlets, particularly in the late 1990s. They are distinguished from the depositions of prisoners undertaken by the party as the framing of the narrative rather than its content. These were framed in the form of narratives of witnessing. They were set up as "truth" telling venues, to speak of stories of great suffering, perseverance, and resistance. For the apostates, they offered a venue to reconvert to the nation, to repent yet again for their "repentance" in Iranian prison camps. Yet, a great deal of the information given in these testimonies drew on depositions of Ba'ath reports, with some crucial differences. Unlike the narrative of the reports, in which the returnee functioned as an informant on other prisoners within the confines of party offices or processing centers, the witnessing of prisoners was invested with very public meanings. The prisoner's biography was meant to tell the story of the Iran-Iraq War as much as it was meant to affect reconciliation, establish difference, and elide some truths. These narratives were venues of retelling publicly what had been largely a hidden story. The juxtaposition of the stories of apostates with Ba'thist prisoners was meant to highlight the heroism and importance of the party as representative of the nation, and the weakness of those who succumbed. Both, however, were victims of the Iranian prison system that had sought to divide Iraqis along sectarian lines. The nation and its leader rewarded the loyalty of those who were steadfast and forgave the transgression of those who had not.

The redemptive and moralistic character of these truth telling narratives concealed and helped mitigate some hard political and social realities in Iraq of the 1990s. The heroism of the Ba'thist commissars in these narratives elided the fact that many Ba'thists, Sunnis, and Shi'is within the prison system had "converted" under pressure of torture and deprivation, a fact that unpublished reports written by Ba'thist commissars highlighted. Furthermore, as the stories of apostates were at all times those of men from the Shi'i south, the narratives of the prisoners who had succumbed served as a metaphor for the transgression of the Shi'i southern population against the regime during the 1991 Intifada. In prison as during the Intifada, they had been victim to the sectarian propaganda of the Iranian government. Finally, the biographies of the prisoners of war stood as a metaphor for Iraqis living the deprivation of sanctions and the betrayal of sections of their own population who were now allied to Iran and the United States. Those who persevere have moral rectitude and those who succumb can repent and return to the fold.

Two testimonies serve to illustrate the highly contextual nature of truth telling. The first appeared in the newspaper in 1997 in the midst of negotiations with Iran over the return of prisoners of war, including those who had fought in the Badr brigade. The apostate in question had joined the Badr brigade and had returned to Iraq despite the pressure by the Iranian government to remain in Iran and his fear of being arrested and tortured by the Iraqi government. These fears had proved unfounded, and the former prisoner was now living among his family and loved ones, had felt no pressure from the Iraqi government, and was enjoying the generosity of Saddam Husayn, who had granted him some form of entitlement.[13]

The testimony is telegraphic, meant to gloss over the troubled history of the Badr brigade, its collaboration with Iran during the Iran-Iraq War, and the implication of its political leadership in the conversion and torture of Iraqi prisoners of war. The purpose of the testimony is to re-integrate the apostate back into Iraqi society, to highlight the lies propagated by Iran, and to position Saddam Husayn as the generous and forgiving father of the nation. While not denying the truth of the prisoner's biography, the testimony is above all a call to forget the political realities and repercussions of the Iran-Iraq War as it is an attempt to rehabilitate its most problematic figure.

The second testimony is drawn from a collection of biographies of prisoners of war that appeared in book form in 1999. Entitled *The Language of Lashes*, it was published by the main government press in Baghdad and was meant to document the testimonies of twelve prisoners of war who had persevered in Iranian prison camps.[14] Not all the prisoners were drawn from the Ba'th party; a few were military leaders and one was a member of the Republican Guard. Some had spent as much as sixteen years in imprisonment, were subjected to many forms of torture, and were moved to high-security prisons because of their participation in hunger strikes and other acts of resistance.

Two aspects of these testimonies distinguished them from the reports. The first is a clear attempt on their part to position their experience in the context of humanitarian law, in large part as a response to the Iraqi government's continued efforts to bring the issue of Iraqi prisoners of war to the United Nations. While the testimonies mention the role of Iraqis in oppressing their countrymen, the narratives highlight prison conditions as well as the Iranians' role in creating and maintaining these conditions. At the same time, not all Iranians within the prison system are portrayed as a unified enemy. Some accounts provide a nuanced picture of prison camps, emphasizing the difference in the treatment of prisoners by those who belonged to the military and those who belonged to the Revolutionary Guard. Some draw attention to the struggle within the Iranian religious establishment in the camps over interpretation of dogma. All mention the lack of sanitation and frequent illnesses that developed among prisoners because of lack of sufficient healthcare and food. All emphasized as well the techniques of torture that prisoners were subjected to, including the use of cables to lash prisoners, solitary confinement, lack of sleep, repeated insults, and myriad other forms of pressure. The second component of these testimonies is their exclusion of narratives by apostates. When the latter appear, they do so as an arm of the oppressive prison system, as a problem that needs to be addressed not through reconciliation but through the careful parsing out of levels of collaboration. Written in the context of a humanitarian crisis brought on by the sanctions regime, and clearly geared to provide the example of Iraqis who survived and resisted under imprisonment, isolation, and great political pressures, these testimonies employed witnessing by heroic prisoners to highlight the ability to persevere against great odds.

Salam Wahb Abbas al-'Ubaydi was imprisoned on March 24, 1982 and repatriated on April 4, 1998. A commander of a brigade, he was taken prisoner outside of Dezful. A high-ranking member of the Ba'th party and member of the National Assembly, clearly he was a prized prisoner to the Iranian authorities, who had been apprised of his identity by apostates and military intelligence. al-'Ubaydi records his interrogation and torture by prison authorities, particularly after he attempts to organize a Ba'th party cell in his prison. More than a year after his imprisonment, he is moved to a new prison camp to isolate him from his comrades, this time one that was almost completely controlled by apostates. Here again, he tries to organize a party cell and is sent to a special court in Tehran, tortured, kept in solitary confinement, and then moved to another prison camp twenty kilometers outside of Mashhad, where he joins 2,000 Iraqi prisoners who had persisted in fomenting rebellion within the prison system. He continues to be moved around throughout the early 1990s and is finally moved to a central prison in 1995, where he was confined until 1998.[15]

al-ʿUbaydi's testimony focuses on resistance, steadfastness, and torture. For a testimony by a Baʿthist commissar, it is remarkably free from the sycophantic vocabulary that peppered the reports of Baʿth party commissars in the depositions mentioned earlier. His attempts at forming Baʿthist cells within the prison system are portrayed as a political act, meant to organize prisoners whose morale was decimated by the continuous attempts to convert them. At the same time, his emphasis on torture and his description of prison conditions brings to light the persistent violation of humanitarian law by the Iranian government.

* * *

The last narrative of imprisonment is an oral interview I conducted in Amman in the summer of 2007.[16] Abu Mukhlis, a reservist who had participated in the war against the Kurds in 1974–75, was called to duty again in 1980. He was taken prisoner at Chalamcha in 1981 after sustaining injuries during battle. His story shares some of the outlines of the reports and the testimonies of the prisoners mentioned above: the hierarchy in prison of collaborators, torture, isolation, and persistent attempts to annihilate identity. However, it is unique because of his position as a refugee who had fled the sectarian conflict in his country. Furthermore, his story is distinctive because it was seldom part of the public narrative on prisoners of war during the 1990s. Perhaps this is due to his marginality both as a Mandaen, a member of a very small minority, and his roots in Maysan province, an area that has been historically difficult to integrate into the nationalist narrative of Baʿthist Iraq. As a Mandaen, he belonged to an ancient community whose religious rituals were tied to Iraq's rivers and whose practices could not be easily subsumed under monotheism of Islam, Christianity or Judaism. *Shrugis*, as the population of Maysan was known, occupied a liminal space in Iraq's national narrative of modernity and integration. Mostly

Shi'a, they were designated by various governments in Iraq as poor and "primitive" marsh dwellers, in need of modernization. Those who migrated to the city of Baghdad, as had Abu Mukhlis' family, resided in the working-class area of Madinat Saddam (currently Sadr City). The Ba'thist government questioned the allegiance of *Shrugis* to the Iraqi state throughout the last two decades of its rule. Maysan had been a haven to deserters throughout the Iran-Iraq War, its population had played a prominent role in the 1991 uprising against the regime, and it was a stronghold for Shi'i Islamist parties. It is within the context of this double marginality and the sectarian conflict in Iraq, particularly of the sectarian killing by Shi'i militants of Iraqi minorities in Sadr City, that Abu Mukhlis' narrative should be situated.

When I interviewed Abu Mukhlis, he had been a refugee in Jordan for two years. He left Iraq after he was kidnapped from his home in Sadr City, where he owned a small jewelry store. For Abu Mukhlis, his captivity in 2005 was a reliving of his thirteen years in Iranian prison camps. He said that his captors in 2005 called him impure (*najis*) and an infidel (*kafir*), just as he and other minorities, Christians, Kakas, and Yazidis, had been called in Iranian prison camps. His narrative is shaped by that identity, and his long captivity and experience are centered on his suffering in prison because he was a minority who refused to convert from his religion. Under different circumstances, he might have told his story emphasizing his refusal to surrender his national identity. Although his narrative had few kind words to say about the Ba'th, he said that the Ba'thist refused to give him his entitlements because he was a *shrugi*; one of the walls in his two-room house had a large picture of Saddam Husayn, the "martyr."

Unlike the reports and testimonies presented earlier, Abu Mukhlis did not address the hierarchy of converts and prison camp officials in the same language as the reports or the public testimonies. He did not use the religious idioms used by the Iranians and the Iraqi Ba'thist within the prison system to describe the hierarchy within the converted population. Nor was he particularly concerned with describing them as traitorous. The prison camp was divided into three groups of Iraqis: those of the advanced and middle ranks within the system who were loyal to the Iranians, and the rest of the prison population who had to survive them. The latter, who were the real prisoners, refused to give the *bay'a* to Khomeini. These included Iraqis from all parts of Iraq, from different sects and ethnicities. However, his narrative above all focuses on the treatment of minorities. For most of his stay, he and other minorities who refused to convert slept, ate, and bathed in separate cells. This was largely owing to matters of purity, as they were regarded as unclean. At the same time, they were subjected to intense pressure to convert, including "debates" with religious scholars who sought to "convince" them to convert. When not convinced, the prisoners were isolated. Abu Mukhlis did get himself in trouble quite often and was known, in his words, as a *mushakis*, a contrarian. He burned the picture of Imam Muhammad Baqir al-Sadr and Bint al-Huda when they were part of the meeting to convert him and others. For that he was placed in isolation after receiving 180 lashes. When he was stationed in Bejort prison, on the borders with the Soviet Union, he hatched a plot to flee with two Christians in his cell. The Christians managed to get close to the border but were arrested. He failed to join them. Nevertheless he was implicated in the plot and punished.

There is another aspect of this narrative that marks it against the others mentioned earlier. Abu Mukhlis could remember with great detail the daily humiliations and deprivations inflicted on him and his cellmates. These were not political, but rather were aimed at subjugating his body: lack of warm clothes, lice, lack of meat in his meals, the half-empty cigarettes given to him and his cellmates, and always the lack of water to bathe. This was particularly painful for a Mandaen, whose rituals were inextricably linked to bathing and notions of purity.

Abu Mukhlis told his story as a victim of sectarian violence in Iraq as part of a linear narrative of victimization by Shi'is that started with his prison camps in Iran. His truth telling is framed within the context of Iraqi politics in the post-Ba'thist period. It is, however, a narrative that consciously attempts to engage the concern of humanitarian agencies and the United Nations High Commission on Refugees (UNHCR) in Jordan about the fate of minorities in Iraq. He presented his repatriation papers from the prison camps at the same time as he showed me a picture of his body, which had been tortured by his captors in 2005. He was planning to submit both to the UNHCR as proof of a consistent pattern of sectarian violence that he had suffered.

Conclusion

The figure of the Iraqi prisoner of war continues to be a controversial one in post-Ba'thist Iraq. As a hero he resisted conversion under inhumane conditions of imprisonment, his life was testament to the resilience of Iraqi national identity and human strength. As a convert he betrayed his nation and his comrades in prison and was an apostate from the nation. While the Ba'thist government had celebrated the former and tried to punish or rehabilitate the latter, the current government of Iraq, whose leaders hold a measure of responsibility in prison camp policies, regards the "converts" as the true patriots who were fighting an oppressive Ba'thist regime by recruiting foot soldiers from the prison population. The continued polarization on the meaning of the figure of the prisoner of war is in large part the result of the state of continuous war that Iraq had experienced for the past three decades. While the Iranian government has successfully forged a modicum of consent over the war as a "sacred defense" under peaceful conditions in the last thirty years, Iraqi governments have not had such luxury. During the 1990s, the Iraqi government assumed that the returnees had come back to a nation that had fought a legitimate war of defense against an Iranian aggressor. The American invasion and occupation brought with it a group of Iraqi political exiles who had spent much of the period of the Iran-Iraq War challenging its legitimacy as a national war, insisting that it was a Ba'thist war, and engaging in recruiting Iraqi prisoners to their cause. The polarization within Iraq about the meaning of the Iran-Iraq War has now taken sectarian and anti-Iranian overtones. Press reports and electronic coverage by various political groups pit the current government and its supporters against those, both Sunni and Shi'i, who insist on seeing the war as one of national defense against a hegemonic and sectarian Iranian enemy with historical designs on Iraq.

The narratives and testimonies of the Iraqi prisoners of war engage this polarized vision of the Iran-Iraq War and the continuous violence that is the legacy of that war. They do not exist apart from it or in opposition to it. What the narratives do, however, is offer a more complicated and specific articulation of "truthfulness" that belies the simple categories of resister and collaborator, victim and perpetrator. The converts became apostates, not because they believed in Khomeini's or the Da'wa's vision of political order, but because they were tortured. At the same time, it is difficult to understand them only as victims, as some of them engaged in the victimization of others. They position themselves in their narratives as victim and perpetrator, informant and repentant, truth telling witness and dissimulator. At the same time, those who steadfastly opposed the prison camp order did so for a variety of reasons. Their public testimonies based on the internal reports to the Ba'th party attest to their loyalty to the party and nation. However, their public testimonies, while based on their experience in the camps, elide their role as informants on other prisoners. Truth telling always involved strategic elisions in the narratives of Iraqi prisoners of war.

NOTES

1 John Quigley, "Iran and Iraq and the Obligations to Release and Repatriate Prisoners of War After the Close of Hostilities," *American University International Law Review* 5, 1(1989), 73–86.

2 Ian Brown, *Khomeini's Forgotten Sons, The Story of Iran's Boy Soldiers* (London: Gray Seal, 1990), pp. 97–117, for Iraqi treatment of Iranian prisoner of war.

3 Ba'th Regional Command Council, Iraq Memory Foundation Archive, Hoover Institution. Hitherto BRCC 01–3665–0001–0006 to 0053.

4 Ervand Abrahamian, *Tortured Confessions, Prison and Public Recantation in Modern Iran* (Berkeley: University of California Press, 1999), offers an insightful analysis of the aim of torture and recantation in a highly ideological regime such as Iran's in the 1980s. Torture used on Iraqi prisoners was similar to that used on political prisoners. Water boarding, solitary confinement, and whipping were some of the methods used.

5 Allen Feldman, "Memory Theaters, Virtual Witnessing, and the Trauma-Aesthetic," *Biography* 27, 1 (2004), 163–201.

6 *al-Qadisiyya*, July 7, 1991, p. 4; November 19, 1991, p. 5; March 21, 1994, p. 5.

7 In March 1997, for example, the government organized activities across for a week to support the return of prisoners of war and highlight their plight. *al-Qadisiyya*, March 16, p. 4; March 24, p. 2; and March 25, p. 4.

8 The use of the term "apostate" by the regime was meant to emphasize that these prisoners had betrayed their sacred duty to their nation and hence deserved their exclusion from rights as citizens. It was up to the Ba'th party and the regime to determine the extent of their inclusion backed by information gathered by its commissars on the individual's level of collaboration within the prison camps.

9 BRCC 01–3665–0001–0013 to 0118.

10 BRCC 01–3688–0034 to 0037.

11 The analysis of these narratives is derived from two box files on prisoners of war, one issued in 1990 and the other in 1999. BRCC 01–3665–0001 and BRCC 01–3856–0001.

12 BRCC 01–3856–0001–0027 to 0043.

13 *al-Qadisiyya*, August 18, 1997, p. 2.

14 Abd al-Mu'min Hamnadi, *Lughat al-Siyat* (Baghdad: Dar al-Huriyya, 1999).

15 Ibid., pp. 47–53.

16 Abu Mukhlis, Amman, August 7, 2007.

6

Stepping Back from the Front

A Glance at Home Front Narratives of the Iran-Iraq War in Persian and Arabic Fiction

AMIR MOOSAVI

In discussions of modern literatures rarely are modern Arabic and Persian fictions brought together in a comparative context. Despite many shared sources and intertwining histories in the classical period and similar trajectories in the development of what are now considered modern literatures, Persian and Arabic literary traditions are seldom brought into conversation with one another. As a result, and despite some more recent attempts to rectify this situation, whether in the form of conferences or publications,[1] scholars and critics of either literature face a lacuna just considering the possibilities of comparison between the two literary traditions, even though both are often housed within the same academic departments.

There are a few reasons for this large gap in comparative work between Persian and Arabic fictions that immediately come to mind. The first is obviously a problem of language; while exceptions certainly exist, few scholars who work on modern literatures function comfortably in both Arabic and Persian. This issue is compounded by the fact that translations of modern literary works rarely cross from Persian into Arabic or vice versa. Translations of modern fiction abound in both languages, but they are largely limited to translations originating from the Americas and Europe. This has meant that there are fairly few pieces of secondary literature in either Arabic or Persian that deal specifically with criticism or the literary history of the other in the modern era. Another reason, perhaps, for the large gap in comparative works is rooted in the differing historical experiences of Iran and many countries in the Arab world. For the countries in the Arab world, the traumas of various colonial encounters, the issue of Palestine and the political currency of pan-Arabism have created different historical markers of major importance from those of Iran, which witnessed the Constitutional Revolution of 1905–1907, the coup against Mosaddeq in 1953, and the 1979 Revolution. This is not to say that events in the Arab world were not felt in Iran or the contrary, but simply to state some of the various ways in which Iran and the Arab world have been on somewhat separate paths over the last century, which complicates the historical grounds for literary comparison.

The Iran-Iraq War, however, does provide an immediate historical context for exploring the possibilities of comparison between Arabic and Persian fiction. The war locked Iraq and Iran into a long and devastating conflict that left incredibly tragic and lasting effects on both nations. During the nearly decade-long conflict, both the Baathist regime in Iraq and the newly established Islamic Republic of Iran embarked on massive campaigns to harness all forms of cultural production and bring them into their war efforts. At the beginning of the 1980s, intellectuals, writers, and artists in both countries often found themselves in difficult positions where they were pressured to produce works in the service of their newly established, 1979 governments' wartime causes or remain silent. To say that a type of government domination of culture existed in both countries to actively support the war effort is an understatement. Indeed, throughout the 1980s both Iraq and Iran witnessed the establishment of two separate "war cultures," to borrow a term and its usage from Patrick Deer's work on British cultural productions during and following the First and Second World Wars.[2] There existed distinct but all-encompassing official war cultures that worked within the discourse of both regimes. The official cultural apparatuses of both countries attempted to exert a process of cultural control similar to that which emerged in the contexts of the First and Second World Wars in Britain, paralleling what Deer observes when stating that "the war planners drew voraciously on whatever lay at hand. Nothing was sacred."[3] Indeed, both nations witnessed states of "total war"—war that stretched from the warfront to the home front, where its proponents sought to engulf all aspects of life.

Shortly after the start of the war in September 1980, the Ba'athist regime in Iraq and the Islamic Republic of Iran each worked to establish cultural arms of their war efforts at the front. Just as the warfront was bombarded with a multitude of weapons by each side, the home front was the site of a cultural and political war that sought to manufacture a unified voice singing the praises of the wartime cause. In addition, each government sought to maintain the unity of their message and righteousness of their cause following the end of hostilities in August 1988. In Iran, this continues until today in a number of ways which will be elaborated upon below. In Iraq, cultural practices related to the war slowed dramatically during the last decade of the twentieth century as Iraq endured crippling sanctions, and came to an abrupt halt in 2003 when the country was invaded by the U.S.-led Coalition of the Willing, toppling Saddam Hussein's regime. Despite the attempts by both sides to create unified war cultures on the home front, independently minded writers, artists, and filmmakers from both countries attempted to present alternative narratives of the war experience that did not harmonize with official narrative. These types of works became increasingly common in the later years of the war and in the postwar period—the focus of this chapter.

In the following pages, after briefly addressing the war cultures established in both Iran and Iraq, I will focus on a few attempts in both Arabic and Persian fiction to write, from the perspective of the home front, about the Iran-Iraq War in the postwar period. I have chosen this period based on the fact that the literary output of both countries throughout the 1980s was almost entirely dominated by the official discourses of both governments. The vast majority of cultural publications, literary or otherwise, that dealt with the war during the years of fighting were commissioned by the governments; what was not directly commissioned was subjected to the terrifyingly Orwellian censors that operated in each country at the time. That said, I am not suggesting that the literary output of the 1980s should be completely ignored, for undoubtedly there were attempts, as rare as they might have been, by writers, critics, filmmakers, and artists—some of which have received some scholarly attention—to show another side of the war. Doubtless, there is plenty of room to explore that era of war narratives in both Arabic and Persian literatures and within other cultural productions; however, that task lies beyond the immediate focus of this chapter. By concentrating on home front writings by both Iraqi and Iranian authors, written in the postwar period, I contend that despite differing historical, social, and political circumstances, Iranian and Iraqi writers have found that, during the postwar period, the shared experience of the war has led to some similar literary techniques that can provide fertile ground for exploration and comparison between the two literary traditions in the context of creating narratives of the Iran-Iraq War.

Writing War into the Revolution

Creating an Official Narrative of the War in Iran

By now, it is well known that the 1979 Revolution in Iran brought about a semiotic reordering of state and national symbols to fit the newly established Islamic Republic's identity and discourse. In the same way, the Iran-Iraq War found its own place within the government's official rhetoric and ideology. Like the official discourse of any other war, the conflict was framed as far more than simply a defense of the homeland. In this conflict, the regime defined the war as the ultimate battle between good and evil, heroes and villains, God and the Devil. The stakes became far greater than simply the border between the two countries. The national defense effort against the Iraqi invasion, in the official rhetoric of the government, connected the war to a larger fight against global, anti-Islamic imperialism. In doing so, the Islamic Republic molded its discourse on the war into a very particular shape, one that drew from a bank of Shiite symbols and Iranian nationalist discourse that were immediately recognizable to the people of the nation. From this bank of Shiite symbolism, three principal concepts constituted an essential part of the government's official war narrative: the story of Karbala, martyrdom, and jihad.

Additionally, the official war discourse portrayed—and continues to portray—inevitable victory (despite necessary hardship and victimhood) for the Islamic forces of the country and characterizes the warfront volunteers as fearless men with an unequivocal fervor and passion for the cause—a duty that was simultaneously religious and national. The official narrative of the conflict clearly told the young volunteers and conscripts that they were emulating what the most highly regarded men in Shiism had done before them: they were making the ultimate sacrifice for their faith. Their deaths—their martyrdoms—which at various points in the war were almost certain, were not for material gain, but for the survival and victory of Islam itself. By writing into this narrative the story of Karbala and the martyrdom of the third Shiite Imam, Husayn, Ayatollah Khomeini, and the other leaders of the regime left no doubt for their followers as to what the war was about. As Peter Chelkowski and Hamid Dabashi have written, "The righteousness of Khomeini's cause in war against Saddam Hussein . . . did not derive from any particular exigency of the situation itself. That righteousness was rooted in a history long before the Iran-Iraq War . . . [it] was rooted in the righteousness of the Imam Hussein's cause against the Umayyad caliph."[4] The authors go on to cite Khomeini himself in one of his sermons during the war. They note:

> If today all those who have power, and all those who simply talk gibberish, write, deliver speeches, or conspire against you and against the Islamic Republic [. . . even] they would not be able to conceal the truth. You are right! Just as Imam [Husayn], the Prince of the Martyrs, was right . . . Although he was martyred, and his children were martyred, he still kept Islam alive . . . you too are Shiites [followers] of His Same Excellency. You too, in such battles as those of Abadan . . . did, something miraculous [sic].[5]

Another essential component of the state narrative of the war was the depictions of women and children on the home front who ardently supported the fighters at the warfront. Oftentimes in a caricature-like fashion, women and children played the role of the Islamic defense on the home front. Without hesitation, wives and mothers encouraged their husbands and sons to fight. A novel such as Qasim 'Ali Farasat's *Nakhl-ha-yi bi Sar* (*Headless Palms*, 1988), for example, exemplifies this. The mother and sister of the protagonist (Nasir) enthusiastically participate in the home front war effort through the relief efforts organized by local mosques. The characters located on the home front, like those on the warfront, both participate in a continual Islamicization of the conflict through constant praise of Imam Khomeini, references to the Karbala story, and an unquestioning commitment to the cause for which the Iranian martyrs die. This reaches its climax as Nasir achieves what ostensibly becomes his goal in the course of the novel—martyrdom—dying at the front, his mother vowing to not mourn his death. Farasat's work embodies many of the crucial aspects of the official narrative of the war which, to the present day, are reflected in myriad state-sponsored literary works on the Iran-Iraq War. Aside from literature—fiction, poetry, and memoirs—scholarly histories, books of criticism, documentaries, films, and art are subject to this discourse.

The 1980s saw this narrative at its peak as the Iranian war machine utilized all available tools at its disposal to disseminate it. In this regard, the Iraqi invasion and occupation of Iranian territory in the first years of the war helped the state in the co-option of writers and intellectuals, even those who were not supporters of the Islamic government.[6] Literature's function, in the view of the official narrative, was to serve the wartime cause. In this way, the 1980s, particularly from the middle of the decade onward, witnessed an explosion of wartime writing that was meant to immediately aid the war effort. A majority of publications during those years, as Hasan Mirabedini documents well in two lengthy chapters devoted to the subject in his *100 Years of Persian Fiction*, do not have much to offer in terms of opening the discourse on the war to various viewpoints, let alone finding texts that we can justifiably call polyphonic in any sense.[7]

However, as previously mentioned, this is not to say that the 1980s failed to produce any successful literary depictions of the war. For, despite all of the Islamic Republic's efforts to control the official war story, it has never been able to maintain complete homogeneity in terms of cultural productions that deal with the subject. A few literary works produced in the 1980s do stand out and are worth mentioning, among them: Ahmad Mahmoud's *Scorched Earth*, Isma'il Fasih's *Zimistan-i Shast-o-do* (*The Winter of 82*) and *Suraya dar Ighma* (*Suraya in a Coma*), as well as Mohsen Makhmalbaf's *Bagh-i Bulur* (*The Crystal Garden*). These should be seen as early attempts to produce literary productions that were not ideologically aligned with the Islamic Republic and its stance on the war. They laid the groundwork, I contend, for more recent works in Persian fiction and film to voice what has now become a quite palpable lack of consent toward the official narrative. Ranging from writers who ignore the official narrative to those who have chosen to contest it, fiction has clearly emerged as a field that seeks to put forth various counternarratives of the conflict. Persian fiction, like its counterpart in Iraq, has slowly emerged as a polyphonic site of alternative narratives of the Iran-Iraq War, particularly in the postwar era.

Saddam Hussein's *Qadisiyya*

Iraq's First Gulf War

The Iraqi experience, although quite different in the aftermath of the war with Iran, finds many points of comparison during the 1980s. Like the Iranian regime's usage of the Karbala story, a poignant ancient myth was revived and the conflict was framed within nationalist as well as religious terminology. *Qadisiyyat Saddam*, or Saddam's *Qadisiyya*, in reference to the Arab Islamic conquest of Sassanid Iran in 637 CE, quickly became the frame of reference wielded by the Baathist regime to support Saddam Hussein's invasion of Iran. The Baathist state after 1979, with nearly all of its power increasingly consolidated under one man, Saddam Hussein, sought to imagine the war as a guaranteed victory over the Persians. In August 1980, Hussein abrogated the 1975 Algiers treaty that established the border between Iran and Iraq and claimed the entire Shatt al-'Arab waterway that divides the two countries. A month later he launched a land and air invasion against Iran, occupying the southern province of Khuzestan. Hoping for a quick victory over the newly established Islamic Republic of Iran, Hussein did not envision the massive mobilization that would take place in Iran and which the regime would use to consolidate its newly acquired control over the next eight years.[8]

The Baathist regime, like its counterpart in Iran, used every cultural apparatus at its disposal to promote the war effort. The co-option of writers, artists, and intellectuals in Iraq during the years of the war was quite possibly greater than what took place in Iran. Thoroughly covering the war years and the 1990s, the Salam Abboud in *Thaqafat al-'Unf fi al-'Iraq (The Culture of Violence in Iraq)*[9] details the level of control and coercion wielded by the Baathist regime in all affairs, but especially toward literary productions related to the war with Iran. In order to garner support for his war effort, Saddam attempted—often successfully—to buy off, coerce, or simply intimidate Iraqi writers, intellectuals, artists, filmmakers, actors, and musicians to promote his cause against the Persians. In terms of literature, the result (as in Iran) was a massive amount of fiction, poetry, and prose devoted to the state's official narrative of the war. The main difference was the degree to which the process of state sponsorship continued in Iran in the postwar years, while largely coming to an end in Iraq.

Consequently, literature and literary criticism written during the war were mostly commissioned by the Baathist regime, and what was not directly commissioned was subjected to a heavy-handed and frightening censor. Miriam Cooke in her *Women and the War Story*[10] has attempted, successfully at times, to uncover buried narratives within some novels and short stories written during the war. Yet, her choice of novels is random and she often dismisses the fact that the official government narrative still dominates the overall storyline and plot of most of the works she highlights. In this regard, Salam Abboud has pulled the pendulum in the other direction and taken a highly critical perspective toward individual writers and critics during much of Saddam Hussein's rule.[11]

Postwar Reflections

The postwar period has undoubtedly witnessed the emergence of more diverse and, by nearly any estimation, more successful, literary narratives that deal with the Iran-Iraq War in both Persian and Arabic. There are many more works that are not subject to the harsh wartime censors that operated in both countries and that feature multiple, alternative, and sometimes even opposing discourses and voices in their narratives. Of course, the historical realities of both countries since the end of the war in 1988 has also meant that very different publishing practices exist among Iranian and Iraqi authors. On the one hand, any discussion of literary works that even broach the topic of the war in Persian fiction must take into consideration the continuation of a vibrant, government-sponsored industry in Iran around what is called *Adabiyat-i Jang-i Muqaddas*, or the Literature of Holy Defense, which involves the production of a number of largely ideological works every year, as well as an annual prize for the best war novel, and a number of smaller literary and book festivals. On the other hand, Iraq has been subjected to two more devastating wars since the conclusion of the war with Iran, as well as some of the most comprehensive sanctions ever leveled against a state. This has meant nearly thirty years of continual warfare for the country, resulting in narratives of the Iran-Iraq War that are now often part of larger storylines that include the experiences of the successive wars, sanctions, political repression, and exile.

The postwar era in Iran has likewise seen a multitude of literary works that treat the war as just one part of recent history, namely as one of the biggest markers of the first decade following the 1979 Revolution. This is perhaps best seen in narratives of the conflict that take place on the home front. In fact, since the earliest and most ferocious years of the war, two significant domains of war narratives have existed in Persian literature: one taking place at the warfront and another on the home front. Generally speaking—and despite the fact that this trend has been slowly changing in recent years—former soldiers, many of them ideologically aligned with the Islamic Republic, have dominated the publication of literary works that take place on the warfront. The vast majority of these publications—fiction, poetry, memoir, or otherwise—are published by the *Howzih-i Hunari* and its publishing house *Surih-yi Mihr*.

However, home front narratives of the Iran-Iraq War in Persian fiction have been, ideologically speaking, written by a far more diverse crowd. While it would clearly be a mistake to categorize the writers of stories that take place on the home front as an *organized* group, per se, one can certainly say that the writers who have written works dealing with the Iran-Iraq War, and who are not ideologically aligned with the Iranian government, tend to be more politically varied, more inclusive of women, and include far more "professional writers," as opposed to those who picked up a pen for the first time when they decided, or were commissioned, to write about the war.

In many of the more recent Iraqi novels and short stories, the home front has also emerged as the setting for narratives of the experience of the Iran-Iraq War in its aftermath. Prominent examples include Muhsin al-Ramli's *Scattered Crumbs* and some of the short stories of Muhammad Khudayir and Ibtisam 'Abd Allah. As is often the case and as demonstrated in the examples below, Iraqi narratives of the war often alternate between memories of the war and more recent experiences of exile and the difficulties of adapting to its harsh living conditions in foreign lands. It is safe to say that war, and especially the war with Iran, has a more prominent position in Iraqi literature written in exile, as opposed to the literary works written by Iranians in exile. Some more prominent examples are 'Alia Mamdouh's *The Loved Ones*, Haifa Zangana's *Women on a Journey*, and two texts treated below: Betool Khedairi's *A Sky so Close* and Iqbal Qazwini's *Zubaiada's Window*.

The first of those two titles, Khedairi's *A Sky so Close*, was first published in 1999 in Beirut under the title *Kam Bada't as-Sama' Qaribatan*. It has since gone through four printings in Arabic and was first translated and published in English in 2001,[12] significantly, before the most recent wave of interest in Iraq, and Iraqi and Muslim women in general following the events of September 11, 2001 and the 2003 US-led invasion. Set in Iraq for much of the first half of the novel, the unnamed narrator—a young woman—grows up in a small village outside Baghdad with her British mother and Iraqi father, a seemingly autobiographically inspired aspect to the novel. The narrator comes of age torn between the clashing values and mores of her mother, who feels increasingly estranged in Iraq, and her Iraqi father, who dies during the narrator's teenage years.

The major turning point in the novel is the beginning of the Iran-Iraq War. It quickly becomes the primary event which shapes the background of the novel, but a background that remains palpable throughout the novel. The story's plot and bildungsroman-like narrative primarily revolve around the narrator, the long time spent at a ballet school in Baghdad, and her mother's cancer diagnosis. Eventually, the two move to England for her treatment and thus begins another story of migration, marked by a sense of frustration and hopelessness coinciding with the televised broadcast of the 1991 Gulf War.

The fact that the novel's narrator is part British, along with the significant focus on the large part that ballet played in her life, steers the novel away from blatant political engagement. Instead, it is largely themed around growing up with a bicultural identity in Iraq during the 1980s, exemplified by the interactions with her father and mother. The narration is peppered with the mention of bombing and destruction and is constantly punctuated by military communiqués that are noticeably ignored and sometimes mocked. Rather than spending much time speaking of the Iran-Iraq War, the narration focuses on the extremely personal and artistic aspect of one girl's life. Here, the prominent role that ballet plays in the novel is quite significant, as it slowly becomes the antithesis of the war—a way for the young men and women in the ballet studio to act in defiance of the war and choose to continue their studies of ballet rather than take part in the war effort surrounding them. Critique of war does arise, but is largely limited to the latter parts of the novel set in England, where the narrator watches the televised American-led air campaigns drop bombs on Iraq during the 1990–91 Gulf War.

The lack of direct engagement with the Iraqi state's war narrative discourse in Khedairi's novel is remarkable. The narrator avoids direct engagement with the Baathist regime, despite her proximity to it, undoubtedly demonstrating a commitment on the part of the author to speak against the efforts of the regime to control all aspects of literary production that deal with the war. It seems to be a tactful move by the narrator, rather than the product of consent or intimidation, as she keenly works around the official war discourse, never allowing herself to be sucked in. When the war, on the other hand, attempts to engage with the text, it is usually ignored and pushed aside. Khedairi successfully depicts the way in which the war disrupted life for those living through it, while also demonstrating how ordinary Iraqis resisted the state's efforts to bring them into the war.

Iqbal al-Qazwini, however, takes an opposite approach in her novella, *Zubaida's Window*, originally published in Amman in 2006 under the title *Mamarrat al-Sukun*. The main character of the novella, Zubaida, in a move that parallels the life of the author, leaves Iraq and settles in East Germany in 1979, from where she narrates the novel.

Zubaida's life in Berlin is a depressing one marked by sadness, gloom, and nostalgia for an Iraq that will never return. Her loneliness suffered in exile is broken up by references to the three wars that Iraq has witnessed since 1980 and through which Zubaida vicariously lives via televised news. The dull and drab background of East Germany intensifies the dreary atmosphere of the novella whose slow progression is given time indicators only through the war references. Epitomizing the mood of the novel and the passage of time in it, the narrator writes: "Gray envelops Berlin, spreading flood over the pavements, the faces of people and trees. The absence of color mixes morning and evening hours, and thus, Zubaida cannot tell time."[13]

The war with Iran, which claims her youngest brother as a victim, marks Zubaida's earliest years in exile, while the war "that did not take place"—the 1991 Gulf War—puts an end to the slight reprieve from international conflict that Iraq felt after the war with Iran came to a close. The final chapters of the novel are dominated by the 2003 invasion. What is not told through reference to war and violence is a nostalgic view, at times verging on the utopian, of a more pluralistic and non-sectarian past: Jews, Chaldeans, Shiites, and Sunnis seemed to live side by side and in harmony; a harmony that was severely damaged with the rise of Saddam Hussein, and destroyed completely after 2003.

Essential to the novel's narrative is the role that media plays in broadcasting news and images of the wars in Iraq. Because Zubaida has not returned to the country since her initial departure, she experiences the traumas the nation has suffered via the media. In a dreamlike scene in the beginning of the novel, Zubaida finds herself in one of the televised depictions she has previously seen on television:

> Zubaida sinks into a cloud of grief and smoke, enveloped by the din of destruction exploding on the screen. Dazed and in tears she switches off the television . . . Between the satellite pictures and the golden domes, the sky rages with a sand storm as red as blood. Satellite correspondents transmit fresh news and Zubaida smells the odor of spilt blood and drinks bitter tea . . . In a deserted southern city, a very old man walks with the help of a stick. Zubaida sticks her head over the balcony and asks him about the people who have disappeared.
>
> "They're gone! No one is left!"
> "Gone where?"
> "They're fine; all gone the way they chose."
> The piercing sounds of air-raid sirens rouse her. She comes out of the TV screen. (3–5, Zubaida's Window)

The experience is indicative of Zubaida's life in exile, vicariously living the nightmares of war that ordinary Iraqis felt through the media portrayals of it that were broadcast in Germany. Her inability to fully integrate into her new environment after being there for nearly twenty years is just as much connected to her inability to let go of her homeland and accept a new life, far from the tragedy of Iraq. Her personal state is one of constant melancholia.

What we see in these two examples of postwar writing are attempts to reconstruct the lives of ordinary Iraqis who lived through the war, who were greatly affected by it, but who were not directly engaged with the killing on the front. The approaches differ, but by writing the conflict at a distance from the warfront the authors are able to take the focus off of the war solely and address various issues that have affected Iraqis during the years of the conflict as well as the postwar years that have witnessed more violence as well as political oppression.

This is where the comparison between postwar writing in Iran is perhaps most relevant. The two short stories I have chosen to reference here also take similar approaches to the war; they are written in the postwar period, and from the perspective of the home front. Despite the differing historical circumstances in both Iran and Iraq since the end of the war, a story by Amir Hasan Chihiltan, "Munis, Mother of Isfandiyar," and Marjan Riahi's "Eight-Thirty in the Morning," also attempt to narrate the war from noncombatant perspectives that highlight civilian suffering during wartime and ignore the official rhetoric of the conflict.

Chihiltan's short story "Munis, Mother of Isfandiyar" was published in a 1997 collection of short stories entitled *Chizi be Farda Namandast* (*Not Much Left to Tomorrow*).[14] In it, he treats the character of Munis, a mother who refuses to admit that her son, Isfandiyar, has been killed in combat. For eight years she doesn't see or hear anything from him, and following the release of POWs in Iraq he is still unaccounted for. His name doesn't appear in the newspaper or over radio broadcasts. Everyone around her knows what has happened to him, yet Munis denies all of this and instead insists on the presence of her son in her own home. She shoos away visitors on account of Isfandiyar being sick, takes his pants and shirt to be ironed regularly, and talks about how he goes to and from work.

This goes on for the entirety of the story and her neighbors and friends, who all seem to know what has happened, don't tell her. It seems that they can't get themselves to tell an old woman that her child, seemingly her only relative, has been killed. At the same time, they simply don't know what's happened to Isfandiyar. This last point is a larger comment on the status of MIAs and POWs during the war. The absence of a soldier or the remains of his body leaves family and friends in a troubling position, one in which they either have to admit to the death, and thus accept his status of martyr, or remain hopeful that he'll eventually return. Munis' behavior is obviously an extreme version of the latter category.

Aside from depicting the painful suffering of a mother who loses her only son, what Chihiltan's story does is fight the tendency toward the official discourse's sanctification of martyrdom through portraying a character who actively denies its taking place. As such, it also undercuts the unique status of the martyr in the larger official culture of war by placing more importance on the families of the victim than on the actual martyr himself. In fact, the conclusion of the story plays directly into this notion and upturns what others have called the "martyrdom paradigm" of the war. Munis dies in her house, alone. The story ends with a typical mourning ceremony for her, not for Isfandiyar. After a few days the neighbors break in and find her body in a bedroom. The scene reads:

> They saw Munis who had sat on the ground at the foot of the bed with clean, untouched sheets, her forehead stuck to the mattress. On the bed were an ironed shirt, pajamas, and a clean undershirt carefully placed next to each other. They lifted Munis' head from the mattress and saw bloodstains the size of the palm on the white sheets. (73)

The loneliness of Munis and her refusal to accept the tragic loss of her son brings to mind the suffering and trauma that Qazwini's Zubaida goes through. More than anything else, they attempt to hold on to a past, forever lost, wrecked by war which they wanted nothing to do with.

Marjan Riahi, another Iranian author writing in the postwar period, also takes up the war in her short story entitled "Eight-Thirty in the Morning." Translated and published in a collection of Persian short stories entitled *Sohrab's Wars*,[15] the narrator is a young woman in Isfahan waiting for her fiancé to return from the front. As she reminisces about the little time they had together as an engaged couple she mentions, multiple times, the hour "8:30 in the morning," which for the narrator is a seemingly perfect time of the day "when everything is alive." It is a love story and quite short, but in the course of a few pages the narrator is able to completely reorient time around herself and the wait for her fiancé to return. The narration lies completely outside the state ideology.

The references that the story makes to the war are almost entirely within the context of the fiancé's return from the front. He comes back once during the war, clearly traumatized by his experiences fighting, and then goes back to the front. His next return is in a coffin. The narrator tells us: "We waited for him. Many people were waiting. And they came. No one's shoulders were empty. In the morning, at eight-thirty, they buried him."[16]

The success of this story is in its ability to write the tragedy of the home front completely outside the terms of the conflict set by the official narrative. The story makes a prominent disengagement from the state narrative by remaining absolutely unwilling to participate in the discourse of the war, particularly concerning the issue of martyrdom. This can be seen clearly at one point earlier in the story as coffins pass over Isfahan's famous Si-o-Seh Bridge. The narrator's fiancé, back temporarily from the front, sees them and cries. Yet both the narrator and her fiancé refrain from speaking about the war, the cause, or the deaths of the men in the coffins. There are no martyrs and no heroes, only tragedy. Here, we can see a deliberate move by Riahi to keep the text ideologically unengaged. As a result, for its entirety and despite being totally framed by the Iran-Iraq War, "Eight-Thirty in the Morning" is entirely devoid of the ideological discourse of the regime.

In this way, Riahi's work finds common ground with Khedairi's *A Sky so Close*, as both authors approach the war through a literary lens, yet successfully keep its official narrative out of their own writings. This technique is rarely found during the years of the war in either country. Rather than engaging with the official narrative, either in support or opposition, these two fictional texts remain silent. Yet, in an atmosphere such as Baathist Iraq or the Islamic Republic of Iran, choosing to remain silent on an issue as politicized or ideologically charged as the Iran-Iraq War was tantamount to dissent.

In a different fashion, a short story like Chihiltan's "Munis, Mother of Isfandiyar" attempts to write against the official narrative of the war using the very language that the official narrative is steeped in. By giving martyrdom such a centrality in his story, Chihiltan, more actively than Khedairi or Riahi, uses literature as a vehicle of contention to challenge one of the essential aspects of the state's narrative of the war; the literary sphere becomes an ideological site of struggle over the meaning of the war and the author attempts to re-signify martyrdom by associating it with defeat and loss rather than victory.

Iqbal Qazwini's approach to writing about Iraq's tragic experience with warfare over the past thirty years is by far the most straightforward, aggressive, and critical challenge to the official state narrative of war. Her position as a refugee living in Germany, far from the reaches of Saddam Hussein's government, undoubtedly allows her to write in such unforgiving terms of the Iraqi regime. The harsh political criticism found in *Zubaida's Window*, however, is indicative of a type of Iraqi fiction that is politically engaged, critical, and was written at a distance far from Saddam Hussein's oppressive government. The novella successfully depicts the quotidian frustrations of living in exile while demonstrating the deep feelings of loss shared by many Iraqis today for a country that is now forever gone.

Home front writings in the postwar period in both Arabic and Persian, of which this chapter is merely a short introduction, have added significantly to our understandings of the experience of war by citizens of both countries. Far from focusing solely on the fighting and destruction that the war caused, home front narratives, in both Arabic and Persian, have moved the focus away from fighting and have highlighted the larger human catastrophe that the war created and continues to produce. In both countries, the officially sanctioned literature of the Iran-Iraq War primarily centered on the experience of combat, depicting bravery, heroism, and victory, while often vilifying the enemy forces. Home front writings, on the other hand, have tended to focus on the innocent victims of senseless fighting: young conscripts who never return, widows, refugees, bereaved parents of "martyrs," and a large group not even mentioned in this short chapter—veterans. Home front narratives, particularly those written in the postwar period in both literatures, successfully prompt readers to consider the long-term consequences of this conflict much more than many of the action-packed, violent narratives of the warfront.

Admittedly, much more can, and indeed should, be said about the diverse array of literary narratives produced as a result of the Iran-Iraq War in both Arabic and Persian, not to mention other languages. The magnitude of literature produced in Iraq, Iran, and by the diaspora communities of both countries points to the immense importance that this war has had on the lives of the people of both countries. At the same time, the myriad ways in which Iranian and Iraqi writers have responded beg for a much larger, comparative study to be undertaken. Further investigation into the shared aesthetic responses of writers, artists, and filmmakers to the violent reality that they, along with millions of others, were forced to experience and in many cases are still coming to terms with today, is sure to reveal much more about the production of literature in contemporary Iraq and Iran as well as highlight new intersections between Arabic and Persian literatures today.

NOTES

1 For examples of academic and critical works that treat both modern literatures, see Kamran Rastegar, *Literary Modernity between the Middle East and Europe: Textual Transactions in Nineteenth and Twentieth Century Arabic, Persian and English Literatures* (New York and London: Routledge, 2007) for an excellent look at the early-modern period. Kamran Talattof's final chapter in *The Politics of Writing in Iran: A History of Modern Persian Literature* (Syracuse, NY: Syracuse University Press, 2000) attempts to bring together modern Iranian and Arabic literatures.

2 See Patrick Deer, *Culture in Camouflage: War, Empire and Modern British Literature* (New York: Oxford University Press, 2009).

3 Ibid., 2.

4 Chelkowski and Dabashi, 273–274.

5 Ibid., 274. Abadan, an oil refining city in Southwestern Iran, was the site of some of the most ferocious fighting between Iranian and Iraqi forces, especially in the earliest years of the war.

6 A particularly striking example of this can be found in the case of well-known, leftist author of social-realism, Ahmad Mahmoud. In an interview published in 1995, he speaks about his well-known novel, *Zamin-i Sukhtih* (Scorched Earth) and the overtly anti-Iraqi, nationalist positions of the novel's main characters. After stating that he was accused of war-mongering at the time, he says, "At any rate, if this is what warmongering is, then I'm still one. So long as I know that the enemy is on our land I believe that we should fight. Until the time when they are driven out I am a warmonger. I see no reason for giving up our territory and remaining silent . . . before anything else I'm a nationalist and then an internationalist. See Leyli Golestan, *Hikayat-i Hal: Goftigu ba Ahmad-i Mahmud.* Tehran: Ketab-e Mahnaz, 1995, pp.158–9, translation my own.

7 Hasan Mirabedini, *Sad Sal Dastan Nevisi.* Tehran: Nashr-i Chishmih, 2007. 890–891.

8 Charles Tripp, *A History of Iraq*. Cambridge: Cambridge University Press, 2007.

9 Abboud, *Thaqafat al-'Unf fi al-'Iraq*. Koln, Germany: Al-Kamel Verag, 2002.

10 See Miriam Cooke, *Women and the War Story*, and especially the chapter entitled "Flames of Fire in Qadisiya," 220–264. Cooke's selection of novels and short stories from Iraq is based solely on what her friend, author Daisy al-Amir, sent her "in two gunny sacks . . . filled with novels, short stories and volumes of criticism produced by the Iraq Ministry of Culture and Information in the last four years of the war" (223).

11 'Abboud, *Thaqafat al-'Unf fi al-'Iraq*, 2002.

12 See Betool Khedairi, *A Sky so Close* (New York: Pantheon Books, 2001).

13 Iqbal Qazwini, *Zubaida's Window: A Novel of Iraqi Exile*, 59.

14 Amir Hasan Chihiltan, *Chizi be Fardah Namandast*. Tehran: Entesharat-e Negah, 1999.

15 Mohammad Mehdi Khorrami, *Sohrab's Wars*. Costa Mesa, CA: Mazda Publishers, 2008.

16 Ibid., 46.

7

Not a Manifesto

The Languages of Aggression

MICHAEL BEARD

Suave etiam belli certamina magna tueri
Per campos instructa tua sine parte pericli.
—Lucretius, *De rerum natura* 2.5–6

How pleasant it is to behold great encounters of
warfare arrayed over the plains, taking no part in the peril.

There is a genre of landscape painting that developed in the late six-teenth century, notably in a series of six etchings Jacques Callot drew depicting the Spanish Siege of Jeda (1624–25). We know that Callot was commissioned by the Spanish government to memorialize their victory, and this may account for its visual orientation. In the foreground we see, from behind, a cluster of warships gliding toward the shore. We see ahead of them, inland, further up the picture, their Dutch opponents, much smaller, smaller in fact than perspective requires. Perspective is distorted further still as the eye moves up the rectangular space. The rest of the picture is a map, which is close enough to show the walled city, scattered fortifications, and defending soldiers in formation, not yet deployed. The detail suggests the view we might see out of an airplane window a few moments before touching down. (It is more detail than television viewers ever got in news coverage of the Iran-Iraq War.) We, who are more familiar with aerial views, may still experience the dis-orientation. The upper space, perhaps four fifths of the page, is tipped up ninety degrees from the foreground, vertiginously. "This clash of modes," says the art historian Julie Anne Plax about this genre, "seemed to cause no discomfort, and, indeed, it was a commonly understood manner of conveying diverse kinds of information" (Plax 2000, 62).

Nonetheless, it requires an act of visualization that seems more than we should be able to take in. It would be difficult to say whether we can see it without a feeling of disorientation. It may be in its way as disturbing as "Les Misères et les malheurs de la Guerre," drawn eight years later.

I find it difficult to determine whether I should be seeing it as propaganda or as a disinterested portrayal. We are clearly seeing from the Spanish point of view, and perhaps it demeans the defenders to distance and shrink them. Callot's miniature is framed by a frieze of mannered sculptural shapes, tiny scenes of combatants in a row, portraits, architecture. It may have appealed to Callot's Spanish patrons that the scene of violence was made static and beautiful, an extreme of Olympian detachment.

A scene of war portrayed in narrative is contracted generically to convey a sense of motion, and the necessity of establishing an observer's point of view may be as strong as that in representational painting. The third chapter of Voltaire's *Candide* opens with a battle scene, presumably an indirect fictional representation of the Seven Years' War.

> Nothing could have been so fine, so brisk, so brilliant, so well-drilled [],
> as the two armies. The trumpets, the fifes, the oboes, the drums, and the
> cannon produced such a harmony as was never heard in hell. First the
> cannons battered down about six thousand men on each side; then vol-
> leys of musket fire removed from the best of worlds about nine or ten
> thousand rascals who were cluttering up its surface. The bayonet was a
> sufficient reason for the demise of several others. Total casualties might
> well amount to thirty thousand men or so. Candide, who was trembling
> like a philosopher, hid himself as best he could [] while this heroic butch-
> ery was going on. (*Candide*, chapter 5; *Romans & Contes*, 153–154)

What is likely to strike us first is something discordant: praise for the armies juxtaposed with the horrific, inhuman intensity of the violence. It is a description of war, but we don't feel the violence. The musical instruments seem part of the same list with the cannons, musket fire, and bayonets. It all comes to us as praise.

There is a word for this style: We are likely to be aware of it before I say it. It is irony, and we are also likely to know that irony is a volatile substance. As with many rhetorical devices, we hear the message before we are aware of it as a rhetorical device. (Rhetorical devices are particularly persuasive when we don't notice them.) Feigned praise governs the book to an extent that, whenever you hear something praised, you become suspicious. But the constant threat of irony is that a reader may take it seriously. Voltaire's tactic is to make the irony break at intervals. "Such a harmony as was never heard in hell." (Read "*even* in hell.") The second is the phrase "heroic butchery." "Heroic" is ironic; "butchery" isn't. "Trembling like a philosopher" is a cunning example (not ironic) in which we are told, as if it could pass without saying, that philosophers are cowards.

Let's leave aside the question whether a satirical vision of war is persuasive, moral, or realistic. Instead I want to point out another literary device—again a device we feel before we become aware of it. Candide has in the first two chapters been a victim: he's been expelled from the castle where he grew up; he has been drafted by the local army; he has been punished brutally in training. And yet here by virtue of his desertion he does not suffer the fate of the thirty thousand colleagues who were dispatched in the first five sentences. The book hardly ever invites us to feel the pain, either the pain Candide has undergone or the pain he has witnessed. (The exception is in chapter 19, the scene in Surinam when he encounters the mutilated laborer in the sugar mill.) In chapter 3 there is an additional reason for us to feel narratorial distance: Candide is observing the action from outside. And if Candide were not a survivor we wouldn't have access to the story at all.

If we suspect that Voltaire's distanced portrayal of war is atypical, we might ask what the alternatives might be, and how many there are. The only plan I have is to catalogue them, understanding the objection that we can't catalogue everything, that only provisional conclusions are possible. An observer, whether narrator or character, can be close to the action or distant. We can even trace a spectrum of fictional scenarios, from distant to close-up. If we catalogue them according to their position on this spectrum, from those which, like Voltaire's in *Candide*, see the war at a distance, to those that describe it from the inside, we can attempt to devise a conceptual box to put them in.

It may be a narrow box. War is a big subject, but the presentation of it may be a much smaller one. "In practice," Fredric Jameson suggests, "we can enumerate some seven or eight situations, which more or less exhaust the genre" ("War & Representation," 1533). As with narrative situations, so with narrative points of view and the sensibility of the observer. We may feel we are free in the formal devices we use to describe war; more likely the possibilities are finite, and possibly we can track the built-in limits as we try to imagine ourselves closer and closer to the violence.

The vista of war can be distant. I believe it was George Steiner who observed of Jane Austen's novels that political context hardly seemed to exist, yet all those eligible army officers who showed up in genteel drawing rooms must have been on leave from the Napoleonic wars. In Don DeLillo's early novel *End Zone* (1972), the war in question is, strictly speaking, only a possibility. A college football player, closet intellectual, undergoes a crisis brought on by his reading:

> I liked playing football and I knew . . . that I'd have trouble finding another school that would take me. But I had to leave. It started with a book, an immense volume about the possibilities of nuclear war— assigned reading for a course I was taking on modes of disaster technology. The problem was simple and terrible: I enjoyed the book. I liked reading about the deaths of tens of millions of people. I liked dwelling on the destruction of great cities. Five to twenty million dead. Fifty to a hundred million dead. Ninety percent population loss. Seattle wiped out by mistake. . . . I liked to think of huge buildings toppling, of firestorms, of bridges collapsing, survivors roaming the charred countryside. (DeLillo 1972, 20–21)

It is an experience many of us may have undergone—not the experience of war but the experience of imagining it. War conceived from a distance can fascinate, as in war movies and video games. It may be an act of heroism just to acknowledge our fascination, but once we've done that it haunts instead of fascinates. There is a moment in *End Zone* when the narrator, in a conversation with another closet intellectual on his football team, asks:

> "Does the silence bother you?"
> "What silence?" he said.
> "The silence. The big metallic noise."

DeLillo catches the anxiety not just of contemplating war, of contemplating a war at the limit of comprehension, but realizing that there can be pleasure in it. An unnatural sound just beyond the horizon of experience makes that anxiety accessible in all its ambiguity. La Rochefoucauld's maxim is an unsettling truth, "Nous avons tous assez de force pour supporter les maux d'autrui" (We all have strength enough to bear the misfortunes of others). (To look ahead at what I shall be saying, it foreshadows the problem of anyone who writes fiction about war: Fiction cannot *simply* cause pain. In order to draw a reader in, even to a vista of horror, there has to be some pleasure in the representation.)

It is a natural next step to that point of view in which the battle is going on, but elsewhere. Still, there is an actual war and the outside observer feels threatened by it. The observer can become a participant instantly. And here memoirs of the Iran-Iraq War provide particularly telling examples.

Shirin Ebadi's memoir, *Iran Awakening*, not fiction but narrative using the same rhetorical devices, describes the Iran-Iraq War in some detail through the medium of newspaper and television information, comments on strategy, the relation between internal politics and the war. Accounts in the media are safe. They present pre-processed information which distances us. This is balanced by experience from a distance: Ebadi's office looks down at a courtyard where mass funerals for the war dead were convened. "I hid my face, turning it to the wall so the tears could stream down without my secretary seeing. I didn't want her to think I was so weak, crying at the funeral of strangers" (62). Seeing daily funerals leads to a distanced vista of war, which is effective in a way that the historical overviews are not. The war comes even closer as bombing makes the spectators actual victims:

> One morning in this period I went downtown to run some errands, and stood at a busy intersection, waiting for a taxi. After about fifteen minutes, sick from the fumes of the chugging buses, I started walking. I hadn't even reached the other end of the long block when a deafening boom resounded, the ground beneath me heaved, and I saw the pavement below me pass in a blur. The force threw me against the concrete side of a building, and I lay there slumped, blinking at the commotion around me. People were shouting and pointing toward the corner where

I had been standing. I limped back, pushing my way through the crowd, past charred, smoking cars, and stared into a large crater, full of rubble and injured bodies. (Ebadi 2007, 84)

Again, it is a trade-off whether a representation of the war is more vivid to us when we hear of atrocities in the newspaper or when we hear the account of an eyewitness. The one can be precise and complete; the other brings us closer in.

As noncombatants are drawn into war, it may not be surprising how many accounts of the bombing of Tehran emphasize the innocence of the observer. Limited comprehension hyperbolizes, and thus a focus on the perceptions of children can be particularly effective. It may even be a generic necessity, simply because the child's point of view focuses and intensifies the anxiety. Abbas Milani's memoir, *Tales of Two Cities* (1996), provides a good example.

> By the time the war reached Tehran, Ameh had learned to accept food shortages; she had grown accustomed to streets bereft of young faces, and to the gradual increase of those with damaged limbs, often on crutches, haunting the crowded avenues. But when the first Iraqi rockets hit Tehran, Ameh changed. . . .
>
> Ameh was not the only one changed by the war. The whole fabric of the city changed. A sense of dread became a fact of life. Rocket attacks were a permanent fixture of our lives. My young son's painting grew grimmer by the day. Every house he drew was a target of menacing bombs that floated in the air. (Milani 1996, 235)

Adults can evoke sympathy; children seem particularly susceptible to pain; our sympathy intensifies. The juxtaposition without comment of two observable facts: the rocket attacks and the child's painting, evokes pain in itself.

Marjane Satrapi's graphic novel *Persepolis: The Story of a Childhood* (2001) describes the Iran-Iraq War from the point of view of a child observer in a wealthy Tehran family. As with the previous two examples, we never watch the violence from up close, but we feel more nearly on the scene. It's hard to say why. Like any graphic novel it proceeds in fragments of narrative. Satrapi's particular contribution to the form is a minimalist sensibility, with stylized, rounded human forms whose only real expression is widening and narrowing eyes, set against backgrounds without texture. The effect of a narrative expressed in a sequence of static images is that the eye sweeps across them quickly. The flat squares, oddly, allow conceptual depth. The young girl's family learns about the war watching television during a vacation in Spain, wondering at first if it is a weather report (78). There is a map on the television screen, but not like Callot's: it is minimal, crude, with place names (Irak, Golfo persico) in their Spanish versions. One result is that the reader finds the family, at this point, comic and naïve; another is that the war looms up gradually, starting with the narrow confines of that television screen and widening until it surrounds her. A memoir can describe their vision of war in intense vignettes, but Satrapi's vignettes are personal; they hardly ever leave a child's point of view. The images of war are scattered. Nine squares show the child visiting her father's office, hearing a sonic boom, identifying the airplanes as F 14s, verifying it on the radio, running around the office in rage (80–81). As more news of the battle front comes in, the point of the vignettes, their dark humor, depends on her immature reactions, her grotesque enthusiasm, sympathy that alternates with inappropriate responses: petty disagreements, children's jokes, manic games.

There is a contrast here which might come across as a contradiction. On the one hand the narrative point is the child's misreading of what she sees. This can come across as comic. On the other hand, there are two scenes in which her imagination coincides with historical reality. She sees at school the keys child soldiers are given as keys to heaven and in a half-page freeze-frame we see silhouettes of children's bodies blown in the air, keys in hand (102). The next frame shows her at her first pre-teen party. Fourteen pages further on another full-page war scene shows adult soldiers—again a page full of bodies in silhouette (I count 27 of them). Again the figures are suspended in the air as if the bomb has just gone off. They are framed by a background of cartoon half-circles representing smoke, a full-page war scene in simple, unpretentious silhouettes (116). We know it is her imagination, because the battle scene is superimposed on the stairs of her basement as she descends. At the top of the picture she begins descending the stairs and we read her soliloquy. Its voice is adult: "They eventually admitted that the survival of the regime depended on the war." At the bottom, underneath the war scene, we see her form, again at the bottom of the stairs and see the soliloquy continued: "When I think we could have avoided it all . . . it just makes me sick. A million people would still be alive" (116). The adult voice is momentary. She's still an immature observer, and her reaction on the next page is to smoke her first cigarette. But against the backdrop of her limited perception those scenes of realistic violence, even filtered through her imagination, carry a real shock.

Another graphic novel, Joe Sacco's *Footnotes in Gaza* (2009), is closer to the scene of war, an autobiographical account of a visit to the scene of violence, previously the violence of war, currently the violence of occupation. Sacco chronicles trips to Rafah and Khan al-Yousef (in 2002 and 2003), at the southern tip of Ghâza, observing the experience of occupation and reconstructing the events of a 1956 massacre. The drawings are realistic, hardly cartoons at all, and a historian's seriousness is visible even in the visual layout: there are more words on the page than readers of graphic narrative are used to, in balloons and in inset narrative rectangles. There are maps as detailed as Callot's etching of the Siege of Jena. There is violence everywhere in the book, reconstructed through personal interviews. There are more scenes of rubble than of combat. The scenes of combat are embedded narrative, accounts of war remembered by informants.

Gérard Genette observes that an analepsis, a flashback in narrative, never feels like the past. It occupies the foreground and becomes the reader's present (Genette 1980, 66). Reading Joe Sacco we are still not faced with a direct portrayal of war, but flashbacks recounted by on-the-scene narrators. Their accounts, however, are so clear, so effective, so present to us, that we see the violence with unusual clarity. We see how war is never a phenomenon with sharp edges, never an event that can be limited to an army. This tactic of representation makes violence encroach on the present as it represents the violence which encroaches on the lives of noncombatants.

Sacco's informants are participants in remembered violence. He is at one remove from the events themselves. A representation of war can be located across generations. A. S. Byatt's poem "Trench Names" (2009) visits the scene of the trenches left from World War I. It is not the kind of analepsis that fills the foreground, but nonetheless something vivid about life in the trenches emerges:

> We gouge out tunnels in the sleeping fields.
> We turn the clay and slice the turf, and make
> A scheme of cross-roads, orderly and mad,
> Under and through, like moles, like monstrous worms.

What follows is a disembodied map seen from the present, its form a list of names. Those names make tangible the imagination of combatants—sometimes realistic sometimes escapist, regularly ironic.

> . . . English men
> Imposed a ghostly English map on French
> Crushed ruined harvests and polluted streams.
>
> So here run Piccadilly, Regent Street,
> Oxford Street, Bond Street, Tothill Fields, Tower Bridge,
> And Kentish places, Dover, Tunbridge Wells,
> Entering wider hauntings, resonant,
> The Boggart Hole, Bleak House, Deep Doom and Gloom.
>
> Remembering boyhood, soldier poets recall
> The desperate deeds of Lost Boys, Peter Pan,
> Hook Copse, and Wendy Cottage. Horrors lurk
> In Jekyll Copse and Hyde Copse. (Byatt 2009, 54–55)

Strictly speaking, the melancholy of a battlefield seen in serenity years after, when the violence is less than a memory, might be the antithesis of a battle scene, but names have a power that can persist. The recital of Palestinian village names in Émile Habiby's *Pessoptimist* (*Mutashâ'il*, 1974) place names no longer on maps, carries a different kind of melancholy. The point is their antiquity, their unacknowledged, rooted legitimacy. We can't know who named them. By contrast, the names of trenches are heard as an act of will. Both are memorials of violence that take the form of anonymous speech acts more intimate than we expect.

Proper history is usually contracted to take an omniscient view of the war. It probes to the center of the action but sees it from above, in a kind of aerial view. Historical fiction takes an omniscient overview less frequently, but when it does it may seem a little like Callot's "Siege of Breda," vertiginous. An example is the account of Napoleon's defeat in Russia, the events of 1812, in *War & Peace*. Tolstoy begins that passage in the role of a historian, tactician, apologist for the Russian side.

> The battle of Borodinó, with the occupation of Moscow that followed it and flight of the French without further conflicts, is one of the most instructive phenomena in history.
>
> All historians agree that the external activity of states and nations in their conflict with one another is expressed in wars, and that as a direct result of greater or less success in war the political strength of states and nations increases or decreases. (Tolstoi 1966, 1145)

There are individual observers. It is a novel after all, but we encounter them in a series of fragments, a mosaic of self-sufficient scenes.

> The small bands that had started their activities long before and had already observed the French closely considered things possible which the commanders of the big detachments did not dare to contemplate. The Cossacks and peasants who crept in among the French now considered everything possible.
>
> On October 22, Denísov (who was one of the irregulars) was with his group at the height of the guerrilla enthusiasm. Since early morning he and his part had been on the move. (1150–1151)

It's a solution with its limits: as he changes camera angles from one group to another, from a distant view to a close-up, the omniscient narrator intervenes to patch the garments together, and the reader feels a secure distance.

It is a truism that we can say the words "Battle of Waterloo" and attach the date 1815, but the reality is too amorphous, scattered between too many points of view to be portrayed. A possible solution occurs in Stendhal's *Charterhouse of Parma*, in the series of scenes in which the naïve young Fabrice leaves Italy and comes on his own to join

Napoleon's army and attempts to enlist, or at least to take part in the fighting as a kind of free agent.

One distinction between Tolstoy's account of the Battle of Borodinó and Stendhal's Waterloo is that Stendhal comes closer to portraying the sense of risk. He shows us the action, , focalized through the eyes of a particular character. It is a widespread, perhaps inevitable device in third person narrative: we are shown what a particular character sees.

A standard reading says that the attitude toward Fabrice, as we sense it behind Fabrice's observations, is confined to mockery. Fabrice doesn't even realize something the reader knows immediately, that he's present at a turning point in history. We are shown through his eyes only what an uninformed observer might perceive, and his motives are divided between anti-royalist commitment and his adolescent desire to prove himself. His guide is a woman who sells food from a cart to passing soldiers, who takes an interest in him because he is good-looking and obviously wealthy. She suggests to him that he should enter the battle the next morning, but he insists on proving himself on the spot:

> "On the contrary, I want to start fighting at once," said our hero in a somber tone that seemed to the *vivandière* to augur well. The noise of the guns grew twice as loud and seemed to be coming nearer. The explosions were beginning to form a sort of figured bass; there was no interval between one explosion and the next, and above this figured bass, which resembled the roar of a torrent in the distance, the sound of musketry firing could be clearly distinguished. (Stendhal 1958, 54)

Readers of *Candide* are likely to feel that this description is derivative. The sounds of battle are framed in almost the same words, but we experience a point of view that rides through them, toward the action, desperate to participate. With momentary exceptions (as in that opening phrase clearly interior to the *vivandière*) we are limited to what he sees, with the same lack of comprehension. However we feel about Fabrice, we see that he is riding into the battle, with a determination that validates his desire for experience: "'Now,' thought Fabrice, 'I shall see whether I am a coward.'"

He attaches himself to a group of officers and, riding with them, experiences a scene that is close to the action, or inside it.

Fabrice saw, twenty paces ahead of him, a piece of tilled land that was being ploughed up in a singular fashion [*qui était remuée d'une façon singulière* i.86]. The bottoms of the rows were full of water, and the very damp soil that formed the ridges of these furrows was flying about in little black lumps flung three or four feet into the air. Fabrice noted this curious effect as he was passing . . . He heard a sharp cry close by him; it was two hussars falling struck by shot; and when he looked round at them, they were already twenty paces behind the escort. What seemed to him horrible was a horse streaming with blood that was writhing on the ploughed land, its hooves entangled in its own entrails. (58–59)

If Fabrice has noticed that he was under fire, that the pieces of dirt thrown into the air were thrown by bullets, we don't know it: The narrator doesn't tell us. And yet what he notices is what we would be likely to notice. We are seeing in 1839 the contemporary distinction between showing and telling which has since become a fundamental value in courses on creative writing: that the narrator never tells us what a character is like. The reader derives it from specific, neutral detail. Stendhal is among the nineteenth-century writers who pioneer this style. For contemporary writing, showing rather than telling is an item of faith, a stylistic tick. For Stendhal style works in the service of a political point, that war is experienced only in fragments, rarely understood by its own participants.

It may be that the more realistic and detailed a presentation of war becomes, the more serious it is about the war's historical importance, the more it strives toward neutrality, and showing increasingly overcomes telling. A refusal to heroize the war requires a determination to refuse judgment, i.e., to minimize telling. Stendhal represents war with photographic accuracy. It surrounds the reader, but Fabrice's role as our focalizing figure compromises the sense of risk. The serious and heroic figures (some of them historical) are in the background. At this point in the novel we know Fabrice as a comic figure, naïve and not completely serious. (Stendhal has a wider project, a depiction of the cynical political world that succeeded the Napoleonic era. The experience of 1815 functions as preparation.) More fundamentally, we know from the start that Fabrice will survive the experience intact. The reader is never allowed to feel that the danger to our point-of-view character is real.

I suggest that this is the contradictory limit of narration. The ultimate power of representing war should be identification with a character inside it. But the rules of narrative require the observing character to be alive. The presence of death which defines war is available only to survivors. The victims are dead and not available to us. (There are of course narratives with dead narrators, most famously Chaucer's Troilus in the closing scene of *Troilus and Cressida*, who looks down on the siege of Troy from his perch in heaven and laughs. This is not a common narrative device, in part because, once we observe from heaven, narrative tension is no longer a possibility.)

The tension between the scene of risk and the reader's certainty that we are hearing a survivor speak is particularly intense in Ahmad Dehqan's *Safar be garâ-ye divist-u haftâd darajeh*, 1996 (in Paul Sprachman's translation *Journey to Heading 270 degrees*). Dehqan shows the reader a scene set in the middle of the Iran-Iraq War so dispassionately and vividly, it may be a limit. He describes a particular campaign in Ahwaz from close up, i.e., from inside. It is as much memoir as fiction, based on a military operation called Karbala 5, one of a series of campaigns to take Shalamcheh, a community just across the border from Basra. And yet it is striking how that testimony avoids the tone of a personal account.

Dehqan outdoes Stendhal's insistence on presenting war in its detail, refusing altogether to frame the experience as anything but individual, personally observed, neutral, and stripped of national sentiment. It unrolls in the present tense, which minimizes the possibility of narrative anticipation. There is something else that resembles Fabrice's experience in the *Charterhouse*: It resists the collective point of view. It even avoids attributing to the hero any emotional reactions. We hear no patriotism, no sense of a bigger picture. We see because we are shown, not told, his loyalty to his own companions. As he goes to war the sense of anticipation is barely present. Even when he is wounded, his own account is so distant we may forget he is describing himself:

The truck driver is holding his RPG so tightly to his side that it is digging into his shirtless skin. The veins in his neck are taut and the whites of his eyes are crimson from the blood flowing through them. As the enemy fires at us relentlessly, he senses a chance to get up and fire, but, as he does so, a mortar round hits the rim of the trench, sending a sharp piece of shrapnel [*tarkesh*] deep into my throat. I become flushed and when the smoke and dust clear, I see fresh blood dripping from between my fingers onto the ground.

Rasool balls up my keffiyeh and hands it to me. My hands are covered with blood. I wrap the keffiyeh around the wound and notice that there is something in my hand, something like a bone. I spit out blood and bits of shattered teeth onto the ground. Moving my hand out from under the keffiyeh, I finger my lips, which are split and the stumps of my teeth, which have been honed to a point by the shrapnel. (Dehqan 2006, 164)

Another index of his neutrality is the way he presents a rare occurrence of humor. I take the following example to be dark comedy, but comedy that remains unacknowledged:

Mehdi is shouting from beside the meeting tent. We get up. Me, Ali, Abdollah, and Mirza, who has withdrawn within himself. We start to move and Rasool empties a pail of water behind us. He splatters the back of our clothes with water and mud. His moonlight [*sic*] face turns red. Mirza scowls at him. Ali sniggers. They have put a banner in front of the bus: [*Jubhe-hâ-ye Junuub. Dabirestân-e Kamâli-ye Isfahâni*–90] Tour of the Southern Front. Kamali High School of Esfahan. Mehdi explains, "It's to fool the Iraqi spies." (58)

We can see that it *is* humor, but it is not the narrator's humor, and the reader may feel that there is a competition between the moment of lightness and the degree-zero, neutral voice. The neutral narration wins. The bus is just another observed object, and if we were tempted to laugh we have Mehdi's exclamation. The humor has a military use.

The withdrawal of affect may or may not be a symptom of posttraumatic stress, but more important is its interface with history. Paul Sprachman suggests that *Journey to Heading 270 Degrees* became so popular in part because it accorded with a widespread disillusionment in the aftermath of the war that the nation's patriotic commitment had been exploited. In other words, Dehqan's insistence on showing rather than telling obviates any explicit political commitment. Neutrality can itself be a political statement. ("Look, I've avoided the standard ideology.") I'm not sure whether it is more moving when read as a novel or as a memoir.

We are certainly inside the process of war when we read letters by participants. Even letters drawn from the historical record, however moving, take on the status of fragments absorbed by the esthetics of representation. The famous 1861 letter by Sullivan Ballou to his wife on the eve of the first battle of Bull Run (made famous in the 1991 documentary of Ken Burns) has the power of its historical reality and the stoic bravery obvious in its tone, but, as it was presented in the documentary (as a disconnected sound bite with a violin tune devised to sound as if it came from the period), there was no choice but to consume it as an esthetic object.

I began this chapter watching, as I'm sure many of us have done, the television coverage of the events in Tunisia, in Egypt, in Libya. Memories of Iran two years earlier came to mind. What struck all of us I suspect were the images sent by cell phones in the middle of the events, hand-held images in real time, unedited, spontaneous, filmed without any visible shaping that could be called esthetic. Some, of course, like the death of the Iranian woman Nada, were so wrenching they seemed our own experience. They did not seem esthetic, even with the esthetics of tragedy. It would be wrong to call these images a genre, but it certainly fits into this discussion because once those spontaneous and unscripted hand-held scenes arrived in new venues—television, YouTube, discussion between friends—they lost their fragmented isolation and became components of a controlled dialogue. They became, inevitably, embedded images, narratives framed by an interpreter. They are in other words raw footage absorbed by measured discourse. I can't complain about that loss of immediacy; without the commentary, the observer wouldn't know how to process them. What else could we do with them?

Images sent to us via cell phone tend to show us civilian casualties. Our literary representations do not seem to be as good at representing them. Civilian casualties are a subject we learn to ignore. The Trojan wars end with the death and humiliation of the citizens who were previously observers. We know this violence occurs, but usually by implication. It takes place offstage, after the events we see in *The Iliad*. Even the pro-Trojan account of defeated Troy in Book ii of Virgil's *Aeneid* focuses on the Trojan heroes waking up in the night to fight, outnumbered, in the streets of Troy. t We follow the refugees, and what happens afterward Virgil leaves us to imagine for ourselves. An unusually influential representation of imagined warfare, the movie *Star Wars* (1977), perhaps definitive of war for an entire generation of Americans, has for its climactic scene the heroic destruction of the Death Star with what seem to be nuclear weapons. It is by now a commonplace to point out that the Death Star is inhabited by noncombatants. Their destruction is crucial to the plot all right, but we're invited not to care about it.

There are of course noncombatants in the folds of war whose anxiety and cunning can evoke both sympathy and skepticism. The title figure of Brecht's *Mother Courage and Her Children* (1939) makes a living inside the war, a noncombatant (like the *vivandière* in Stendhal's *Charterhouse*), selling odds and ends to the soldiers of the Thirty Years' War (1618–1648). The tutelary figure is Jaroslav Hašek's *Good Soldier Shvejk*. Shvejk is a conscripted soldier who doesn't quite experience the First World War because he finds one cunning device after another to avoid it, from boarding the wrong train to fictional illnesses. He is not so much in the folds of war as continually managing to locate the fringes.

The armies of An Lushan's rebellion reached Chang-an (the present-day Xian, the capital of the emperor Xuangzong), in 755 CE. The poet Du Fu (712–770), at that time affiliated with the court, was left unprotected. One of the most celebrated poems of the Táng period describes the scene where he walks past the battle lines with his family.

In Stephen Owen's translation:

> I remember when first we fled the rebellion.
> Hurrying north, we passed through hardship and danger.
> The night deep on the Beng-ya Road,
> And the moon was shining on Whitewater Mountain.
> The whole family had been traveling long on foot—
> Most whom we met seemed to have no shame.
> Here and there birds of the valley sang.
> We saw no travelers going the other way. (Lawall 2002, 1385–86)

It is a great poem, but the fact that it is a poem may not be crucial to its effect. It comes across well in translation, and we can tell in translation that the violence is present only by indirection. It is traditional to represent the melancholy of a natural scene interrupted by humans, but Du Fu's example intensifies it. The background of war produces a second order of interruption. The human world is also disrupted. It emphasizes both the beauty of the scene and the pathos of the slow escape: "The whole family had been traveling long on foot." The natural world provides its own commentary: "Here and there birds of the valley sang," and as for the human world, "We saw no travelers going the other way." There are forty-six lines in all, and only a few speak of the reason they are here at all. We suspect the narrator is seeing atrocities, but our evidence is understatement: "Most whom we met seemed to have no shame." The final purpose of the poem is to thank Sun Tsai, a friend who took them in. "His great goodness reached the tiers of cloud—welcomed us as night's blackness was falling." And yet it is the journey we remember.

The absence of heroism in Du Fu's account adds to its power. Heroism, bravery, dependability in the face of danger: They're all desirable qualities. As Reinhold Niebuhr has observed, in *The Irony of American History*, such values may be admirable in the individual, less so in the aggregate. In narrative terms they are qualities that can deaden the reader's sympathies. We are able to identify with Fabrice in *Charterhouse* or with Du Fu in a way that we cannot with Aeneas, Rustam, Imr al-Qays, Audie Murphy, or Henry V.

There are, I should add, ways to make the death of a heroic or larger than life character seem a real death. Virgil, it is sometimes observed, very rarely uses the words "to be." It is a mark of the muscularity and dynamism of his style in *The Aeneid*. The exception is the way he traditionally portrays death. He will conclude a death scene with the past tense of "to be," *fuit. Fuit*, "he was." By implication "he entered the past tense." His understatement forces the reader to supply what is implied.

Without really intending it, I've been portraying the rules that shape representation as limitations. My examples of eloquence have been the eloquence of understatement. My impression is that, attempting to represent war, language lets us down. We find it inadequate, incompetent, insubstantial. Those who have experienced war are no doubt more aware of this than I am. Our examples suggest that turning down the volume, recognizing the limitations of eloquence, is probably the most expressive tactic available for a writer determined to convince.

And yet, if we set aside accuracy and neutrality as our goal, abandoning the goal of representing risk, we can acknowledge occasions in which language is very effective indeed. When it acts as an exhortation to war we find it is capable of mobilizing its consumer adequately, competently, tangibly, evoking not just commitment but a willingness to risk one's life. In this mode the goal is not accuracy but persuasion. And in this mode its power may have no limit. Incomplete or misleading representations probably carry out this duty better than the accurate portrayals we have been searching for. We speak of patriotism and war fever as physical experiences, a shudder in the viewer, a catch in the throat, and yet it can come only from one place, its representation in language. We may speak of the enthusiasm of music, of the concision with which a flag, logo, decorative ribbon, or poster can compel us. I recently watched an Iranian film from the early 1980s. Brass and percussion without a voice-over, a screen full of rifles and pennants, faces wearing expressions of determination, a parade. I felt momentarily that I wanted to enlist in that war. Revolutionary posters, sometimes works of considerable esthetic appeal, can have the same effect as persuasive language. Even something so basic as a name for the war (*Jang-e tahmîlî* in Iran, the war imposed on us), or on the other side the Qâdisiyyah, alluding to the Arab defeat of the Sassanians in 636 CE, is a speech act with power.

Public advertisements, pamphlets, political speeches, and op-ed pieces in newspapers are not sufficient cause for war, but it is hard to imagine a war without a discourse to make it possible. The minimal case is the royal decree, the declaration of war, the notice of conscription that enforces it legally. Sun-zi's first fundamental factor of war is "that which causes the people to be in harmony with their leaders" (Lao Tsu 1963, 64). It can only be a result of language. This is true when the occasion for violence is fabricated or spurious, but just as true when it is the expression of legitimate grievances (minorities abused, property appropriated, borders broached—we can all think of examples). Victims of violence or oppression may combine to protect themselves without the help of a government. They may have an unofficial protector. If they don't have access to collective language they will suffer in silence.

In a historical moment when demonstrations in streets and public squares have proven powerful enough to bring down regimes, the slogans and signs that characterize them have demonstrated that there is a powerful alternative to the statements of governments. They do not seem so much exhortations as statements of identity: Here's who we are. Here are the situations that bring us here. To my perception they are a big subject, fortunately outside the subject of this chapter.

I taught a class not long ago on the topic of violence in literature. In the course of class discussions it became clear that violence was easy to find. Literature is marbled with violence, both in its plots and in the way narrators approach their subjects. The class became very good at spotting moments of aggression in pretty much everything they read. There was in the syllabus a gentle second-century pastoral romance, Longus's *Daphnis and Chloe*, an account of two shepherds who fall in love and overcome obstacles to unite. It was my test case, my challenge to the class, and it took them no time at all to see a subplot of constant threats to the couple (pirates) and moments of manipulation between the two protagonists (e.g., Daphnis's sexual apprenticeship with a local widow and the widow's advice, which insists that Chloe's sexual initiation will be painful). I asked them to write analyses of violence they found elsewhere in the syllabus, and found in their analyses a repudiation of the violence they had found. One after another I read in their assignments manifestos against violence, manifestos in which the dominant tone was outrage and, oddly, verbal aggression. This elicited from me a follow-up in which they were asked to comment as neutral observers, and this they found very difficult. The will to non-aggression always seemed to wind up in the form of a manifesto. It was a cautionary tale for this chapter. The will to understand the representation of violence presupposes the will to read neutrally. Whitman's determination in part 26 of "Song of Myself"—"Now I will do nothing but listen"—is strictly speaking a rhetorical fiction, but it is in its way a heroic goal. It will fail. But if the will to neutrality is a desperate salmon-swim against the current, it is also a process that can make the current audible. And what I hear in my accumulation of examples is a dimension of violence that resists representation. To reiterate, the moments of authenticity seem to occur when language becomes aware of itself, in self-conscious understatement or the admission of futility. But those are also moments that require the intervention of the narrating self, that persistent voice that can never just listen, that can describe the constitutive feature of war, the experience of death, only from outside.

Video games are designed to produce fantasies of control, of superhuman power and, when you press the replay option, immortality. I know of two exceptions, "You Only Live Once" (from Raitendo) and "One Chance" (Newgrounds), which have been designed for one-time use. There is no replay option. There are numerous ways to die there, but the player will experience only one (except of course by signing on from another computer). It is said that game players find this an anxious experience. You don't learn how to play it better; you learn something else. At least for the period of the gamer's on-screen life, the frame allows the mimesis of experiencing total risk. This is not, I think, a stratagem available to written narrative, for readers rather than gamers, where language cannot portray death from the inside.

Description requires a point of view, but the point of view can change. *War and Peace* and John Hersey's *Hiroshima* are effective examples. There are more intense examples of disorientation. Margot Norris writes of Michael Herr that his memoir *Dispatches* "produced prose that veered like a hand-held camera in dizzying implication at what is narratively seen—a technique that strongly influenced Francis Ford Coppola's surrealistic cinematic style in parts of *Apocalypse Now*, and gave Steven Spielberg's opening sequence in *Saving Private Ryan* much of its visceral impact" (*Writing War*, 25). And yet there is always a spot from which we are looking, an observer through whose eyes we get our information. Observer suggests survivor. It can't represent the risk; it can't represent with neutrality.

In the novel *1919*, the second book of Dos Passos's America trilogy (1930–36), there is a scene set on the day of the Armistice. A soldier named Joe Williams finds himself getting drunk with his girlfriend Jeanette, celebrating the end of the war. A fight breaks out, which we see from Joe's point of view:

> Everybody was yelling and jabbering. Jeanette was trying to get between Joe and the waiter and got a sock in the jaw that knocked her flat. Joe laid out a couple of frogs and was backing off towards the door, when he saw in the mirror that a big guy in a blouse was bringing down a bottle on his

head held with both hands. He tried to swing around, but he didn't have time. The bottle crashed his skull and he was out. (Dos Passos 1961, 256)

With those words the chapter ends, turns to a new scene, and we never hear of Joe again. Again, death is portrayed by an absence, a withdrawal of representation. (But even here we don't lose the narrator altogether: Dos Passos feels it necessary to add a summational sentence not in Joe's point of view: "The bottle crashed his skull and he was out.")

Film may have the option of a more abrupt, vivid sense of closure. If the film ends with the screen going black as the final character dies, we may be as close as we can get to a narrative portrayal of violent death. In the final scene of *The Wrestler* (2008), the screen goes black as Mickey Rourke dives off the ropes into the ring. Viewers disagree whether or not that moment marks his death, but the tactic is effective either way. (I believe Ousmane Sembène's *Emitaï* [1971] may be a clearer example, ending more emphatically, with a rifle shot initiating the sudden darkness on the screen.)

A writer can lower the volume but never completely. The necessary intrusion of a point-of-view character can be silenced only so far. A scene in Cormac McCarthy's novel *The Road* (2006) must be very near the limit. The central character is not killed violently, but his death is disturbing. The setting of *The Road* is the aftermath of violence that is never specified. It may or may not have been a war that has devastated the countryside of America, but it's clear there remain only rubble, wasted trees, abandoned dwellings, and little bands of humans who have descended into bestiality and cannibalism. One could speak about *The Road* at great length for its style, its pathos, its close attention to the hardening sensibility of the focal character, a man alone with his son, walking through the multiple dangers, in part natural, in part human. He attempts to reinforce in his son a sense of human values. They are, they keep repeating, "the good guys." We look at the son through his eyes, wondering what the son feels at every new horror and wondering if the lesson will take.

The father knows he is dying, walking alone with his son day after day down a barren road. His last words, as he lies by the side of the road, offer advice:

You can talk to me and I'll talk to you. You'll see.

Will I hear you?

Yes. You will. You have to make it like talk that you imagine. And you'll hear me. You have to practice. Just don't give up, Okay?

Okay.

Okay.

I'm really scared Papa.

I know. But you'll be okay. You're going to be lucky. I know you are. I've got to stop talking. I'm going to start coughing again.

It's okay, Papa. You don't have to talk. It's okay.

He went down the road as far as he dared and then he came back. His father was asleep. He sat with him under the plywood and watched him. He closed his eyes and talked to him and he kept his eyes closed and listened then he tried again. He went down the road as far as he dared. (MC Carthy 2006, 279–80)

Before the brief dialogue we have been seeing only what the father sees. Every moment of the 278 pages of the book that precede this point (with 6 pages to go) has been focalized through his eyes. After the dialogue the son has taken his place. From now on "he" will mean the son. We know that the father has died and left him behind, alone, but we know it by elimination, indirectly, because the transition has taken place in narrative silence. There is nothing reassuring in the survivor's point of view. The son has survived, but tentatively: "He went down the road as far as he dared and then he came back." He asserts himself so slightly, he has to do it twice.

NOTE
Thanks to Georgia Coward, Professor of Art History at Case Western Reserve University, for help understanding Callot. Thanks to Rex Sorgatz for technical advice. And thanks to Anika Aichbhaumik for her timing.

BIBLIOGRAPHY
Byatt, A. S. "Trench Names." *New Yorker*, April 6, 2009, 54–55.
Dehqan, Ahmad. *Journey to Heading 270 Degrees*, trans. Paul Sprachman. Costa Mesa, CA: Mazda, 2006.

Dehqan, Ahmad. *Safar beh Garâ-ye 270 Darajeh*. Tehran: Nashr-e Sarîr, 1375.

DeLillo, Don. *End Zone*. New York: Penguin, 1972.

Department of Art, Brown University. *Jacques Callot: 1592–1635*. Providence, Rhode Island. Exhibitions prepared by Graduate Students at the History of Art, Brown University, 1970.

Dos Passos, John. *1919*. New York: Washington Square Press, 1961.

Ebadi, Shirin, with Azadeh Moaveni. *Iran Awakening: One Women's Journey to Reclaim her Life and Country*. New York: Random House, 2007.

Genette, Gérard. *Narrative Discourse: An Essay in Method*, trans. Jane E. Lewin. Ithaca, NY: Cornell University Press, 1980.

Jameson, Fredric. "War and Representation." *PMLA* 124.5 (October 2009): 1532–1547.

Lawall, Sarah, ed. *The Norton Anthology of World Literature*, 2nd ed., vol. B. New York: W.W. Norton, 2002.

Lucretius. *De Rerum Natura*, with an English translation by W.H.D. Rouse. London: William Heinemann, 1931.

McCarthy, Cormac. *The Road*. New York: Vintage, 2006.

Milani, Abbas. *Tales of Two Cities: A Persian Memoir*. Washington, DC: Mage, 1996.

Norris, Margot. *Writing War in the Twentieth Century*. Charlottesville and London: University Press of Virginia, 2000.

Plax, Julie Anne. *Watteau and the Cultural Politics of Eighteenth-Century France*. Cambridge: Cambridge University Press, 2000.

La Rochefoucauld. *Maximes et Réflexions Diverses*, ed. Jacques Truchet. Paris: Garnet-Flammarion, 1977.

Sacco, Joe. *Footnotes in Gaza*. New York: Henry Holt & Co., 2009.

Satrapi, Marjane. *Persepolis: The Story of a Childhood*. New York: Pantheon, 2003.

Stendhal. *The Charterhouse of Parma*, trans. Margaret R. B. Shaw. New York: Penguin, 1958.

Sun Tzu (Sun-zi). *The Art of War*, trans. Samuel B. Griffith. Oxford: Oxford University Press, 1963.

Tolstoy, Leo. *War and Peace: The Maude Translation, Backgrounds and Sources, Essays in Criticism*, trans. Louise and Aylmer Maude, ed. George Gibian. New York: W.W. Norton, 1966.

Voltaire. *Romans et contes*, ed. René Groos. Paris: Gallimard, 1954.

———. *Candide, or Optimism*, trans. Robert Adams. New York: W.W. Norton, 1991.

PART III

War through Visual Representations

8

All's Not Quiet on the Western Front

Graphic Arts in the Iranian War Effort

PETER CHELKOWSKI

In the summer of 1999, I was invited to a conference on "Shii Rituals" in Shiraz. Since I had to see many people, I was assigned a car with a driver. In such instances, it is my custom to sit next to the driver and chat. On this occasion the driver, whose name was Mohammad, was not what I expected of a Shirazi man; the Shirazis are generally easy-going and cheerful. He was sad, and not very communicative. During our conversation, which was mainly a monologue on my part, I asked him about the war with Iraq and whether he had been a participant in it. He very briskly answered, "Yes." I responded, "Thank God you have returned alive from the front." His reply astonished me. "Unfortunately," he said. I asked him what he meant and he tried to cut the conversation short, but I persisted and asked him again.

He finally responded, "My brother Rasul and I enlisted together in the Basij. We were sent to the front, but we were not in the same unit. After nine months, we had leave, but not at the same time. My brother arrived home before me and bought air tickets to Mashhad for himself and our mother to go on pilgrimage: *ziyarat*. Upon arrival there, almost immediately, they went to the shrine of Imam Reza. In the *haram* (inner sanctum) Rasul turned to my mother and asked her to pray to the holy Imam that he would become a martyr on the battlefield. My mother was shocked and refused to pray for such a thing. They returned to the inn next to the shrine and then, in the late afternoon, went back to the shrine mosque. My mother again refused to pray for her son's death. "Throughout the day, my brother Rasul continued to entreat my mother to pray for his martyrdom. Finally, the next morning, they went back to the shrine and my mother prayed to Imam Reza to grant my brother's wish, without, however, specifically mentioning death or martyrdom. Rasul went back to the front when his leave was over and six weeks later was killed in action, achieving the martyrdom which he had desired so fervently. I, who had the same desire as my brother to sacrifice my life in combat, was not granted this honor."

Like many young Iranians, these two brothers had answered the call to arms to defend their country and faith against Saddam Hussein's aggression, which began in September 1980. The protracted war with Iraq required immense sacrifice, determination, and supreme heroism from the men, women, and children of Iran. Graphic artists played an important role in mobilizing the masses and comforting the bereaved. Countless posters, murals, paintings, illustrations, and cartoons were dedicated to the war effort.

The Ayatollah Khomeini focused his military efforts on building up the Revolutionary Guards, which were originally conceived as a revolutionary militia; he didn't trust the Shah's forces and had many of the Shah's officers executed. Based on a photograph of a band of Revolutionary Guards proudly marching forward wearing red bandanas, which invoke various Shi'i adages, Ahmad Yarri Rad created an image that was so popular, it appeared on posters and postage stamps, and also

Figure 8.1

Figure 8.2

on a huge 19×24-meter tile mural in Tehran (figure 8.1). During the war, it became a common practice to utilize images in a variety of media. Kazem Chalipa created a poster called "The Guards of the Anemone Fields," representing a mosaic of the ethnic groups of Iran defending the oilfields of Khuzestan, unified in their fight against Saddam. Khomeini appears above, watching over them (figure 8.2).

Figure 8.3

In the initial phase of the war, Iranian casualties were extremely high and the Iraqis occupied Iranian territory along the western border. Cemeteries all over the country rapidly filled up with the bodies of the fallen, who were referred to as "martyrs." Abolfazl 'Aali created a poster, entitled "Behesht-e Zahra," depicting the famous cemetery south of Tehran. Over each tomb is a stand holding a photograph of the soldier buried beneath. The atmosphere is not tragic, but triumphant—above a golden glow surrounding the burial ground, we see the souls of the departed ascending to heaven (figure 8.3). In another Behesht-e Zahra poster intended to comfort bereaved women, a group of mourning women in chadors are sitting around a tomb strewn with flowers. They are joined by a glowing, veiled apparition of Fatimeh Zahra, who has come to commiserate with them (figure 8.4).

Since so many Iranian men were killed in the trenches, the armed forces started to recruit teenagers for the front lines. Basij units were created for young and old. In the poster by Kazem Chalipa entitled "Guards of Light," a wounded guardsman continues forward toward the battle, while a woman guides a boy in the same direction. The young combatant carries a grenade in one hand and a Molotov cocktail in the other. Khomeini is seen hovering above the trio and overseeing their march toward the battlefield.

In Shii culture, particularly in the Shii Iranian tradition, Moharram rituals are observed with great reverence. The philosophy behind these rituals is based on the removal of time and space constraints so that spectators can identify with the suffering of Imam Hussein. Ta'ziyeh, the Shii passion play, recounts many episodes from Hussein's life, and during the war, provided inspiration to soldiers and citizens alike.

Figure 8.4

Figure 8.5

Self-mortification is also an important part of the Moharram observances; it helps the participants to identify with the martyrs of Karbala. Boys of age twelve and older march in Moharram and Safar parades, beating their backs with chains. During the war, there were weekly rallies and marches of this type honoring the heroes of the trenches who were then fighting. Young boys carried plastic grenades in these processions, but soon they went to the front carrying real weapons. Photographs of such parades were popular and were widely published.

The most famous of these young war heroes was Hossein Fahmideh. A postage stamp with his photograph was created to honor him (figure 8.5).

Text inscribed next to the photograph quotes Khomeini, "Our *rahbar* [leader] is that youth of twelve years whose valiant little heart can be justly described neither by a hundred tongues nor a hundred pens. He attached grenades to his body and threw himself under the enemy tank and destroyed it and he himself drank the sweet elixir of martyrdom." *Rahbar* was a title reserved for Khomeini alone. The repetition of this sentiment may be seen in a poster produced by the Art Center of the Islamic Propagation Organization depicting a young soldier bidding farewell, presumably to his sister, as he leaves for the front. Graffiti on the wall behind them reproduces part of the above quote with additional text from Khomeini asking that he not be called *rahbar*, but rather, "servant of the nation." Hossein Fahmideh's image also appeared as a watermark in bank notes. He was further immortalized in a giant mural painting in Tehran on Avenue Enqelab. In this painting, the disabled tank appears along with Khomeini's famous quote. The same mural was repainted between 2004 and 2009 by the Office of Beautification of the City of Tehran, but this time, the quote and tank have been removed and the colors are more cheerful.

During the eight years of fighting against Iraq, every available space and surface was used to promote the war effort. The most striking graphic creations were the colossal murals that appeared on the sides of buildings. Almost thirty years later, many of the giant murals in Tehran still pay tribute to the martyrs of the war against Iraq, and to the Revolution. Kazem Chalipa's poster entitled "Self Sacrifice," which also appeared as a postage stamp, was one of the first such large-scale murals created during the war (figure 8.6). It adorns a building not far from the site of the American Embassy and depicts a woman holding a fallen soldier in her outstretched arms. The lower half of her body is shaped like a red tulip. The red tulip in Iranian tradition is the flower of love and sacrifice. On her right, a line of tulip buds, each holding an unborn child, stretches away into the distance, while on her left a progression of soldiers marches off to war. The background shows an army of shrouded heroes representing the martyrs of Karbala. The entire scene is framed by a *mihrab*, a niche that points toward Mecca. The arch of the niche is covered with verses from the Qur'an, such as, "To him who fights in the cause of Allah, whether he is slain or victorious, soon shall we give him a reward of great value" (4:74). The image is a tribute to the heroes of the Iran-Iraq War, but at the same time is also a tribute to the Iranian women who readily sacrificed their children for the cause.

The series of posters devoted to women under the rubric, "The Way of Zaynab"—the sister of Imam Hussein and the granddaughter of the Prophet—idealizes the role of women in society. In particular, the poster created by Mohammad Khazai entitled, "O Zahra," emphasizes this idealization. One of a crowd of veiled women carries a sign inscribed, "Man Goes to Heaven from the Lap of Woman." The meaning of this sentiment is that if a woman raises a man properly, he goes to Paradise. Another woman carries a vibrant portrait of Ayatollah Khomeini with his arm raised, blessing the crowd. Above the procession of chador-clad women hovers the huge image of another woman amidst floating flags in symbolic colors, exhorting the multitude onward. This is a very good example of how a photograph can be enhanced in another form (figure 8.7).

Figure 8.6

Figure 8.7

Figure 8.8

The glorification of martyrdom both in narrative and illustration played a major role in the art of persuasion during the war. In the mural from Qazvin, the right-hand side proclaims, "The only way to happiness (heavenly bliss) is faith, *jihad*, and *shahadat* (martyrdom)." The left-hand side of the mural illustrates the text shown in figure 8.8.

There were many surfaces available for murals of this type since the traditional Iranian dwelling is surrounded by an adobe or brick wall. A wall in Andimeshk has a combination of murals and graffiti on its surface. One of the slogans, written in bold calligraphy, proclaims, "The martyr is the heart of history." When the Iranian armed forces finally gained the upper hand in the conflict with Iraq, and not only regained lost territory but moved into that of their enemy, quite a number of murals appeared, saying, "Forward towards Hossein's sanctuary (Karbala)." Such sentiments provided justification for a switch from a defensive stance to an offensive campaign.

The so-called Imposed War between Iraq and Iran was the longest conventional war of the twentieth century. It did not involve the *blitzkrieg* tactics of World War II, but, rather, the trench warfare of World War I. The front, which was mainly static, was covered by thousands of billboards with inspirational slogans intended to boost the morale of the combatants. A typical billboard displayed one of Khomeini's famous quotes, "From afar, I kiss the hand of you fighters, shielded as it is, by the hand of God, and I take pride in this obedient kiss."

Human rights were stressed in a photograph showing two children fleeing from an Iraqi bombardment during the war. The fear that is so evident on the faces of the girl and the little boy she is carrying is powerful and moving. It can be compared to the famous photo of a naked Vietnamese girl fleeing a village under a napalm attack. Ahmad Agha Qulizadeh created a poster based on the image of the two Iranian children and incorporated the details of a second photograph showing a town in ruins in the background. His poster, however, has neither the immediacy nor the emotional impact of the photograph.

Taking into consideration that during the revolution and war, illiteracy in Iran was still very high, posters concentrated on images with minimal text. Calligraphy, however, was and is one of the major Islamic art forms and therefore it was impossible to completely neglect it. The poster depicted in figure 8.9 is an excellent example of how calligraphy in its simplicity can deliver a powerful message. The word *Basij*, meaning "mobilization," but also referring to the Iranian military units made up of volunteers, is written in a bold green against a black background. The letter *jim* appears as a sickle cutting the Iraqi flag in two.

Figure 8.9

Figure 8.10

(At a certain moment in the war, the Iraqis realized that religion could add an important dimension to their propaganda and thereafter included the invocation, 'Allah u Akbar,' on their flag.)

In the tradition of Persian miniature painting, we see an image of Ayatollah Khomeini moving through the various stages of his life and finally entering the gates of Paradise. Just before his death, he is depicted comforting the families of those slain in war (figure 8.10).

The decade of revolution and war in Iran was a flourishing period for the graphic arts. An army of painters and photographers worked day and night to create images that would inspire the people and boost the morale of the Iranian armed forces and the revolutionary fighters. There were many art centers in various ministries and militia units. Despite the fact that today it is the giant murals that overwhelm passersby with their grandiose scale, the poster is the outstanding mode of artistic expression to emerge from that time of bloodshed and sacrifice.

BIBLIOGRAPHY

'Aali, Abolfazl. *A Decade with the Graphists of the Islamic Revolution, 1979–1989.* Tehran: Art Center of the Islamic Propagation Organization, 1989.

Chelkowski, Peter and Hamid Dabashi. *Staging a Revolution, The Art of Persuasion in the Islamic Republic of Iran.* New York: New York University Press, 1999.

Goodarzi, Mustafa. *A Decade with Painters of the Islamic Revolution 1979–1989.* Tehran: Art Center of the Islamic Propagation Organization, 1989.

The Imposed War: Defense vs. Aggression. Vol. 1, War Information Headquarters, Supreme Defense Council of the Islamic Republic of Iran, Tehran, February 1983.

———. Vol. 2, April 1984.

———. Vol. 3, September 1985.

———. Vol. 4, September 1986.

———. Vol. 5, September 1987.

9

Shadows of War

An Overview of Iranian War Films from 1980 to 1988

MARJAN RIAHI

Translated by Arta Khakpour

In 1979, the Iranian monarchy collapsed and the Ayatollah Khomeini assumed leadership of the Revolution, resulting in the transformation of Iran's government from a monarchy to an Islamic republic. On September 22, 1980, while this fledgling government was still facing numerous domestic difficulties, Iran officially entered a state of war with its western neighbor, Iraq. Lasting eight years, it would be the second longest war of the twentieth century after the Vietnam War. During the Iraqi army's first campaign upon Iranian soil, approximately 30,000 square kilometers were occupied by the invading forces. The casualty count released by the Iranian government indicated 213,255 dead. Iran's major cities were subject to aerial bombardment on numerous occasions. Border cities such as Abadan, Khorramshahr, and Susangerd suffered destruction at rates higher than 70 percent of their area. The city of Dezful was subject to more than seven hundred rocket attacks. Finally, in July 1988, a ceasefire agreement was signed by both parties. One year later, negotiations for the release of POWs began—negotiations that would take more than twelve years and that left many families forever awaiting their missing-in-action loved ones.

Now, twenty-two years after the ceasefire, victims of chemical weapons continue to die from long-term fatal illnesses, minefields on the border have not been completely cleared, investigations continue for the remains of war dead, and the social and psychological ramifications of the war continue to cast a shadow upon the daily lives of the Iranian people.

Meanwhile, art, born of experience and introspection, has been one of the narrators of this history. Among the seven arts, cinema is the subject of this chapter, which will address aesthetic developments in Iranian war cinema, with the intent of defining and identifying what is known today in Iran as the "cinema of the sacred defense." Accordingly, this chapter will address developments between the years 1980 and 1989. For the purposes of this presentation, professional cinema will be defined as 35mm fictional films intended to be played in Iranian cinemas.

Because the Revolution and the Iran-Iraq War occurred in such close proximity, this chapter will also provide a brief overview of developments in Iranian cinema during 1978 and 1979.

Spring 1978–Winter 1979

Although the spring and summer of 1978 witnessed scattered strikes and demonstrations against the monarchic government, Iranian cinemas generally continued about their usual business, and even the arson fires of several cinemas did not bring about a general halt in the movie industry.

There were 450 active cinemas in Iran at this point. The films that were shown on their screens came from three major sources. (1) Seven American companies who had the largest share of film exports to Iran. (2) A number of Iranian and non-Iranian merchants who, in addition to their other wares, imported foreign films to Iran. (3) Domestic productions, which made up the smallest share, and which mostly fell into the category of "Film Farsi" due to their pulp style and popular appeal (*Kayhan* newspaper, June 27, 1978).

The next sixth months, and particularly the period after the regime fired on protesters on September 8, 1978, witnessed a deterioration in the state of affairs. Cinemas were attacked in several cities and cinema owners were among the first business owners compelled to shut their doors.

After February 11, 1979, and the official victory of the Islamic Revolution, cinema owners were able to resume their business. However, the heightened religious sensibilities that resulted from the leadership of a cleric of course meant that cinema owners refrained from showing films that would offend these sensibilities. Film Farsi's days were over and movie importers sought films that would be compatible with the people's revolutionary fervor. On March 7, *Kayhan* newspaper's headline announced in bold: "Women must wear the hijab to work." Sensitivities regarding women and veiling affected the importation of foreign films and their censorship.

Filmmakers who were active at that time were hurt by their association with the previous regime. The fledgling revolution lacked filmmakers of its own to offer as an alternative, and the elder filmmakers faced constant scrutiny for allegedly having Western and anti-Islamic influences.

1979

On 12 Farvardin (April), the Islamic Republic was elected by referendum as the official government of Iran, and the issue of Islamicization attained urgency at all levels of society. The most salient news items of the day were the executions of regime forces and other opposition militants, and pictures of the dead were published on the front pages. Meanwhile, movie ads were deleted from the newspapers. From spring 1979 until October 12 of that year, *Kayhan* printed no movie ads. The first ad after this hiatus featured an image of the leading man, Dariush Eqbali, a popular pop singer who was rumored to be a regime opponent.

Filmmakers who were inclined to produce under such conditions continued to do so, and their results could be seen in the coming years. In the first phase, some filmmakers attempted to make films without female actors, and to form the plot in such a way that the presence of women would not be required. When this strategy failed, women were relegated to marginal roles in films. This line of thinking prevailed in war cinema, more or less, throughout the first decade, but other genres proceeded along a different course. Foreign films, both of the light entertainment variety and the more weighty social and political material, were all that kept Iranian cinemas functioning in this period. Meanwhile local filmmakers, operating in the atmosphere of the time and the post-crisis chaos, filmed screenplays that were populated entirely by good or evil characters. These films were unable to satisfy even the revolutionary audiences of their time.

Revolutionary subject matter for films included any manner of conflict between feudal landholders, smugglers, thugs, and corrupt politicians from the Shah's regime on one side and innocent, oppressed people on the other. Other directors focused on drug addiction and presented it as a legacy of the previous regime and a Western ploy to afflict the country's youth. Meanwhile, private and governmental funding of the film industry was still disorganized, and occasionally, public relations divisions of government ministries would enter the filmmaking business.

1980

In 1980, the Cultural Revolution was initiated, with the aim of purging Westernized students and professors and islamicizing the universities. Practically speaking, the way was closed for the education of new innovators in the field of cinema. With the nation embroiled in internal conflict, including the assassination of public officials and serious divisions between opposition groups, cinemas secured their livelihood by addressing the topics of the day.

On September 22, 1980, after months of conflict, Iraq invaded Iran.

The war and the revolution shared certain characteristics in the Iranian political sphere. Both were considered to have been necessitated by the conspiracies of the enemies of Iran and Islam. Both required self-sacrifice and martyrdom for victory. Thus, filmmakers began this period by expressing these general political sentiments, and they addressed the war directly less often. Of course, the war differed from the revolution in several ways. First, only a portion of Iran's land was in daily struggle, whereas the rest of the population was exposed to the war through the news. The number of those martyred in the war was several degrees higher than during the revolution, and in time, the war's effects would spread to every city. Moreover, the war caused complications for which historical memory did not provide analogies and that were not easily remedied. These included events such as the usage of chemical weapons against several regions and the sudden emigration of residents of war-afflicted cities.

The war initially targeted the province of Khuzestan. While Iranians in other regions of the country continued their daily lives, Khorramshahr fell and Abadan was besieged. Other cities in Khuzestan were subjected to constant Iraqi attacks. Khuzestan had thirty-eight cinemas at the time, Abadan having the largest share, fourteen. The province's other cities with cinemas included Ahvaz with nine, Khorramshahr with five, Dezful, Masjed Suleiman, Behbahan, and Andimeshk with two each, and Shushtar, Ramhormoz, and Susangerd with one each. The province's cinemas were largely shut down for the duration of the war, but the tragedy that was inflicted upon the people of this region did not cease for a moment and would eventually motivate people to speak its story through film.

Foreign films that played in Iran this year included *The Day that Shook the World*; *The Case is Closed, Forget It*; *Operacion Ogro*; *Robin Hood*; and *The Purple Plain*.

1980–1981

The siege of Abadan was broken during the month of Mehr (September–October) in 1981. Subsequent to this important event on the battlefield, and in commemoration of the anniversary of the revolution, sixteen films that had been produced between 1979 and 1980 were shown in theaters throughout the country during January and February. All cinemas were required to suspend their regular programming and show these sixteen films.

The characteristics of these films demonstrate that the anniversary event's organizers were primarily interested in showcasing cinematic accomplishments, and they were willing to screen whatever films were at their disposal without attention to the usual categorizations of time period or genre (such as fiction or documentary).

Revolutionary themes, rather than war, were still dominant in these films. Both private individuals and the government were involved in their production and funding. Among these, only the film *Marz* (Border) can be seriously considered the genesis of Iranian war cinema. These films appear very weak in comparison with their foreign counterparts, due to their transparent duality of good and innocent people versus evil and demonic enemies, and their weakness in constructing a plot.

During this time, there was still no "war cinema" as a film genre. There was no name for it, not "war cinema" and not "cinema of the sacred defense." This latter title was only applied later to films that dealt with the Iran-Iraq War. On March 15, 1981, *Kayhan* newspaper published a quote placing the number of Iranian films produced in 1974 at 67, 1975 at 79, 1977 at 54, and 1978 at 16. While the number of domestic productions in 1981 remained at 16, 340 foreign films were dominating the movie screens.

Being in such a weak state, which to a large extent was the result of the economic crisis, the Iranian film industry was not able to address the normal cinematic needs of the country, let alone be able to create new, native genres of film.

In 1981, the film *Command* (Farman), directed by Hadi Meshkat and dealing with the situation in Kurdistan, was released in cinemas. The film's distribution was managed by the Foundation of the Oppressed. This organization would go on to play an active role in the production and distribution of films in the 1980s.[1]

Renamed "Islamic Republic Foundation of the Oppressed and Disabled" in 1989, the Foundation maintains a website at www.irmf.ir where one can find a list of the organization's activities in the cinematic realm.

In Tehran alone, the Foundation ran the following theaters: Shahr-e Farang (Azadi), Laleh, Jomhuri, Shahr-e qesseh, Felestin, Qods, Enqelab, Esteqlal, Afriqa, Qiyam, Payam, Shahed, Kuch, and Homay. Showtimes for these cinemas were published virtually every day next to and distinct from those of other cinemas in the nation's afternoon newspapers.

In 1981, the Korean film *The Florist's Daughter* was released by the Foundation and became the best-selling film of the year. After its initial run and subsequent television airplay, it was released for a second run, although only in the less well-known cinemas of the country. The film deals with the life of a girl separated from her family during the Korean conflict and partition. Although the events of the film were superficially similar to the experiences of hundreds of Iranian refugees who were separated from their families, the melodrama wasn't able to meaningfully connect with the lives of millions of other Iranians who were able to continue their daily routines more or less throughout the war. The status attained by this film is therefore more a reflection on the weakness of Iran's domestic film industry and its inability to palpably portray the lives of Iranians during the war.

Foreign films screened in Iran included the Norman Wisdom film *On the Beat, Oliver Twist*, Disney's *Cinderella*, and the Algerian film *December*.

1982

On April 25, 1982, the deputy minister of cinematic affairs, Mehdi Kalhor, stated in an interview that the number of Iranian cinema screening rooms had grown from 400 to 1,500. He did not indicate whether these screening rooms were actually of "cinema" caliber or which films they would be playing. It bears mentioning that Mehdi Kalhor has been Ahmadinejad's arts and culture advisor from the beginning of his presidential term.

The same year, the Department of Islamic Art and Thought, later renamed the Ministry of Islamic Propagation, became active as a producer and distributer of films. Other organizations, including the Cultural Foundation of the Martyrs and the Cooperative Film Council, began work in film distribution as well, but not nearly to the extent of the Foundation of the Oppressed.

Later this year, while *The Florist's Daughter* was still playing in cinemas, another Korean film was released and distributed by the Foundation. This film, entitled *Years of Separation*, enjoyed a twenty-five-week run in cinemas and dealt, once again, with the topic of families separated during the partition of Korea.

On May 23, 1982, Khorramshahr was liberated. The anniversary of this event is still celebrated yearly. A Libyan war movie was released later in the year and enjoyed little success in theaters.

Throughout the year, universities remained closed and Mohammad Khatami presided as head of the Ministry of Culture and Islamic Guidance. On December 29, 1982, the Islamic Center for Filmmaking Education was founded at the Bagh-e Ferdows palace in northern Tehran. Its stated goal was to promote specialized expertise in its field. The center's head stated at the opening that "Between 1966 and 1972, 2,260 films were played in Iran. Between 1972 and 1982, that number was 2,197 and between 1977 and 1980 alone, 2,100. From 1980 on, only 142 films were shown in Iranian cinemas, 90 percent of which were foreign. Domestic film production is presently around 10 films a year, of which 2 to 4 never make it to the screens." This news item was printed in *Kayhan*, without indicating the name of the center spokesman.

Later that year, Kamal Tabrizi became the educational director of the center, where he remained active until 1983. He changed careers to become a professional filmmaker afterward, and in 1995, seven years after the ceasefire, created the first Iranian war-comedy film, *Leili is With Me*, which became the best-selling film of the year and propelled Tabrizi to fame. In 2004, his film *The Lizard* was tremendously successful despite being banned soon after its release. The Center for Filmmaking Education later added editing, screenwriting, and set design to its curriculum. In 2000, however, poor management led to its closing. The center's headquarters is now a film museum.

In the winter of 1982, the complete schedule of the first Fajr Film and Theater Festival was announced. No part of the agenda was dedicated to war cinema, and the theme of war did not have a notable presence in the festival, even though three years had passed since the beginning of the conflict. Revolutionary films from Cuba, and films dealing with the oppression of Native Americans and blacks, became analogies for revolutionary Iran.

1983

In 1983, *Bridge of Freedom*, directed by Mehdi Madani, was released. The film, which tells the story of the liberation of Khorramshahr, was produced by the Ministry of Islamic Propagation and distributed by the Foundation of the Meek. This same year, universities gradually reopened. The Minister of Culture and Higher Education promised that all humanities departments would reopen this year. He made no mention of the arts. The education of experts thus began, three years after the start of the war.

Although the war inflicted great losses upon the country, the cinematic market enjoyed a particular boom. Several films were produced that dealt with the war theme, but the film that captured the attention of audiences was *Two Blind Eyes*, directed by Mohsen Makhmalbaf and produced by the artistic bureau of the Organization of Islamic Propagation.

This film tells the story of a gung ho war supporter who, despite his best efforts, is not able to make it to the front. In return, however, his child's blindness is cured by the Shiite holy figure Imam Reza.

1984

In 1984, the third Fajr film festival was held. Mohammad Khatami, who was at the time Minister of Culture and Islamic Guidance, participated in the final ceremonies of the festival. He spoke on the fact that thus far, their work had been of a negative nature, meaning aimed against anti-Islamic activities in the arts. Islamic art, however, was not limited to the negation of the anti-Islamic, he argued; it must also have a positive dimension as the messenger of Islam and the Revolution. If we want to grade an artistic work, he said, we have to devote 90 points to message and content, and 10 points to technique.

In this speech, Khatami made no mention of war cinema, and presented the government line in general terms. The organizers of the festival did not address the topic of war. In the short film section, however, the name of Ibrahim Hatamikia was heard for the first time. He received honors for his short film *The Path*, and was recognized by the judges for excellence in presenting a theme related to the war.

In 1981, Hatamikia (as cameraman) joined Morteza Avini, who was the biggest documentarian of the war, to travel to the front. Hatamikia is a director recognized as the storyteller of the war in Iranian cinema. All of his films deal with the war, and are most notable for their attention to social changes brought about by the war. He began his work in 35mm film in 1985 with the film *Identity*. In *Joining of the Righteous*, he treats the topic of war-torn families. In *Karkheh to the Rhine*, he deals with a victim of a chemical weapons attack. In *The Scent of Joseph's Shirt*, produced after the war's end, he deals with the return of POWs.

Morteza Avini is the most prominent documentary filmmaker of the war. His series, *Chronicles of Victory*, has been aired many times on Iranian television. He traveled to the various fronts of the war and covered issues ranging from the front line to logistical operations. In 1993, while filming, Avini stepped on a landmine and was killed. He was a major proponent of the war and the Islamic Republic and, in his works, presented the war as a sacred and purifying event.

1985

Mr. Khamenei, on 2 Ordibehesht (April) 1985, during his term as president of Iran, declared in an interview that anything, such as cinema, that receives inspiration from Islamic thought, will necessarily serve Islamic thought. Two days later, Mr. Rafsanjani, as chairman of the parliament, said in an interview that the importance of cinema requires that the government support it sufficiently and in such a way that people of true faith will enter the cinematic field.

These declarations show the unity of the government perspective regarding expectations from cinema, from Khatami to other government heads. War films were produced this year as well, but the films that achieved acclaim were *The City of Mice* and *Chrysanthemums*, by Rasul Sadr Ameli. The former is a children's movie and the latter is a love story about a blind couple.

1987–1988

In 1987, the sixth annual Fajr Film Festival was held. No award for best film was presented, but judges' special prizes were given to *Little Birds of Good Fortune* by Puran Derakhshandeh and *Kani Manga* by Seif Ala Dad. *Kani Manga* is a war film, and, precisely one year before the end of the war, it became the first war film to win a major domestic prize.

The year started with the bombing of several Iranian cities. The bombardment brought greater suffering upon the populace compared to previous years, and became known as the "war of the cities."

Most of the cities that had not experienced bombardment before, or that had suffered less damage, came under constant Iraqi attack. Residents of major cities took refuge in the countryside. Isfahan, Tehran, Rasht, and even Mashhad, located some 2,000 miles from the front, came under air attack. Public tolerance for this eight-year war of attrition had come to an end. A generation of young boys either had been killed in the war or had left the country. Under these circumstances, support for peace negotiations increased and the public was hopeful that the war might soon end. The slogan, "One must pass through Karbala to liberate Jerusalem," had lost its effect and, on graffiti, "War, war until victory" was changed to "War, war, where is victory?"

Many cities witnessed the expansion of their cemeteries and, likewise, the number of grieving families, which contributed to public unrest. Students were sent to war via their schools, and there were reports of children as young as ten and twelve years old being sent to the front after a twenty-five-day training session.

During the month of Khordad, *Kani Manga* was released and received moderate audience acclaim. *Maybe Another Time*, a film by Bahram Beyzdi which tells the story of a pair of reunited twins, was released the same month, however, and surpassed it to become the bestseller of the year.

Peace accords were signed during the month of Mordad (July–August). The cinema of the war, like other genres, can be criticized because of its weakness in terms of content and fictional structure, and its emulation of foreign films. With the end of the war, however, and the resulting talks concerning the release of POWs, war cinema took on a new form. Filmmakers and producers began tackling the aftermath of the war and its complications.

1989–1990

During the month of Mordad, the first group of POWs was released. At the eighth Fajr Festival, three war films were shown, but *Hamoun*, the story of the philosophical conflicts of a student and his love for his wife, won best picture.

Throughout the decade following the revolution and the outbreak of war, Iranian cinema was faced with several difficulties that hindered the production of films narrating the war. First, lack of budget and equipment prevented these films from being able to compete with the visceral documentary footage shown on nightly television, particularly the work of Morteza Avini.

A large percentage of the urban population of Khuzestan was forced to migrate to the central cities, and throughout eight years of war, no cinematic narrative was made of their plight. After the peace accords, however, filmmakers who were interested in the war turned to stories that could show the war's aftermath and complications, and did not require the difficult and expensive depiction of the conflict itself. In fact, the golden age of war cinema began after the peace accords.

Cinema of the Sacred Defense

Until the end of the war, this cinematic genre had no name and, in fact, the word "war" alone was not used by the press and in political circles. Instead, "imposed war" was used. After the war, however, the word "war" gradually gave way to "defense," and the word "imposed" gradually became "sacred," such that after the signing of the peace accords, the "sacred defense" was born. War cinema was thus named "cinema of the sacred defense."

The usage of the sacred, despite its connotation of purification and its tendency to stifle criticism, was never able to prevent domestic criticism regarding the quality of such cinema in Iran. Filmmakers who aimed to work in this field, however, had no choice but to show their characters as having undergone spiritual transformations, and to show the war, as much as they could, as a spiritually cleansing event with heroes who were pious and god-fearing. One cannot find a single work in this genre that questions the sacredness of the war. Either the pain and suffering of the war is shown to transform ordinary individuals into martyrs, or else the film's characters are shown to be transcendent figures, distinct from the outset from the general public.

Proponents of the cinema of the sacred defense distinguish it from war cinema. Their point of view is exemplified by Morteza Avini, who said, "All war is evil except for jihad in the path of God. Because the sacred defense was the place of the slaughter of lovers, and played host to truth-worshipping heroes such as Hemmat and Kharrazi and others who defended the station of the divine deputy of man, our cinema of the sacred defense is clearly distinct from other cinemas. If it were not so, it would have been incumbent upon filmmakers to have made, instead of *The Refugee* and *The Scout* and *Journey to Chazzabeh* [Iranian war films], films like *Full Metal Jacket* in order to ridicule the nihilistic armies of the world."

According to this viewpoint, the cinema of the sacred defense is completely different from "war cinema," in terms of content and theorization of values. In other words, the tradition of the cinema of the sacred defense rejects certain structures and elements inherent to the war genre. Films of the war genre, particularly World War I and World War II films, encompass the bitter events of death at the war front while presenting epic scenes of heroism and myth-making. The essence of the sacred defense genre, however, presents the courage and sacrifice and spiritual condition of the warriors at the front.

Accordingly, critics who share this viewpoint do not consider Mohsen Makhmalbaf's *Wedding of the Blessed* to fall within the category of sacred defense cinema, because it presents the darkness and ugliness of war, while sacred defense cinema is full of the filmmaker's transcendental view that war is a beautiful thing and associated with heaven. This can be seen in Morteza Avini's films and the zeal they show for going to the front, which Avini sees as the truth of the sacred defense.

An example of this line of thinking is the banning of Mohsen Makhmalbaf's film *Nights of Zayandehrud*, which approached the aftermath of the war in a different and more documentarian way. The likely justification was that the film showed the suicide of a Basiji militia member. This work was never considered a work of sacred defense cinema.

On 12 Mehr (October) 1990, the Foundation for the Preservation of the Works and Values of the Sacred Defense was founded. It established independent offices throughout the country, held literary competitions, and produced literature, film, and theater related to the war. The government sponsorship of this organization was clear. The weakness of filmmaking inherent in its field, however, was to such an extent that despite holding a film festival for the sacred defense every other year between 1992 and 2002, after 2002 there was a three-year gap and then a five-year gap between the two subsequent festivals.

In order to create facilities for filmmakers, the Sacred Defense Cinema Village was created on kilometer 35 between Tehran and Qom. The village covers approximately 700 hectares and provides for the needs of war filmmakers, and is thus recognized as the most essential institution in support of the cinema of the sacred defense. The village provides locations and sets for sacred defense films, and filmmakers must obtain tanks, helicopters, airplanes, and other necessities from the relevant organizations.

Between 1994 and 2002, approximately 250 films, serials, and clips were produced at the village. Currently, it is under the auspices of the Basij Resistance Forces of the Revolutionary Guards, but it is managed by the Foundation of the Chronicles of Victory. The Association of Revolutionary and Sacred Defense Cinema is another of its sponsors.

Most of these films are made either through the direct intervention of government agencies or indirectly through government loans. In light of the fact that the likelihood of a capital return is very small, the production of these films is practically impossible without government support.

The fate of war cinema in Iran, like in other countries, moves forward, and as society becomes concerned with various issues, it relinquishes its audience to other spaces. However, the prevailing political atmosphere in Iran is insistent upon keeping the war alive and in accord with the government's taste.

Cinematic storytelling of the war, for all its relative success in Iran, was never successful in narrating the war from a neutral point of view, and documentary film is still the best and most communicative source of war narrative.

War cinema in Iran, given that it exists solely as the cinema of the sacred defense, limits expression regarding the war and its aftermath. Producers in the private sphere are reluctant to invest due to the small likelihood of capital return. Producers in the government sphere, or those able to obtain government funds for producing war films, only support a certain range of filmmakers. Therefore, despite all the publicity and even the complaining regarding cinema of the sacred defense, this cinema is becoming duller and more lifeless with each day. The framework of the sacred, in terms of subject matter and the analysis of fictional narrative, has constrained this cinema to such an extent that it has rendered the cinematic narrative of the war an incomplete one—a narrative only certain sides of which have been told.

NOTE

1 The Foundation of the Oppressed was established in 1979 and placed under the auspices of a council selected by the Supreme Leader, including Khamenei, Hashemi Rafsanjani, Mousavi-Ardabeli, Jalali, Mas'oudi, and Mehdi Sanjabi. The Foundation's stated aims were to improve the material and spiritual lives of the less fortunate, to maximize economic growth and efficiency, and to sponsor the growth and development of human capital. In 1981, the Foundation owned 164 businesses, 101 industrial offices, 34 mines, 18 cultural institutions, 12 building firms, and a large number of shops, means of transport, and fixed and moveable assets. The Foundation also had at its disposal all assets seized by the revolutionary courts. Between 1981 and 1989, by decree of Ayatollah Khomeini, Prime Minister Mir Hossein Mousavi was in charge of the Foundation's activities.

PART IV

Literary Narratives of War

10

Representation of the Iran-Iraq War in Kurdish Fiction

MARDIN AMINPOUR

This chapter investigates some of the perspectives modern Kurdish literature has generally adopted vis-à-vis the phenomenon of war and the Kurds' prolonged struggle for independence, with a narrower focus on examination of some of the notions and impressions of war inform-ing the Kurdish fictional narratives that deal with the question of the Iran-Iraq War. Speaking in broad terms, nationalism has served as an interface between modern Kurdish literature and the Kurdish struggle for independence, establishing a dual-natured interaction between the two spheres such that, despite their unanimity of purpose, they have also confronted one another now and then. Conterminous with the political awakening of Kurds in the early twentieth century, a consid-erable sum of modern Kurdish fiction, naturally, came to share the concerns of the participants in the Kurdish war of independence. As can be expected, nationalist and sentimental propaganda and lauda-tion of guerilla warfare monopolized a remarkable portion of literary themes and perspectives in the early periods of the rise of nationalism in the early twentieth century. In other words, the early period exhib-ited a strong tendency toward glorification of war as the only viable means of liberation of Kurdistan from the tyrannical rule of the modern Arab, Turkish, and Persian nation-states that each controlled a differ-ent part of Kurdistan. The early nationalist fervor that had ensured the support of the populations at large to the nationalist cause impacted literature too. Thus the advocacy of the Kurdish nationalist resistance movements was to retain its vigorous appeal as a literary theme in litera-ture, especially in fictional narratives as late as the late 1960s, when the ravaging consequences of the often erroneous and costly miscalcula-tions of the movement leadership had planted seeds of doubt within the affected civilian populations, a discontent that gradually began to draw criticism from literary circles as well. This new development quickly gained momentum in the wake of the devastating eight-year-long war between Iran and Iraq. Straddling the border between the two countries at war, the Kurdish communities under a politically immature and factional leadership with shifting loyalties bore the brunt of the war, a fact that embittered large numbers of Kurds and alienated many intellectuals and writers from the nationalist movement. This chapter seeks to examine a number of fictional narratives that have looked back at the Iran-Iraq War with an investigative eye that has viewed the role of the Kurds in the war from an unconventional standpoint while it has also shown the general reluctance of the Kurdish civilians to take part in the war, one that was largely seen as a conflict between two foreign powers with awful repercussions for the Kurds. The critical attitude toward the nationalist movement becomes more acerbic when it comes to the leadership, which is typically deemed the real culprit for bringing about such war atrocities as the large-scale, atrocious massacre of Kurdish civilians at the hands of Saddam Hussein in the Iraqi-Kurdish border town of Halabja. Before discussing the fictional narratives that held an unconventional perspective on the Iran-Iraq War, and also, in order to gain a better understanding of the context within which the antiwar sentiments grew and found expression in literature, a more thorough investigation of the broader context of modern Kurdish literature seems important. It should be noted that this critical perspective is measured against the established conventional view that predominantly informed literary themes and notions of war since the rise of nationalist movements.

One of the early literary works written in Kurdish which later in the twentieth century drew a remarkable amount of attention from the Kurdish nationalists was Ahmade Khani's romance *Mam u Zin*. Much ahead of its time in terms of developing a nationalist tendency, Ahmade Khani (1650–1707), a seventeenth-century mystical poet and philosopher, wrote *Mam u Zin*, as he suggested in the preface to the poem, "as a reaction against the growing nationalism of Ottoman and Safavid empires, proclaiming the individuality of the Kurds and their rights to independence and freedom."[1] This ambitious literary project is an exemplary case of a narrative that exhibited early signs of nascent Kurdish nationalist aspirations of national recognition that were to escalate into a full-fledged struggle for independence much later in the early decades of the twentieth century. Khani's romantic epic follows the traditions of romances and epics, which typically related the adventures of a man of high status who embarked on a dangerous quest after accomplishment of a great feat. This long poem is similarly based on the popular romance of Mame Alan, a Kurdish prince, who meets his tragic death after uniting with the Kurdish beloved he sought and found far away from his kingdom in another part of Kurdistan. Despite containing "national symbolism, and patriotic declarations of faith,"[2] the striking popularity of the book among advocates of the Kurdish nationalist cause in the twentieth century owed much to the author's express nationalist remarks in the preface that resonated with the pro-self-rule Kurds. Khani's criticism of the divisive tribal nature of Kurdish community came to be shared by many modern intellectuals and activists. His critical remarks regarding the tribal and divisive lifestyle of his contemporary Kurdish communities, the cause of whose misery he diagnoses to be grounded in their ignorant willingness to persist in their inferiority as loyal subjects of either Arab, Turkish, or Persian rulers, made perfect sense to the twentieth-century nationalist intellectuals and men of letters. Needless to say, his romantic poem about a Kurdish prince, a man of high status, naturally conjured up images of the good old days, when Kurdistan was ruled by semi-autonomous Kurdish municipalities.

The nationalist attitude informing Ahmade Khani's romance turned this literary work into a source of inspiration that reinforced Kurdish consciousness of the dire need for unification. Impressed by the popularity and effectiveness of Ahmade Khani's work in propelling nationalism, most of the Kurdish literature that chose contemporary issues as matters of concern were inspired to write in support of unification and liberation of Kurdistan. In other words, they wrote in advocacy of the nationalist cause spearheaded by the Kurdish nationalist movements that sought to materialize this ideal through challenging on the battlefield the authority of the sovereign states under which they lived.

Kurdistan had long been split into two spheres of influence between the rivaling Ottoman-Safavid empires, but the Kurds still enjoyed ample latitude when it came to their cross-border seasonal migrations in search of pasture for their herds. The real division came after the conclusion of World War I, when the Allies saw it fit and in accordance with their interests in the area to divide the Kurds among four countries, each ruled by an ethnic majority different from the Kurds. Thus the Kurds found themselves citizens of states that generally held a hostile attitude toward them.[3] The partition, being coterminous with the wide propagation of nation-building ideologies among the peoples of the Middle East, led to the demand by Kurdish nationalists and also Kurdish literature of similar rights for the Kurds that Ahmad Khani had long before endorsed. Given the egregious economic and political underrepresentation of the Kurds within the newly formed modern states, it was only natural that such themes as encouragement of the persistence in the struggle and praise of Kurdish peshmarga (guerrilla) warfare become a major theme informing much of the engaged and committed Kurdish literature of the time as late as the 1960s, when numerous experiences of defeat, for which the Kurdish leadership was partially to blame, gradually planted doubts concerning the righteousness of the movement and the hefty prices the Kurdish civilians had had to pay.

In the early phases of the rise of nationalism in Kurdistan, most of the Kurdish literature—poetry in particular—was strongly inclined toward the advocacy of the struggle, as the majority of it was produced by individuals who were also participants in the struggle. The literature of this period, for instance the poetry of such Iranian Kurdish poets as Hejar (Abdulrahman Sharafkani, 1920–91) and Hemin (Muhammad Amin Shaykhul Islam, 1921–86)—called the Poets of the Nation—who were also active members of the elite party that established the Republic of Mahabad in 1946, was heavily charged with nationalist sentiments and ideological propaganda.[4] Their poetry became a medium through which they introduced new nationalist ideas to the educated minority and the illiterate masses at large.[5] Thanks to the lyrical quality their ideologically driven writings enjoyed, modern ideas and concepts such as freedom, independence, love of homeland, and the awareness of the existence of a distinct Kurdish identity entered the collective consciousness of the Kurdish tribal community on a much broader scale. Moving away from the classical themes of mystical love and moral advice, the literary productions of these engaged intellectuals and men of letters paralleled the rise of the Kurdish press, both of which made major contributions to fostering a sense of nationalist pride, through redefining various aspects of the Kurdish culture as constituents of Kurdish identity. In other words, literature in this period served as the chief bastion from which disseminating nationalist propaganda of various political parties and entities such as the short-lived Republic of Mahabad poured into the public. A notable example of the nationalist poetry of the period is a short poem, *Ey Raqib* (*O Enemy*) by Dildar (Yunis Mala Rauf, 1918–48), that "became the National Anthem of the Autonomous Republic of Kurdistan (1946) and was subsequently adopted by all Kurdish nationalists."[6] Old literary ideals and the classical universal beloved were substituted by the praise of peshmargas (Kurdish freedom fighters) and women who cast off their hijab to join the struggle.

Similarly, in fictional narratives, which came about at a much later stage than collections of poetry, mainly due to financial challenges, printing difficulties, and a narrow readership, national and political ideologies were of paramount importance among literary themes and perspectives.[7] Most of the fiction written in this period consisted of personal accounts of first-hand experience of either witnessing or active participation shaping the political developments in Kurdistan. For instance, *Peshmarga*[8] (first published in 1961), one of the earliest novels written in Sorani Kurdish, in the literary dialect of Iraqi and Iranian Kurds, is a novel by the political activist Rahim Qazi, who was sent by the Republic to study in the Soviet Union. The novel describes the birth and demise of the Republic in 1946.[9] Likewise, *Dimdim*,[10] a novel originally published in 1966 in Yerevan by Erab Shamilov, is a nationalist book of fiction that traces the root of the Kurdish question in the early history of Ottoman-Safavid rivalry. The novel is based on an epic poem that narrates the story of the prince of Baradost, known as the Khan of the Golden Arm, who from the castle of Dimdim valiantly battled the Safavid invaders to the last drop of his blood.[11] His courage and nobility are accentuated by his womenfolk's choosing suicide over shameful captivity in the hands of the aggressors. The message Shamilov tries to send to his Kurdish readers is that Kurdistan and the Kurdish people, represented by the besieged Castle of Dimdim and its residents, have long been beleaguered and bullied by the aggressive neighbors seeking to annex Kurdistan to their territory.

Besides the omnipresent Kurdish nationalist themes and the tyranny of the occupying powers in the literature of this period, the themes of internal oppression of the Kurdish peasants at the hands of the despotic

Kurdish feudal lords, who are also often portrayed as betrayers to the Kurdish cause through their siding with the occupiers of Kurdistan, are also popular. Hasan Qizilji's *Pekanini Gada*[12] belongs in this category. The novel demonstrates the harsh life of the wretched peasants and subjects, who are forced into exile by the oppression of Kurdish despotic *aghas* (feudal lords) and khans, crossing the borders from one part of Kurdistan to another only to die of desperation and homelessness. These landlords and generally anyone affiliating himself with the state against the Kurdish liberation movement come to be referred to by the derogatory title of *Jash*, a term used commonly during the Iran-Iraq War to brand any Kurd who collaborated with either the Iranian or Iraqi regimes.

The oppression of the Kurds, denial of their identity coupled with their marginalization and exclusion from the political participation available to the other majority citizens in the countries in which they resided gave vigor to their subsequent struggle, which had not been without taxing consequences for the Kurdish populations. These deprivations and the subsequent losses later turned into the main concerns of the literature produced in retrospect. The prolonged Kurdish struggle for independence, the political games the Shah of Iran and the Baathist regime of Iraq played on the helpless Kurdish nationalist parties, and the credulous nature of the immature leadership of the nationalist movement, along with its exposed naiveté, led to frequent inter-fighting among Kurdish rivaling parties, factors that wreaked havoc on the allegiance of the Kurdish masses to the nationalist cause. The nationalist parties' leadership suffered heavier losses to their credibility among the populace during the Iran-Iraq War, when the two parties, namely the Kurdish Democratic Party and the Patriotic Union of Kurdistan, both based in Iraqi Kurdistan, egregiously sided with the two countries at war. The result was further alienation of the Kurdish civilians from the struggle. This critical disposition found expression in some of the contemporary fiction and the narratives that looked back at the developments in hindsight.

In spite of the instabilities the war brought to Kurdistan, as early as 1985, when the Iran-Iraq War was still raging, a number of critical narratives appeared. Fazil Karim Ahmad's 1985 short story *Amro Zamawand Agerin* (Their Wedding Is Today),[13] is certainly representative of this category. This short story voices a strong condemnation of the atrocities committed by the peshmargas—the Kurdish guerillas, against civilians, including fellow Kurds and the Arab sympathizers with the Kurdish cause. "Their Wedding Is Today" relates the tragic story of two Arab lovers, possibly Shiites, who during the war flee the Baathist-controlled territories to fight on the side of the Kurds in the so-called liberated Kurdistan, where they are put to death along with hundreds of other Kurdish civilians, ironically at the hands of the Kurds themselves. Shero, the chief commander of the purported PUK-led offensive against the Kurdish-populated village of Pishtashan in 1983,[14] massacres in cold blood all the civilians in the village, including the wounded and the captives. When Qays and Lamis, the two Arab lovers, who are busy tending to the wounded in a makeshift hospital, announce their wedding ceremony to be on that same day, Shero calls them foreigners and occupiers of the holy land of Kurdistan. He yells out his intention to be ridding Kurdistan of all kinds of "vermin," Kurds or Arabs. Witnessing the brutal killings of other defenseless civilians before their eyes, Qays and Lamis become convinced of his inhumane intention and hug each other before reeling in their own blood. The story is a timely attack on the political immaturity and self-serving objectives of the rivaling Kurdish parties that use nationalist rhetoric to advance their party interests. The fascistic face of the Kurdish struggle is laid bare when Shero, despite Mala Hedi's efforts to convince him of the illegitimacy of his decision to kill innocent people, disregards him and proceeds to callously enforce the "Great Leader's" orders. Here, there is clearly a break with the tradition of glorification of war and guerrilla warfare, which was the subject of much praise in earlier literature. In this story, the struggle is not only presented as being far from a holy war of independence, but it is also depicted as a totally absurd phenomenon that results in the destruction of the lives of innocent people.

Through war, the picturesque mountainous scenery of Kurdistan, once trodden by gallant Kurdish cavalry that either won a victory or died honorably on the battleground against the occupying powers, has now turned into a desolate land covered in mines or smoke from constant bombardment. Halabja, the town that came under chemical gas attack toward the closing days of the Iran-Iraq War, becomes the epicenter of later war narratives. Due to its strategic location near the mountainous border, Halabja had traditionally served as a peshmarga stronghold, from where they often led surprise attacks against the advancing Iraqi army equipped with artillery. Therefore, this war-stricken town, where bloodshed and loss of human life were common facts of life, becomes a recurring literary locus of many narratives.

Hamma Dostan's voluminous novel, *Black Wind from the Kurdish Hills*[15] (2005) published in Sweden, is a fictionalized account of the author's life in Halabja up to 1975, the year he leaves Iraq for Europe. The novel features a handful of neighborhood boys, who are born into the lingering war between the Iraqi regimes and the peshmargas, grow up in it, and die in it. The narrative unfolds in such a matter-of-fact tone that the cruel savage reality of war slaps the reader across the face. War is depicted as if it were a normal fact of life and the Kurds living through it were machines that were there only to ensure it would carry on. Throughout this poignant account of war and bloodshed, the question concerning the purpose of waging the war leaps out of every page of the book. Female characters play an especially significant role in voicing the opposing view to the conventional nationalist standpoint and con- demnation of the war and its absurdity. In this novel also, the nationalist venture advanced by the peshmarga forces is presented as equally fascist in nature as the ideological state apparatus of the Baathist regime. The leadership is represented by individual opportunists, who use national- ist propaganda sentiments to subdue all opposition. Consequently, in this type of fiction most of the traditionally sanctified concepts, such as the courageous, selfless freedom fighter, martyrdom, and national independence, are seriously brought into question. Unlike in earlier narratives, in Dostan's novel, the Kurds are left with no choice but to become peshmargas; they do not volunteer to save the homeland, rather they join the peshmarga forces either because the war seems like the only option before them or they are simply forced to enlist or face the dire consequences. Far from glorified, the war and its ravaging conse- quences are made clear in *Black Wind from Kurdish Hills* in unequivocal words that are as sharp as the bullets that cut through the human flesh.

Similar to Hama Dostan's narrative in *Black Wind from Kurdish Hills*, *My Father's Rifle*, a memoir by Henar Salim, recounts in the same vein a personal experience of events and developments leading up to the Iran- Iraq War. Despite the focus of these two narratives on the events prior to the war between Iran and Iraq, they are very much representative of a decent amount of war literature that puts the blame for the destruction of Halabja and the lives of its residents during the war not far from the leadership in charge of advancing the nationalist cause. Moreover, in both of these narratives, the role of the Shah of Iran and the Baath regime in pitting the Kurdish parties against each other is also pronounced, and the former heroic Kurdish guerrillas are viewed through the doubtful and disappointed perspective that Fazil Karim Ahmad formed in "Their Wedding Is Today."

In a similar fashion, in recent years, many retrospective narratives that reflect on the atrocities that took place in Halabja during Iran-Iraq War raise similar questions vis-à-vis the Kurdish involvement in the war, which is seen as an outsiders' war imposed on the Kurds. In other words, these narratives also do not hesitate to expose the miscalculations of the Kurdish leadership that helped cause the atrocities against the people in Kurdistan in general and in Halabja, in particular.

Margi Bekota, translated as *The Never-ending Death* (2002), by Rizgar Karim, is a war saga that relates the many disasters Halabja and its residents experienced over several decades. This narrative also depicts a nightmarish world in which people seem to have accepted war as a natural part of their everyday lives. Many characters appear and disappear in the war that never ends. The people of the town are frequently forced to abandon their homes for unknown destinations. At times, they end up taking refuge in the Iranian territory across the border, where SAVAK, the Iranian security and intelligence organization, keeps the Kurdish activists such as Mahmud, the main character of the story, under constant surveillance. "What a misery," Mahmud says, "to run away from the oppression of the Baathists only to face a more horrifying fate at the hands of the Shah."[16] Resonating popular leftist ideologies of the time, the teacher, Mahmud, as the spokesperson of the author, maintains that the only possible way to salvage Kurdistan is through refashioning the Kurdish personality anew through education.

Mahmud is totally disappointed in the success of the nationalist struggle of his people after witnessing numerous Kurds who collaborate for different reasons with the government of the Shah of Iran against their own fellow activist Kurds in Iran. Back in Iraq from the refugee camp in Iran, Mahmud and other people of the town face constant harassment at the hands of the *Jashes*, Kurdish collaborators with the Baath regime. In fact, it is the Kurdish *Jashes* who are in the Kurdish war-stricken zone and fight and kill other Kurds. In other words, the Iran-Iraq War becomes the war between Kurdish factions funded by the two regimes at war.

Similar to much of Persian and Iraqi Arabic fiction about the war, the narratives written in Kurdish on the subject of the Iran-Iraq War are mostly based on autobiographical accounts written by people who had personal experience as war veterans or guerrillas in the case of the Kurds or were eyewitnesses to the war. Therefore, the literature that has been written in the postwar years in retrospect typically follows a chronological order in narrating the events. Some of the Kurdish war narratives are so faithful to the factuality of the events or the order in which they occurred and affected their personal lives that most of the time it brings them closer to memoir rather than fiction. Moreover, the authors, by virtue of their involvement with the struggle and being personally affected by the war, often find it hard to keep their own persona and personal beliefs out of the narrative. After all, the authors were also emotionally invested, and for most of them, writing an account of the war was a means of seeking ways of coping with and making sense of the war and the many losses that came as a result of it. Not surprisingly, many of the narratives are dedicated to commentary, reflection, or to rally support for one party against the other, especially because the war was part of the ongoing struggle for independence, which seems not to have become any less destructive than the war period. It did not take long after the war and the establishment of the no-fly zone in Iraqi Kurdistan following the Gulf War that the two Kurdish parties, namely OUK and KDP, declared war against each other.

One of the other major themes that informed much of the Kurdish partisan or nationalist fiction was the oppression of the Kurds by foreign powers as described by Erab Shamilov in his novel *Dimdim*. Following in the footsteps of Shamilov, many Kurdish writers treated the subject of war from this perspective, i.e., as a phenomenon imposed on the Kurds from outside. Thus, portraying the Kurds as pawns in the hands of the Iranian and Iraqi regimes is a familiar theme that surfaces frequently in a majority of the narratives with nationalist motivations behind their writing. For instance, in *The Never-ending Death*, Mahmud addresses an Arab colleague, who is a sympathizer with the Kurdish cause, as such: "The misery of the Kurds is the greatest since Kurdistan has been divided among four states that oppress their Kurdish citizens." "Halabja," he supports his argument, "on one hand is ruled by the iron fist of the Baathist regime while, on the other hand, it is on the receiving end of daily bombardment from the Iranian artillery."[17] Pinning the Kurds' problem on the Ottoman-Safavid rivalry that led to resolving territorial disputes in Kurdistan, Mahmud believes that the Kurds, plagued by the legacy of this rivalry, are stuck at a point where they have no option other than taking sides. Mahmud sees the core of the problem in the Kurds' financial reliance on these states for survival and above all in the political incompetence and immaturity of the Kurdish leadership. The latter justification that Mahmud mentions as a crucial cause factoring in the Kurds' failure is either completely unprecedented in the earlier fiction or has at best figured minimally. So, arguably, much of the Iran-Iraq War fiction written in Kurdish usually serves as testimonial to the unconstructive role of the Kurds as *Jash* collaborators, who competed with the Baathist agents in adopting the most repressive measures against their own compatriots. Referring to the novel *The Neverending Death* again, a poor Kurdish shepherd is abducted and beheaded in cold blood by a *Jash* collaborator, who, hoping to get financial reward in return, presents his head as that of an Iranian Revolutionary Guard to the Baathists. In Rizgar Karim's novel, the outrageous bilateralism of the Kurdish collaboration is stanchly slashed by having this act represented by a religious figure who is popularly expected to exemplify trustworthiness among people. The leading cleric of the main mosque in the town, Mullah Izzedin, ironically epitomizes the exact opposite of trustworthiness by leading a successful life as a double agent for both the Baath security forces in town and the Iranian army stationed at Ramadan Military Base in the vicinity.[18]

The shockingly brutal chauvinism of the Baath represented by their total disregard of Kurds as human beings and creating a bloodbath in Halabja becomes more horrifying when the Kurdish leadership, characterized by their "fascist" mentality, simple-minded nationalism, and blind emotionalism, proceed to duplicate the Baathist policies. In the closing chapter of the novel, the ruinous naiveté and collaborationism of the Kurdish peshmargas are scathingly criticized through simply narrating the historical facts that led to the massacre of the majority of the residents of Halabja in a matter of hours of its chemical bombardment. The novel ends on a tragic note as it paints the last scene of the Iranian army's march into the town and their completion of Saddam's act of violence by stripping the lifeless residents of the town of their meager belongings as war spoils.

The conclusion of the novel, *The Never-ending Death*, which describes the destroyed town of Halabja as the battleground of the Iranian and Iraqi regimes, both backed by the Kurdish parties, indicates the rise of increasingly popular antiwar tendencies and oppositions against Kurdish nationalism among Kurds. These tendencies have arguably informed the majority of fictional war narratives written in the wake of the Iran-Iraq War that had ravaging consequences for the Kurds. With war being an almost common scene in Kurdistan, especially the Iraqi Kurdistan, a great number of narratives have inevitably reflected on the phenomenon of war and the difficulties of continuing the Kurdish struggle. Concurrent with the dominant traditions of glorification of heroism of warriors in the classical Persian and Arabic literature, Kurdish literature, having a much shorter literary history, sought to form and enrich a tradition of fashioning national heroes in the conventional sense yet imbued with a modern consciousness introduced from the West. Ahmade Khani's *Mam u Zin* is an exemplary instance of an epic that is constructed in the traditional fashion yet with a somewhat contemporary intention of defining the identity of his people against others with a more established culture and identity. Khani became a role model for many writers who followed his example of strengthening the Kurdish national identity. Nevertheless, as the nationalist endeavor of the Kurds dragged on with no promising and reassuring results in sight for the Kurds other than the myriad hardships it brought them, the most tragic and outstanding embodiment of which was the large-scale massacre of Kurdish civilians in Halabja during the final days of the Iran-Iraq War, doubts regarding the burdensome nationalist struggle through war began to embolden the opposing opinion against war and the struggle. This chapter does not argue that Kurdish literature is entirely alienated and has completely divorced itself from subscription to the Kurdish nationalist cause. Relying on the works studied here, this chapter suggests that an opposing perspective against the war, which was unprecedented in the earlier fiction developed in the late 1960s and became much more pronounced after the long-lasting nationalist struggle resulted in such great atrocities as the massacre of civilians in Halabja, for which the Kurdish nationalist leadership was not without blame.

NOTES

1 Philip G. Kreyenbroek, Ulrich Marzolph, and Ehsan Yarshater, *Oral Literature of Iranian Languages, Companion II: Kurdish, Pashto, Balochi, Ossetic, Persian and Tajik* (London: I.B.Tauris & Co. Ltd., 2010), p. 6.

2 Ibid.

3 For more information regarding the partition of Kurdistan after World War I, see David McDowall, *A Modern History of the Kurds* (London, I.B. Tauris, 2004).

4 Farideh Koohi-Kamali, *The Political Development of the Kurds in Iran: Pastoral Nationalism* (New York; Basingstoke, Hampshire: Palgrave Macmillan, 2003), p. 113.

5 Hejar, *Bo Kurdistan* (Hewlêr [Kurdistan, Iraq]: Dezgay Çap u Biławkirdnewey Aras, 2001); Hemin Mukriyani, *Diwani Hemin Mukriyani* (Sweden: Kitebfiroshi Herzan, 2003).

6 Kreyenbroek et al., *Oral Literature*, p. 6.

7 See Hashem Ahmadzadeh's *Nation and Novel: A Study of Persian and Kurdish Narrative Discourse* (Uppsala: Acta Universitatis Upsaliensis, 2003).

8 Rahim Qazi, *Peshmarga* ([Iran]: Tīshk, 1980).

9 Kreyenbroek et al., *Oral Literature*, p. 22.

10 Arab Shamilov, *Dimdim* (Sweden: Weşanēn Roja Nu, 1983).

11 Kreyenbroek et al., *Oral Literature*, p. 17. Also see Loqman Polat's *Bist Romanen Kurdi* (Stockholm: Peknotryck Ofsset, 2004).

12 Hesen Qizilci, *Peganeni Gada* [The Beggar's Laughter] (Baghdad: Chapkhanay Ala, 1985).

13 This is a short story in a collection of short stories by Fadil Karim Ahmad, *La Gejawda* [In a Whirlpool] (Stockhołm: Binkey Hengaw bo Biławkirdnewey Rosinbiri Kurdi, 1988).

14 Hama Said Hasan, *Nawaroku Shewa la Chiroki Kurdida* [Content and Form in Kurdish Stories] (Sweden: Apec-Tryck & Förlag, 1992), p. 39.

15 Hama Dostan, trans. Paul Conlon, *Black Wind from the Kurdish Hills* (London: Janus Publishing, 2005).

16 Rizgar Karim, *Margi Bekota* [The Never-ending Death] ([S.I.]: [s.n.], 2002), accessed January 13, 2012. www.pertwk.com, p. 320.

17 Ibid., p. 413.

18 Ibid., p. 469.

11

Editing (Virayesh) as a Movement of Resistance during the Iran-Iraq War

FARZANEH FARAHZAD

The role of language in shaping collective and national identities is of prime importance in socio-linguistic studies. The issue gains special significance in the case of Iran. There are at least three reasons for this. The first is that Iran has historically been in constant contact with *the foreign* through political as well as economic, literary, and cultural interactions. The second is that it accommodates a variety of ethnic groups, minority languages, and dialects still spoken in different parts of the country. And the third is that, since its conversion to Islam, Iran was exposed to Arabic, both as the language of religion and of the Moslem Self, and at the same time as the language of the Other.

For Persians, it seems, conversion to Islam was different from submission to Arab domination. Iranians contributed to the expansion of the religion through employing their language as the second vehicle of Islam. Yet, they resisted the hegemony of the Arab nation(s) as the Other, whose presence was, strangely enough, justified through the religion they brought to Iranians and later shared with them. The dilemma, it seems, created a tension between the national identity of Iranians and their identity as Moslems and the *Umma* of Islam in some historical periods.

Modernization, together with the development of a modern sense of nationalism in Iran in the early twentieth century, required a definition of identity and of the Self to fit the new situation. This in turn meant identifying the Other(s), and by extension, Otherizing whatever threatened the solidarity of the Self. Goudarzi (2005) believes that in the Pahlavi era, some of the elite and intellectuals resorted to antiquity in search of this definition, retrieving nostalgically the memory of a

Golden Age of ancient Persia. Calling this attitude "a romantic national-ism," Goudarzi (2005:102–3) claims that this definition:

a. created a perception of the Iranian/Persian identity which rejected or trivialized anything foreign,
b. assigned a pivotal role to the Persian language and literature in securing the Iranian/Persian identity,
c. considered the ethnic and cultural diversity and multiplicity of regional vernaculars in Iran a threat to national solidarity,
d. defined national unity in terms of cultural and linguistic unity,
e. aimed at resisting Islam as the Other,
f. gave way to Western values.

Mollanazar (personal communication, November 12, 2011) believes that among the many Others perceived and identified in and after the Qajar era, Europe was the most legitimized. He argues, "as Iranians we were convinced that we were underdeveloped, had to distant ourselves from the *Arab* Other and follow the *European* Other instead." To him, mod-ernization, Westernization, and nationalism went hand in hand in Iran in the early twentieth century.

The Islamic Revolution in 1979 required a re-definition of Iranian identity, this time in line with a mixture of Islamicization, nationalism, and patriotism which marked the revolution as different from many oth-ers. On the one hand, the religious aspect of the revolution legitimized the presence of Arabic and recognized it as a strong aspect of the revo-lutionary Moslem identity. On the other hand, the attitude against the Arabic language as the Other, which had its roots in the pre-revolution eras, persisted, and was even somehow intensified when the so-called Iran-Iraq War[1] started, because ironically Arabic turned out to be the language of the enemy as well. This slowly led to a subtle, hidden, and untold tension between those who foregrounded the religious aspect of their shaping identity and those who underscored its historical-national aspect. It took a few years for the state to resolve the issue. According to Mollanazar (personal communication, November 12, 2011), Arabic was soon proclaimed "the second language of the country" because of its wide distribution and the great number of its speakers in the southern parts of Iran, because it began being taught as the second language with improved curriculum and syllabuses in schools[2] and was categorized as "the second, and not *a/the foreign*, language" in the language teaching university programs in Iran. Gradually Arabic was excluded from the list of Others, although it is still hard to speak of its possible assimilation into the Self. At the same time, the nationalistic aspect of the shaping identity started to be intensified with the onset of the war. This required enhancement of patriotic sentiments which combined with religious devotion to protect the country. The nationalistic aspect of the forming identity manifested itself in various dimensions, of which the linguistic is the concern of this chapter.

In April and May 1980, about a year after the revolution and in fact a few months before the start of the Iran-Iraq War, the universities were closed down all over Iran for the so-called Cultural Revolution. One of the major aims was to reform and re-design university curricula and produce teaching materials in line with the social, political, religious, and ideological changes in the country. This meant that faculty members in all universities would not be teaching for some time (which was about four years in the case of humanities), but were entitled to their monthly salaries. They were therefore asked to send proposals to the Cultural Revolution Committee (*Setad-e Enghelab-e Farhangi*), which was then recently established as the academic authority in the country, for writing or translating books in their fields of study and expertise. Upon approval of the proposal, the faculty member would start the work, report on the progress of the project each month to the department (s)he worked in and to the Committee, and receive the salary. The problem then was that, under those conditions, writing became a difficult, not to say impossible, task. In fact how could one write for absent students and empty classrooms? Consequently, almost all academics all over the country began translating university textbooks and reference materials. Translation became an alternative to writing and gradually occupied a primary position in academic productions.

Soon after this, in September 1980, the Translation, Writing and Editing Committee was established. According to Pourjavadi (1979, pp. 4–7) it was an extension of the Cultural Revolution Committee, and its goal was to encourage academic production in the post-revolution society. The name of the committee suggests that at that time translation was assigned greater importance than writing and editing, perhaps for the very realistic reason that it was hard to write in the absence of both students and research funds which were impossible to afford at that time. In line with this translation project, Iran University Press (*Markaz-e Nashre Daneshghahi*), a state-sponsored publishing house, was established, which started work at about the same time the war broke out, to publish and distribute the products of this huge activity. By 1983, a number of translated books were waiting to be published by the Press. But close examination of the quality of the translations showed that a huge volume of them required substantial correction and editing. The major problem was the unnatural and very often incomprehensible translational language that emerged and rendered many of the works produced in this project unpublishable.

The translational problems were due to one or more of the following:

1. poor knowledge of the source language(s) (normally English and French);
2. poor knowledge of Persian, as the target language, particularly its potentials for terminology;
3. inadequate writing practice in Persian on the part of the academics;
4. poor knowledge of the subject area;
5. lack of what is known today as "transfer competence" in Translation Studies literature and which distinguishes a bilingual from a translator;
6. lack of up-to-date bilingual dictionaries and reference books.

All of the above resulted in literal translation, calque, and incorrect renderings, which paved the way for the direct transfer of foreign structures and terms. The translational errors were basically grammatical and lexical. Grammatical errors ranged from inappropriate use of prepositions to transfer of foreign syntactic patterns into Persian. Lexical errors concerned the use of inappropriate equivalents for ordinary words and of course for technical terms.

To make the translations publishable, Markaze-Nashr took three initiatives. First it set up terminology groups in many fields. Specialists in different areas, some of whom were already fired from university positions for their political orientations, worked in these groups and started publishing small bilingual glossaries. Second, it established an Editing Committee in 1983 which created publishing guidelines for proper writing in Persian, appearing first in the form of articles, and later as manuals and style sheets for writers and translators. Third, it initiated editing courses to train editors and improve the quality of the translations. One of the first outcomes then was the coinage of the words *virayesh* and *virastar* (derived from the root *pirastan* in old Persian), to mean *editing* and *editor*[3] respectively. The work of *virastars* (editors) then covered a wide variety of areas, ranging from copy editing to content modification, securing terminological consistency, use of standard and eloquent Persian and linguistic improvement.

The last two categories listed above were gradually accentuated in the editing style sheets, because the language that emerged in this nationwide translation project turned out to be a mixture of Persian and some foreign source language(s), filled with painfully literal translations, borrowed words and structures, and incorrect, non-cohesive target texts. The emerging language was therefore unnatural, incomprehensible, and far from eloquent. One way to improve the situation and save the Persian language against the foreign, it seemed, was to explore and employ all its potentials. This solution soon turned into an urge for a linguistic purism, which rested on nationalist and patriotic sentiments of the people in a rapidly changing post-revolution society who woke up one day to find their country at war. In this process, the translationese began to be interpreted as a threat against the Persian language and by extension against Iranian identity. In addition to the enemy confronted in the fronts, a second enemy was recognized. It was the body of foreign languages that was threatening the Persian language through translations, and whose agents were translators. The role of translators remained in focus ever since, so much so that several years later, Najafi (1987: 7), in his monumental book *Ghalat Nanevisim* (*Let's Not Write Incorrectly*),[4] a manual for writers and translators, said: "any threat against the Persian language is posed by inexpert translators, particularly news translators who, due to haste, resort to literal translation of foreign words, compounds and structures and who are copied unwittingly by some writers."

The threat became central to all discussions of translation and editing in the early years of the war, pioneered by Najafi and the Iran University Press. In a seminal article entitled[5] "Is the Persian Language in Danger?" Najafi (1986: 4) said: "The impact of foreign language(s) becomes a concern when the grammar gets affected . . . Grammar is, of course, resistant to foreign influence, but is not undefeatable." To him, the major threat was "the drastic changes" that Persian grammar and structure would undergo if constantly influenced by foreign languages. Further, he said: "This will in turn have at least two negative outcomes. One is losing contact with our cultural heritage recorded in the works of the past. The other is failure to communicate with other members of our society" (p. 5). In the light of such discourse, translation strategies required a rethinking. Najafi (pp. 4–5) believed that borrowing and literal translation of terms posed no threat to the language, whereas calque, as a literal transfer of foreign structures, did. In this linguistic-nationalist context, Najafi's monumental book *Ghalat Nanevisim* (*Let's Not Write Incorrectly*) sold 10,000 copies in the first month of its publication, received more than ten excellent and positive reviews in the same period, and was discussed extensively in radio broadcasts inside the country and outside the borders. One major reason for this success was perhaps its appeal to patriotic sentiments. According to a review published a few months after the first printing of the book in the Iran University Press journal, *Nashr-e Danesh* (1988: 85), the success was due to the fact that "the focus of the book is the Persian language, and the love of Iranians for this language and its protection." The book has since gone through numerous reprints.

Suddenly everybody became conscious of the foreign words and structures in Persian translations and writings which metaphorically represented the presence of the Other. The situation called for action. Foreign presence had to be fought, the same way the enemy was fought at the fronts. The military war to protect the borders was paralleled by a linguistic war to protect the language and the identity. To achieve this, first all foreign languages were targeted as the Other. But gradually Arabic was excluded from the list because of its religious significance. European languages, particularly English, French, and German, however, remained on the list as the Others. Meanwhile, the Persian language, which was already under the pressure of adapting itself to the post-revolution discourse, filled with long lists of new words and concepts, coinages, and changing meanings, had to become stronger to enter this war and resist the foreign presence in texts. Seminars were held for exploring the potentials of the Persian language in dealing with the so-called invading foreign terms and structures. Examples are the proceedings of a conference titled *Farsi, Zaban-e Elm* (*Persian, the Language of Science*) and a series of articles on the morphological potentials of Persian by Ali Ashraf Sadeghi in the *Nashr-e Danesh* journal. A sort of linguistic purism was thus encouraged. All this highlighted not only the role of *virayesh* (editing) in resisting the foreign and in securing national unity, but also the role of *virastars* (editors) as mediators of this ideology.

Virayesh gradually snowballed into a movement by extending in scope and range beyond academic translations and writings to almost all other types of linguistic productions in the country. What started during the war as an act of resistance in academia developed into a nationalist movement, inspiring several other activities that targeted the whole nation and went on for some time even after the war. Of all of these, four were major. The first was the establishment of a *Virayesh Council* in IRIB (Islamic Republic of Iran Broadcasting). The second was the inclusion of some major *virayesh* principles in high school textbooks and syllabuses all over the country. The third was the establishment of *virayesh* courses. The last was the establishment of the third Academy of Persian Language and Literature. These are discussed below.

In 1988, a conference was held in Tehran on the poor quality of the language used in IRIB and ways of improving it. This concerned not only the translated material in IRIB, but also the authentic, non-translated Persian texts presented orally or produced spontaneously in live programs. The causes of the problem were identified as calque, unnecessary use of formal and flowery language, verbiage, poor logical coherence, and poor knowledge of rhetoric on the part of those who wrote or performed the programs. To improve the quality, three years later:

a. a *Virayesh* Council was established in IRIB,
b. short-term *Virayesh* courses were held to train *virastars* (editors) for radio and TV programs,
c. *virayesh* guidelines and style sheets were published by IRIB for all those involved in the radio and TV programs,
d. a number of trained *virastars* were employed through administration of *virayesh* tests.

The incentive behind the establishment of the Council was stated (1991a: 2) as follows:

> [T]he Persian language is the carrier of the ancient and glorious culture of Islam and Iran, and if it degenerates our cultural ties will lose strength and the potential of the language for performing its historically critical role will degenerate as well.[6]

The goals of the Council were announced (1991a: 2–3) as follows:

a. to protect standard Persian and provide a remedy for the dangerous illness which was said to threaten the language and unity and solidarity of the country,
b. to equip IRIB programs with a fine, eloquent, and purified language.

The Council received financial support from the President's Office. The patronage contributed to the authority of the Council in IRIB, where all its guidelines had to be followed.

In line with all this, in 1991 and 1992 a series of short TV clips were broadcasted every night as part of a TV program entitled *Farsi ra paas bedarim* (*Let's Protect Persian*). In each episode one incorrect Persian sentence, usually a calque, appeared in a frame. Then the reason why it was incorrect in terms of *virayesh* rules was given, and finally the correct form of the sentence was given. The program received a lot of attention from the public, who were being sensitized to both the emerging and the current errors, coming from an inappropriate mixture of foreign words and structures with Persian in the everyday language. Some of the clips were devoted to the incorrect use of Arabic roots and grammatical markers in Persian, such as, for instance, the use of *tanvin* (an adverb marker in Arabic) with Persian words. Others concerned the literal transfer of grammatical patterns from English, French, and German. The program contributed to the development of a nationwide discourse concerning the Persian language and Iranian identity.

The second achievement of the movement was that some of the basic principles of *virayesh* entered high school textbooks of Persian grammar in the 1990s and students were warned against the incorrect use of the language. The concepts of calque and borrowing were elaborately discussed and the ways to avoid them were introduced and practiced in classrooms all over the country.

The third concerned training of *virastars*. Since 1986 a great number of *virayesh* courses were being offered by different government and nongovernment organizations, including Iran University Press, who pioneered the movement, and the Ministry of Guidance and Islamic Culture, the highest authority which controlled the publication and the book market in the country. A great number of *virastars* were thus trained, and started to work with the press and the publishers, who were now more conscious about the quality of the language in their works than ever before.

The last was the establishment of the third Academy of Persian Language and Literature, which was founded in 1989 and officially started work in 1991.[7] It was later recognized as a research institute working under the auspices of the President's Office. In its constitution (1991: 1–2), the Persian language is referred to as "the second language of Islam," "the key to the huge and invaluable scientific and literary heritage of Islamic civilization" and "the building block of the cultural identity of the Iranian nation." The major goals to be achieved by the Academy are listed as follows:

a. preserving the strength and originality of the Persian language as a manifestation of our national identity, as the second language of the Islamic world and as the vehicle of Islamic culture and knowledge
b. protecting the Persian language
c. improving its potential to meet cultural, scientific, and technological needs
d. establishing the Academy as an internationally recognized authority in Persian language.

The nationalistic and religious incentives behind the establishment of the Academy contributed to a redefined Iranian Moslem identity in the same way that the other three measures did.

Conclusion

Translation both shaped *virayesh* and was shaped by it. *Virayesh* developed in line with translation, and as an offshoot of the nationwide translation project launched in and by the academia in Iran in the early years of the revolution and of the Iran-Iraq War. The project was originally designed to introduce recent foreign knowledge into the country in all fields of science and technology. However, the transfer of such material through translation led to the transfer of foreign discourse and foreign structures, which in turn resulted in a consciousness against the foreign as the Other. Improving the translations gradually came to mean protecting and strengthening the religious and national aspects of Iranian identity as the Self by resisting the Other in text and discourse. Two solutions to the problem were sought. One was to encourage Self-promoting translation strategies, such as naturalness, which became the norm for translation of science and technology as the major topics in the translation project. Interestingly, as the *virayesh* movement extended beyond the translation project to the translation market outside of academia, naturalness was practiced in the form of domestication in literary translation, aiming to erase or at least conceal traces of the Other in translated literature. The other solution was to encourage linguistic purism, which started being practiced as *virayesh*. But this linguistic purism was in serious conflict with translation in its essence. Translation takes place when people want to know about the foreign, and rewriting the foreign inevitably introduces and carries over the foreign discourse, which *virayesh* stood against. The conflict was never resolved, but throughout time *virayesh* became a movement of resistance against the Other. It targeted the foreign discourse, structures, and words, which were thought to reflect the presence of the Other, first linguistically and then ideologically, and threaten national identity. Resisting foreign structures as a focal point in *virayesh* became a metaphor for resisting foreign powers and a metaphor for nationalism. *Virayesh* grew into an elite movement of nationalism and resistance. The movement redefined the history of the nation and the nation itself in the new postrevolutionary context. It also redefined the subject of the nation-state in terms other than religion.

NOTES

1 The phrase *Iran-Iraq War* is used in here in its common form and sense. One might as well use *Iraq-Iran War* instead, with a totally different ideological implication, which is not the concern of this chapter.

2 Before the revolution, English was taught in schools as the second language.

3 The words *virayesh* and *virastars* are used here to mark the difference between the concepts of *editing* and *editor* in English and the local use of the concepts in Iran in the 1980s.

4 The Persian title is *Ghalat na-nevisim: Farhang-e Doshvariha-ye Zaban-e Farsi*, which can be translated into "Let's not write incorrectly: a dictionary of the difficulties in the Persian language." It was a manual for writers and translators.

5 The Persian title is: *Aya Zaban-e Farsi dar Khatar Ast?*.

6 All translations from Persian are my own.

7 The first was established in 1935, but closed down after few years. The second was established in 1969, and was again closed down after the revolution.

REFERENCES

Goudarzi, H. 2005. *goftarha-yi dar bareh-ye zaban va hoviat-e irani*. Tamadon-e Irani Publications: Tehran.

Ma'soumi Hamedani, H. 1981. "bimaihaye virastari," *Nahsr–e Danesh Journal* 1, Issues 5 and 6, pp. 74–81.

Najafi, A. 1987. *ghalat nanevisim: farhang-e doshvariha-ye zaban-e farsi*. Iran University Press: Tehran.

Najafi, A. 1986. "ayaa Zaban e farsi dar khatar ast?" in N. Pourjavadi, *dar bareh-ye tarjomeh*. Iran University Press: Tehran.

Pourjavadi, N. 1979. "dar bareh-ye comiteh-ye tarjomeh, ta'lif va tas'hih," *Nahsr–e Danesh Journal* 1, Issue 1, pp. 4–7.

Pourjavadi, N. 1979. "dar bareh-ye comiteh-ye tarjomeh, ta'lif va tas'hih," *Nahsr–e Danesh Journal* 4, Issue 3, pp. 66–69.

asas nameh-ye farhangestan-e zaban va adab-e farsi. 2005. Nashr e Aasaar Publication Group: Tehran.

bar-resiy-e zaban-e radio. 1991. IRIB Publication: Tehran.

12

Narratives of Silence

Persian Fiction of the 1980–1988 Iran-Iraq War

MOHAMMAD MEHDI KHORRAMI

In a letter to F. Scott Fitzgerald, Ernest Hemingway called war "the writer's best subject." Hemingway justified this description by saying that "[War] groups the maximum of material and speeds up the action and brings out all sorts of stuff that normally you have to wait a lifetime to get."[1] Keeping in mind the notion of dramatic license, he was probably right. And considering the fact that in the past few centuries the Persian literary tradition has had many chances to experience this "best subject," it is reasonable to expect that many great works of Persian war literature have been produced. But in order for this "best subject" to lead to the creation of literary masterpieces, it is necessary that war literature not be regarded as a part or a continuation of war; or that at least such approaches do not stifle those voices which resist the idea that the creative process must be subordinated to war and function as its extension, and indeed, as one of its weapons.

In the case of Iran, from the very beginning, the naming of the war by the official discourse as *Jang-e Eslam va Kofr* (the Battle of Islam Against Infidelity), *Emtehan-e Elahi* (the Divine Test), *Nabard-e Haq ʿaleyh-e Batel* (the Battle of Right Against Wrong), and later on as *Defaʾ-e Moqaddas* (the Holy or Sacred Defense), and similar appellations, was indicative of the state's decision to conduct the war as a "total war." Here I am thinking about this phrase's connotation after the First World War and its developments by recent scholars such as Patrick Deer, who underlined an approach based on which every element of society was required to participate in the war directly.[2] Naturally, as soon as the Iran-Iraq War is designated as "sacred," it is identified with other dichotomizing grand wars. Examples of such wars are seen especially in religious ones (both real and imaginary), with battles between good and evil waged on a cosmic scale. We can think about the war on Jesus (with his divine attribute, "son of God most high") against Satan, or Moses delivering the Hebrews from Pharaoh's army when God parts the Red Sea; or even the Crusades where the Christian soldiers fight against the infidels (Muslims); or, for that matter, the *Qadesiyyeh* battle of Arabs against Iranians.[3] And of course, it is a very well-known fact, mentioned by many critics and commentators, that Saddam Hussein called his war with Iran the second Battle of *Qadesiyyeh*.

One of the significant consequences of the synthesis of this war with dichotomizing binary systems of good-evil, God-Satan, right-wrong, us-them, religious-infidel, patriot-traitor, and so on is that all the people in the society are defined, one way or another, in terms of their relationship to the war. I believe this matter (involving everyone) was one of the main reasons why the Iranian government decided to call any Iranian killed directly or indirectly in the war a martyr. This is a key concept, especially in the early period of contemporary Persian war literature. Like many other wartime governments, the Islamic Republic employed familiar means to impose its discourse and narratives of war. An examination of these methods is beyond the scope of this chapter, but it is necessary to highlight one point: The Islamic Republic's definition of the Iran-Iraq War as a war between Right/Islam and Wrong/Evil eventually led to the emergence of the war as a religion in itself, which naturally had its own sacred and profane components. The most obvious component that was in this religion, the notion of martyrdom—whose praise in all discourses of all wartime governments is a natural phenomenon—became a sacrosanct requirement, and, as we shall see, any deviation from this requirement was considered a sacrilege. Under such conditions, any mention of peace would be and was considered a blasphemy, treason.[4] But this approach brings about its own difficulties.

For those who experience it, war is a very concrete event; it is immediate; too close and too constant for it to have the mysterious and mystic abstractions that a religion needs. This was one of the major paradoxes with which the Islamic Republic had to grapple. On the one hand, it needed to make the war tangible, constantly present, and part of daily life—especially for those on the home front—so that it would become a total war. On the other hand, this same war had to be defined in abstract enough terms so that its divine characteristics and components (e.g., divine violence—leading to killing not only for the sake of a particular religion but for the religion of war—divine objectives, etc.) would not be sullied by its mundane aspects. In the following, I will refer to samples of structures erected by the dominant discourse to justify the simultaneous function on sacred and profane sites, as well as to guarantee the continuity of this religion.

The inflexible nature of the imposition of this religiosity effectively contributed to the creation of an atmosphere in which it was extremely difficult to develop the particular aesthetics needed for Persian literature of the time to speak convincingly of grey areas; of the enemy's humanity, for example; or of the representation of violence in a language of meta-martyrdom. I maintain that this played a crucial role in barring Persian war literature from any chance to create masterpieces in that worldwide literary genre.

The literary and artistic arm of the official discourse made many attempts to explain this dearth. Following the overtly anti-intellectualist impulses of the post-revolutionary government,[5] Mohammad Reza Sarshar (a.k.a. Mohammad Reza Rahgozar), a powerful policy maker and literary figure in charge of many aspects of post-revolutionary literary and artistic productions, tacitly blamed professional writers. He also faulted the lack of experience of those who, in the absence of professional writers whose works did not reflect the official narratives of war, took it upon themselves to bridge this gap.

> Six years of war have passed, and every single day so many epics are created at the front. But so far not even a few novels or collections of stories which could do them justice have been written . . . When the warriors realized that artists [i.e. professional writers and artists] are not doing anything for the war, they were forced to accept this responsibility as well (creating "true" stories of war). Unfortunately, though, they didn't create artistic work. That's why their writings are just full of feelings and emotions; there isn't much art, technique, or the like.[6]

While mentioning some of these points, independent critics painted a more complex picture of the situation and alluded to other, certainly more important elements to explain this deficiency. In a review of Persian war literature produced during the war and the early years after it, Reza Najafi, one of the few independent critics of war literature, published an article, "Asib Shenasi-ye Tatbiqi-ye Adabiyat-e Paydari dar Iran" (A Comparative Pathology of Resistance Literature in Iran) in which he specifically attempted to examine the reasons for the scarcity of outstanding works in the field of war literature. Having mentioned the sanctification of war literature and consequently tabooing of its pathology, he describes various elements which explain the literary shortcomings of these works. Among these elements, he specifically underlines the governmentalization of this genre, as well as the writers' inexperience and lack of professional experience.

> The absence of professional writers at the war fronts and the government's policies [supporting particular writings] encouraged a number of people who were involved in the war—as well as many others who had not experienced the war but were seeking governmental support—to think of producing literary works about the war. Although these productions on many occasions were earnest and honest, in terms of literary and aesthetic values and maturity they left much to be desired. With regard to the amateurishness of many of these authors, suffice it to say that, based on reports of the Seminar on the Review of War Novels in Iran and in the World (1372/1993), the average age of the writers of our country's war literature was 26 years.

He continues:

> The most important element of harm to the literature of the Sacred Defense is said to have been the governmentalization of this genre; meaning that most of the works about the war were either commissioned by the government or were supported by it, or were produced with direct involvement of government institutions.
>
> The governmentalization of the war literature could have two implications. The fact that a government invests in the production of such works and supports them is not in itself problematic, but the second meaning of this phenomenon, the interference of the government in the production

process in the form of supervision, offering directives and guidelines, censorship and restriction of nongovernmental works and other similar approaches could lead to harmful consequences.

The first damage that this interference would cause is the dependence of the writers on the criteria and tastes of government officials who perhaps lack sufficient knowledge. Worse than that, such an approach would attract opportunists who are not trying to create a work of art but are seeking to acquire financial benefit and fame without any hard work.[7]

Of course these statements are general, at times rudimentary observations that have their own limitations, many of which are due to the restrictions imposed on discussions about such a sensitive topic.

To avoid essentialist implications, therefore, we should consider a larger context. Official war literature requires the formation of collective images and the communication of those images. At the same time, any serious genre or subgenre of literature requires its own aesthetics, and forming these aesthetics is possible only through interaction with characteristics of a given literary tradition and its geo-histories. This requirement, I believe, exists even with regard to serious propagandist literature, if one wants to go beyond the banal aspects of propaganda. This combination, war-related aesthetics or works informed by the existing literary tradition, proved very difficult for the official discourse. It should be remembered that the post-revolutionary government had just begun to consolidate its power, and the project of rewriting histories, in this case literary history, had just begun. As usual, the easiest phase, that is the establishment of a censorship system which effectively put out of commission many trained writers and much writing, both of which by their nature at the time were defined in terms of their counter-discursivity. But more important was the fact that Persian fiction was going through particular stages of its modernist evolution and, perhaps even more than other modernist traditions, was emphasizing the impossibility of communication and the seemingly unsolvable problem of linguistic limits. It was in such a context that the official discourse was demanding absolute clarity from writers of war literature.

Another digression is necessary here. Many critics have argued that the subversiveness of contemporary Persian fiction is a characteristic of modernist Persian fiction. Focusing on different disciplinary and interdisciplinary discourses, some have defined this subversiveness within a political landscape. Others have relied on notions such as self-referentiality and its corresponding aesthetics, or on the ignoring of ideological aesthetics of the dominant discourse to define this characteristic of Persian modernist literature. I maintain that, with regard to the war literature, it is the exaggerated trait of self-referentiality of modernist narration which has led to the rejection of penchants toward the collective narratives that are located at the heart of official discourses. Indeed, it is quite natural that this trait cannot accommodate a precisely defined collectivism. Once again, let us consider the notion of martyrdom as an example that, as a component of the religion of war, no deviation of its obligatory nature, whether it is by the author or his protagonists, is tolerated.

The most well-known of such intolerance is the case of Ahmad Dehqan's novel *Safar beh Gara-ye 270 Darajeh* (*Journey to Heading 270 Degrees*). It was written and published a few years after the end of the war, and I believe this timing shows even more clearly the uncompromising nature of the official war culture.[8] The novel was translated into English a few years ago.[9]

After the translation was completed, there was an event in Iran to celebrate the occasion. The translator was then interviewed by two *Adabiyat-e Dastani* critics, Ahmad Shakeri and Kamran Parsinejad. *Adabiyat-e Dastani* (*Fiction*) is a literary journal basically controlled by *Hozeh-ye Honari* (The Arts Center), a branch of the *Sazman-e Tablighat-e Eslami* (The Organization for Islamic Propaganda), which was created after the 1979 Revolution. *Adabiyat-e Dastani* does not deny that they receive their literary instructions from the Supreme Leader; first Khomeini and then Khamenei. In the interview, Shakeri effectively criticizes the translator for having selected this book from among so many other "good ones." This is his argument:

> If in the Iranian culture there are millions who believe in martyrdom, then how could a work which does not believe in martyrdom be written about this culture? Then the war described in this book is not the Iran war. It is a war of some other place![10]

Almost the whole conversation is based on the idea that since at the end of this book the protagonist is not "martyred," it is therefore not a realistic book about the Iranian approach to the war, and thus is not worthy of translation. Reading the interview and its insistence that the notion of martyrdom must be the main component of the imagery of the Iranian painting of the war, it was quite clear that the interviewers wanted to guide the spectator's eyes toward a particular location on this painting.

There are examples in plenty of obvious variations on the theme of martyrdom. If one is interested in examining some of these literary productions, I suggest Mahmud Golabdarreh-i's *Esmail Esmail* (1360/1981), the story of a teenager from Ahvaz who kills a cowardly traitor who has martyred his father; another would be Akbar Khalili's collection of short stories, *Karun Por az Kolah* (*The Karun River Is Full of Helmets*—1371/1993), which have the theme of martyrdom at their heart. It should also be noted that next to these fictions there are many memoirs, many of which are commissioned and all based on selective memories, which follow the same directive. Examining this genre obviously requires a separate study; suffice it to say, however, that the official discourse has been adamant about promoting this genre, perhaps because its formalistic characteristics make it easier to control. By far, the most famous example of these memoirs is *Da* (*Mother*, 1387/1998), in which a young woman tells the story of the early days of the war in Khorramshahr. The book is narrated by Seyyedeh Zahra Hosseini and is written by Seyyedeh A'zam Hosseini. The book unfailingly draws on official clichés and even fabrications about the war, and in affirming these fabrications, it goes so far as to refer, for example, to the presence of forces from Britain, Germany, Jordan, "and every kind of nationality" among the prisoners of war.[11] This book was mentioned by Ali Khamenei, the Supreme Leader of the Islamic Republic, as a superior text and example of Sacred War literature:

> *Da*, which is really and truly a very good book and worthy of being disseminated in the world, is about a small number of events of the Imposed War and this shows that eight years of Sacred Defense has the capacity of producing thousands of books for the purpose of transferring

to the society and the world the Revolutionary and Islamic values and culture.[12]

Obviously, this endorsement has been coupled with practical support; apparently the book has been reprinted more than 120 times. It is also noteworthy that a large sum of money has been allocated to the translation of this book into English. It is currently being translated by the same translator who worked on *Journey to Heading 270 Degrees*.

Conversely, attempts to challenge these clichés, most importantly, the clearly defined binary systems, have been forced to make use of the most subtle methods. After all, with war being a religion, expressions of "atheism" ought to be uttered very cautiously. Shahriar Mandanipur's "Rang-e Atash-e Nimruzi" (The Color of Fire at Midday) is a good example that merits a closer examination.

The story is narrated by a descendant of a landowner who is telling his guests about a recent event that has happened to him and one of his friends. He begins the story by referring to what he considers to be the central, and for him confusing, node of the event; the "darkness."

> – . . . Darkness . . . ahh, darkness . . . it is so mysterious, the darkness. A man would wonder what to do. But it is clear that man is one species and leopard is another. If they are in each other's vicinity, like it or not, they will confront each other. Then they should fight until only one of them returns and the other one remains on the ground and belongs to the earth, or to the vultures and hyenas which at such times would certainly be around.[13]

He then recounts the event. It is the story of a certain Captain Mina who has served in the Iran-Iraq War. Apparently because of psychological difficulties resulting from the war, the captain, who had been a commander of Special Forces, has been ordered by the military physicians to go on compulsory medical leave. He chooses his friend's village to spend his leave and goes there with his wife and his three-year-old daughter. The narrator and the captain spend most of their days remembering their youth and reminiscing especially about their hunting excursions. One day, they decide to go on a picnic and choose a pleasant site near a waterfall. The two friends are chatting and the captain's wife is taking a nap. The little daughter is running after drag-onflies. Suddenly they hear the scream of the little girl and run after her. They see drops of blood on the ground and shortly after they realize that the girl had been attacked by a leopard who, according to the narrator, because of old age and lack of prey, has been forced to hunt humans. The rest of the fabula is about the chasing of the leop-ard by the captain. At different intervals, he talks about his memories of the war and how he used to kill Iraqi soldiers in a most violent manner without ever having the slightest hesitation, physically or men-tally. It seems that in his mind an effort is being made to identify the leopard with the Iraqi enemy. Finally, the captain and the leopard face each other but, somehow, both leave this face-off alive but injured. It seems that their eye-to-eye moment, as well as the unjustifiability of the captain's hatred of the leopard, have undermined this effort. In a rather meaningful silence, he continues this attempt. The two keep up their chase; this time the captain seems less certain. They use an animal to trap the leopard, more or less the same way the captain and his fellow commandos, like their Iraqi counterparts, used explosives and booby traps. For the second time, the captain faces the leopard. The enemy is standing, almost motionless, eating the prey and very much in range of the captain's rifle. But, as if he has experienced a new level of consciousness after his first encounter with the leopard staring in his eyes, the captain cannot kill the creature. The shouting and even the curses of the narrator to encourage and embolden the captain to shoot at the leopard finally break his silence; he shouts the enemy's problematization:

> It was impossible, . . . It is impossible. My child's flesh is in his body . . . It is impossible . . . My child's blood is in his veins.[14]

As a mere witness to the event, the narrator, who has not experienced this internal revolution, dumbfounded, describes the darkness he referred to at the beginning of his story:

> Maybe darkness is not the right word. I don't know. Things that are not clear and straightforward to me I call darkness. I don't like them. Mun-dane affairs should be obvious. Everyone should know the answers to

different things. Inhale, exhale; thirst, satiation; friendship, friendship; enmity, enmity.[15]

In terms of the story's narrative techniques and also its stylistics, this somewhat analytical synopsis is quite simplified and even reductive. In this story and indeed in many of his writings, Mandanipur uses different points of view and focal positions, together with a fairly complicated language which on many occasions warrants the use of the adjective *inaccessible*. Elsewhere I have discussed the concept of inaccessibility in the context of Persian modernist literature and have argued for it to be considered as one of the outcomes of the evolutionary process of the Persian literary tradition in its transition to modernist writing.[16] The other point relevant to the present discussion is that using convoluted and complex linguistic structures and language and focal positions is undoubtedly one of the methods that has been used in this tradition—as well as many other literary traditions—to undermine the imposed absolutist discourses and achieve a moral/philosophical problematization of the binary system of good-evil, friend-foe.

To end this section it seems appropriate to recall a literary anecdote that demonstrates the usage of multiple narrative layers to undermine concepts which are offered and imposed as religious convictions. This anecdote, which quite likely is untrue, is about a fourteenth-century poet, Hafez, Iran's most celebrated lyric poet. The anecdote is about one of his most well-known ghazals which ends with the following verse:

> If the being a musulman be of this sort that Hafez is,
> Alas, if, after today, be a tomorrow.[17]

It is said that after this verse was heard by some fanatic clergy, they interpreted the usage of the word "if" in the second hemistich as expressing doubts about the existence of the Day of Judgment and Resurrection, and of course such a blasphemous utterance was deemed punishable by death. Being well-versed in Islamic legal laws and its different interpretations, and thus knowing that, according to some interpretations, quoting someone else's blasphemous statement is not blasphemy, Hafez added a new narrative layer by writing a new penultimate verse. The ending of the ghazal, therefore, reads:

How pleasantly to me came this tale when in the morning time, said,
At the door of the wine-house, with drum and reed, a Christian:

"If the being a musulman be of this sort that Hafez is,
Alas, if, after today, be a tomorrow."[18]

* * *

As previously mentioned, the official discourse assigned the status of martyr to all who were killed in the war. Another major function of this approach in the mythic and literary universes should be read as the extension of efforts to sublimate acts of violence.

Sarah Cole, one of the theoreticians of contemporary American and British war literature, has examined war as a site of violent death. She analyzes attempts made to produce meaning for these violent deaths. Obviously, the most famous case in Western culture is the story of the death of Jesus which, if considered out of its context, is a story filled with senseless, unreasonable acts of violence. In the frameworks of the crucifixion and the resurrection, as Cole argues, that same violent death suddenly takes on a timeless, germinal meaning.[19] Stories with similar connotations can be found in most major literary traditions. In Persian literature, a close corresponding example is the death of Siavash in the *Shahnameh*, in which that most innocent hero of the entire epic is killed in a cowardly manner, but then his blood is spilled on the ground. A beautiful flower springs up, reinforcing the germinating effect, and of course the continuity of this martyr is also guaranteed through his son, who becomes one of the most important legendary kings in the *Shahnameh*.

It is of course easy to craft stories for one or two individuals, but when we are dealing with thousands and hundreds of thousands of people whose deaths must become meaningful, then we need prescribed, mass-produced martyrdom stories, to create, or at least to try to create, collective images. Formulaic variations based on the previously mentioned binary systems, as well as the concept of victimization, represent the easiest scheme. In particular, stories by "values writers"[20,21] such as Firuz Jalali or Reza Sarshar, are good examples of clearly defined poles of good and evil. There are also well-known representations, interpretations, and variations of this structure. The above-mentioned

Adabiyat-e dastani is the best source to find a more or less complete list of these writers.

In the same vein, there are cliché stories such as Ali Mo'azzeni's long story *Qasedak* (*dandelion / little messenger*, 1371/1982) or Mehdi Shoja'i's collection of short stories, *Zarih-e Cheshmha-ye to* (*The Shrine of Your Eyes*, 1363/1984), and another collection, *Do Kabutar, do Panjereh, yek parvaz* (*Two doves, two windows, one flight*, 1365/1987). The most famous story of this collection which has given its name to the collection is the story of twin brothers who go to the war together and die together. In all these stories the emphasis is placed on the description of the protagonist as a martyr/victim or martyr/oppressed.[22] Of course we are still within the same framework of binary systems, but in these cases we see a more frequent usage of emotionalism and sensationalism, and of course at times the usually indirect identification of the protagonist with Hossein, the third Shiite Imam and the most important victim in Shiism. As mentioned, there are theoretical studies on the topic of how such victimizations have the added benefit of justifying reciprocal violence. Indeed, how can one deny a young protagonist whose father is brutally murdered by Iraqi soldiers his revenge by killing a traitor (the basic outline of Golabdarre'i's *Esmail, Esmail*)? But this, too, is a topic for another study.

As one can guess, popular religious folklore and beliefs play a significant role in literary works commissioned, encouraged, or sanctioned by the government. As a related point, I believe, many official efforts in this regard could also be placed in the category of creating "Prosthetic Memory" ("experiencing through memories [I would say made-up memories] events through which they themselves did not live"). I have borrowed this term from Alison Landsberg's noteworthy discussion of the notions of mediation and authenticity in relation to war memoirs and memories.[23]

Concepts of prosthetic memories and selective memoirs, which basically all wartime governments, and at times postwar governments, use to impose official narratives, in the case of Iran have become weapons used to justify the idea of continuous war (similar to Trotsky's idea of permanent revolution), now turned into a religion.

Landsberg's discussion could easily be expanded to the field of art and literature. In this context, another interesting example was the usage of the Shiite Messiah and the identification of Iranian soldiers with the Messiah's soldiers. Here is the interesting component: In some memoirs/fictional accounts written by veterans of the Iran-Iraq War, the authors specifically mention that they saw the Imam of the Age wearing a green shawl or outfit, riding a white horse, encouraging them to follow him or simply helping them fight the enemy. As just one example, the very short quasi-memoir of Mohammad Taqi Shokri is very entertaining. He seems to be recounting the memory of one of his fellow soldiers from one of the battles when the enemy was attacking ferociously and "Khomeini's lion-men" were defending valiantly:

> Suddenly he saw a man with green outfit riding a white horse who came from beyond mirrors [*sic*] and stepped on the ground with an Ali-like sword in hand and the neigh of his horse deafened the Earth's ears. After a while there was no sign of canons, tanks, and submarines and in general war instruments. Furthermore, the next day I observed that the enemy has retreated eight kilometers.[24]

Naturally, some have attributed this manifestation of the spirit to hallucination (of course, such an analysis could only be mentioned in private spaces). Others, again in those same private spaces, have maintained that the government—probably relying on the notion of simulacrum—sent a few men in white outfits and green shawls riding white horses to the battlefront to encourage and reassure Iranian soldiers that they were indeed on the side of Right fighting against Wrong and, more importantly, that the ultimate victory was near and that even if they were not alive to celebrate that moment, they would certainly end up in Paradise because they followed the Imam of the Age. And finally, there were also people who really believed that the Hidden Imam (i.e., the Imam of the Age) went to the front so there would be no doubt as to which side was the right one.

What is noteworthy here is the fact that many "memoirs" include such incidents—as far as I know there are at least three large volumes recording miracle-related memoirs—and thus bring up the perennial issue of the "true" or "real" representation of war and its violence.

It has always been one of the goals or dreams of war literature to proffer a true or real and precise picture of war, but in the case of Iran, because of rather unusual restrictions, I suggest that the search for and reading of silent moments and narratives is the most productive way to address this matter.

To be sure, in contemporary Persian war literature, there are many stories filled with photographic descriptions of war, but since most of them are couched in agenda-driven structures, elements of those photos are carefully selected to the point where there is no doubt that they are not even remotely representative of war. We should of course bear in mind that in general the concept of a documentary representation demonstrating the reality of a war—or of any other reality—is extremely problematic, mainly because even in the absence of a blatant imposition of dominant discourses, we are still faced with processes of selection, juxtaposition, allocation of textual space, and usage of many rhetorical devices which undermine the notion of the "documentary."

It is difficult to read about memory-making during and after war and not remember the famous debate about Robert Capa's (1913–54) Spanish civil war photograph. More than eighty years ago, Capa, a war photographer, took a photograph which later came to be known as *The Falling Soldier*. It was supposed to have captured one of the most tragic and real moments of this war; the moment of death of a Loyalist. Since the very moment of its distribution its veracity was questioned. The doubts about whether or not this photo was staged have continued to this day. Of course it is to the credit of the photographer that, if staged, he did not do it in such a way that its illegitimacy in imposing its narrative could be immediately and irrevocably be revealed.

In the case of Persian war literature, the story of staged war narratives goes far beyond that. The official discourse, especially while the war was still being waged, used every means of punishment, propaganda, censorship, threats, and encouragement, to crush direct efforts to describe war-related violence, when these descriptions were not used to justify "sacred violence," or to crush efforts that aimed to find a language to describe violence in order "to expose it and not to elevate it." In "Enchantment, Disenchantment, War, Literature," Cole refers to a post–World War I French critic, Jean Norton Cru, whose sole goal was to find an absolutely testimonial language, devoid of influence from macro policies which had led to war and, more importantly, devoid of influence from the aesthetics of war literature. Jean Cru went so far as to criticize one of the best examples of narratives of silence, *All Quiet on the Western Front* (here I am particularly referring to the last part of the novel, if its irony is read ironically). He accused Erich Maria Remarque of having sacrificed "absolute truth about war" for the sake of aesthetic requirements, like other "professional writers."[25] For reasons discussed above, testimonies such as the ones that Cru had in mind did not have much chance of seeing the light of day during the Iran-Iraq War. In fact, I maintain that works that have contributed to the depiction of "truth about war" (whatever this truth may be) are works that, instead of talking about guns and bullets and missiles and acts of violence done to human flesh, speak about seemingly invisible perspectives that have profoundly changed ordinary lives.

War fundamentally interrupts routines, everyday life, and the normal life span. There are efforts by the power apparatus to present this interruption as normal; at times, this translation succeeds in convincing the populace. Conversely, there are ordinary citizens who strive to protect the ordinary life; in this process, most of the time the end result is a compromise which nevertheless carries within itself an element of confrontation. In this context, sub-narratives begin to emerge; at times the subject matter—of a story or a painting, for example—is treated in such a way that it could give the impression that chaos is the order of the day, while other narratives tend to simply ignore the war and refuse to accept the dominance of chaotic elements.

In other words, the strategic narratives promoted by the official discourse to colonize and monopolize the national imagination are best confronted and challenged by emphasis on everyday life, everyday realities and interactions, while using silence as a "tactic of resistance" against those strategic visions. In the case of Iran, this literary resistance gradually found strength after the war due to, relatively speaking, fewer restrictions on literary spaces representing this resistance. Some of the better-known examples of such war-related fictions: Javad Mojabi's *Shab-e Malakh* (*The Night of the Locust*, 1367/1988), Esmail Fasih's *Zemestan-e 62* (*Winter of 1983*, 1368/1989), Hushang Golshiri's "Naqqash-e Baghani" ("The Baghani Painter," 1372/1997) and Reza Baraheni's *Azadeh Khanom va Nevisandeh-ash* (*Azadeh Khanom and Her Writer*, 1376/1997). Examining the subgenre represented by these texts, which, because of their indirect approach to the war, tackle an extremely wide range of subject matter and employ a variety of narrative techniques, requires a separate study.

To stay within the limits of the present study, I end by making a cursory reference to the synopses of three short stories which I believe are good representatives of a brand of literary resistance informed very subtly by an antiwar lyricism.

The first one is "Sarbaz-e Ghayeb" (The Absent Soldier) by Fereshteh Sari, the story of a young woman whose husband's name is on the list of the Missing in Action. "The whole story is the recounting of the narrator's dropping by her mother's house with her small daughter, and her memories of her childhood alley. In this once busy and lively alley, now only women and children are left, along with a single middle-aged man who has spent all these years inside the house with his mother to avoid the war."[26] This was a young man that the narrator used to be attracted to.

Marjan Riahi's 'Sobh, Sa'at-e Hasht-o Nim" (Eight-thirty in the Morning) is the story of a very young woman, the death of whose fiancé kills her dreams, one of which is to get married and get away from going to school. Riahi's approach can be summarized as ignoring the rules of the game as defined by the official discourse. She uses a bare language without any ornamental or rhetorical devices and creates atmospheres that are completely self-referential and have no relationship to the outside world, whose definition is dominated by the official discourse's narrative of the war. This is an attempt to construct a completely personal sensibility which aims to ignore the outside world.

Another very short story is Mandanipur's "Sara-ye Panjshanbeh" (The Thursday Sara), the story of a man who has lost his legs in the war and a nurse who seems to have been his fiancée. The man lives with his mother; the woman visits him every Thursday (sometimes Tuesdays, too) and they talk for a few hours—mostly about the hospital where she works—then she leaves. That is almost all there is to it. I believe "The Thursday Sara" is one of the best short war stories. What all these stories have in common, which I think is best captured and crystallized in the third example, is that they are ignoring the rules of the binary system game; they are silent about it; yet by creating a vague, indecisive, indescribable, unpredictable, and melancholic atmosphere and set of emotions, especially the last two, they constitute what could be called a counter-discursive lyricism in the time of war.

Theodor Adorno once said that "to write poetry after Auschwitz was barbaric." Later on, he modified the statement and said he meant lyric poetry.[27] But I think that in regard to contemporary Persian war literature, many stories have succeeded, through such lyricism, to create silent narratives about war and its tangible violence which, in the context of the discursive battle waged by the government, have contributed to the outlining of an image of "truth about war."

NOTES

1 Quoted from Kate McLoughlin, *The Cambridge Companion to War Writing*, Cambridge: Cambridge University Press, 2009, p. 1.

2 In his review of Patrick Deer's *Culture in Camouflage: War, Empire, and Modern British Literature*, Paul K. Saint-Amour writes:

> Scholars of peace and conflict have lately been much concerned with "total war," an expression coined in 1916 by Léon Daudet to denote the complete mobilization of a nation's resources in a bid to eliminate its adversary, irrespective of distinctions between combatants and noncombatants. The totality that most occupies Deer, however, is neither the limitless extent of targeting nor the engulfing reach of the war economy; it is, instead, the totalizing energy of official war cultures whose manufactured traditions aimed, as he puts it, to "cure and unite the diverse, fragmented spheres of everyday life" (6).

http://muse.jhu.edu, accessed November 28, 2011.

3 The battle of *Qadesiyyeh* (635 CE) was the first major battle that took place between Iranians and Arabs. While it took about two more decades for the Arabs to defeat the Sassanids, this battle has symbolized the defeat of the Iranians and consequently the beginning of the spread of Islam into Iran.

4 Indeed, this sentiment is quite palpable from Khomeini's speech when he was forced to accept the peace treaty. He said:

> How fortunate those who went with martyrdom! How fortunate those who lost their head and life along this caravan of light! How fortunate those who raised these jewels in their bosoms! Lord, leave this book of martyrdom open to those who still seek it enthusiastically; and do not deprive us from reaching it either.
>
> Lord, our country and our nation are still at the beginning of the road and they need the torch of martyrdom. You be the protector and guardian of this luminous light.

> How fortunate you are; you, men and women! How fortunate are martyrs and captives and those missing and the great families of martyrs! And woe unto me who am still alive and have drunk the poisonous cup of the acceptance of the treaty. I feel ashamed in front of the greatness and sacrifices of this nation. And woe unto those who were not part of this caravan! www.bbc.co.uk, accessed November 21, 2011.

5 A representative example is a speech that Khomeini delivered very shortly after the 1979 Revolution, in the city of Qom, in which he chided the university-educated and intellectuals in general. Here is an excerpt from that speech: "Whatever we are suffering is because of these universities; because of this class which keeps saying that 'we have studied at university; we are intellectuals; we know about law and rights.' Whatever we are suffering is from these people." www.kayhanpublishing. uk.com, accessed December 21, 2011.

6 Hasan Mirabedini, *Sad Sal Dastan Nevisi-e Iran* (*One Hundred Years of Fiction in Iran*), Tehran: Cheshmeh, 1998, v. 3, p. 897.

7 www.tebyan.net, accessed December 18, 2011. As indicated in the article, the data come from Masud Kosari's *Barresi-ye Jame'eh Shenakhti-ye Dastanha-ye Kutah-e Jang* (*A Sociological Review of War's Short Stories*), Tehran: Farhangsara-ye Paydari (The Cultural Center for Resistance), 1382/2003, p. 134.

8 To read more about this concept, see Patrick Deer's *Culture in Camouflage: War, Empire, and Modern British Literature*, New York: Oxford University Press, 2009, pp. 1–14.

9 *Journey to Heading 270 Degrees*, translated by Paul Sprachman, Costa Mesa: Mazda, 2006.

10 "Jashn-e Runami'-ye *Safar beh Gara-ye 270 Darajeh*" (The Ceremony for the Unveiling of *Journey to Heading 270 Degrees*) *Adabiyat-e Dastani*, no. 102, 2006, p. 43.

11 Seyyedeh Zahra Hosseini, *Da*, Tehran: Sureh-ye Mehr, Edition 79, 2009, pp. 464, 465.

12 avinyfilm.ir/, accessed November 21, 2011.

13 "The Color of Fire at Midday," p. 68. Translated by Mohammad Mehdi Khorrami, in *Sohrab's Wars: Counter Discourses of Contemporary Persian Fiction*, Costa Mesa: Mazda, 2008.

14 Ibid., p. 82.

15 Ibid., p. 81.

16 'The Image of Modern Persian Fiction in the Broken Mirror of Neo-Orientalism," in *Oriental Languages in Translation*, v. 3, Proceedings of the International Conference Cracow, Cracow: Polish Academy of Sciences Press, 2008, pp. 105–116.

17 *The Divan by Shams-d-Din Muhammad-i-Hafiz-i-Shirazi*, translated by Wilberforce Clarke, New York: Samuel Weiser, 1970, v. 2, p. 860.

18 Ibid.

19 Sarah Cole, "Enchantment, Disenchantment, War, Literature," in *PMLA* 124, n. 5, 2009, pp. 1632–1647.

20 This is the translation of *nevisandegan-e arzeshi*, commonly used by proponents of the official discourse, which refers to writers who adhere to values promoted by the discourse in power.

21 It should be noted that although most established writers reacted one way or another to the war, apparently they did not produce the kind of works that the official discourse was looking for. As Reza Sarshar (a.k.a. Rahgozar) writes: "Six years of war have passed, and every single day so many epics are created at the front. But so far not even a few novels or collections of stories which could do them justice have been written . . . When the warriors realized that artists [i.e., professional writers and artists] are not doing anything for the war, they were forced to accept this responsibility as well (creating "true" stories of war). Unfortunately, though, they didn't create artistic work. That's why their writings are just full of feelings and emotions; there isn't much art, technique, or things like that in them" (Mirabedini, *Sad Sal Dastan Nevisi-e Iran*, p. 897).

22 Mirabedini's *Sad Sal Dastan Nevisi-e Iran* is a good reference work which alludes to many similar titles.

23 Alison Landsberg, *Prosthetic Memory: The Transformation of American Remembrance in the Age of Mass Culture*, New York: Columbia University Press, 2004.

24 eshgh66.persianblog.ir, accessed November 21, 2011.

25 Cole, "Enchantment, Disenchantment, War, Literature," p. 1638.

26 This story is published in English in *A Feast in the Mirror: Stories by Contemporary Iranian Women*, translated and edited by Mohammad Mehdi Khorrami and Shouleh Vatanabadi, Boulder and London: Lynne Rienner, 2000, p. 4.

27 McLoughlin, *The Cambridge Companion to War Writing*, p. 16.

APPENDIX A

Only the Dead Witnessed the End of the War

ALI BADER

Translated by Amir Moosavi

At the Ajeerda divide, the strip of land that separates the marshes on the eastern side, east of the city of Amarah, we were gathered into deeply dug out positions. Thousands of soldiers, dressed in khaki uniforms, we were packed together, drenched by the rain, with our helmets and weapons. We placed ourselves in many positions, small sandbags placed above them, their exposed sides submerged in water and mud.

The mud was so deep that we sank up to our thighs into it. The rain hadn't stopped for two whole days. The sky rained down on us relentlessly and covered the area with a nightmare of water. Before we joined this battle—nearly ten days ago—the soldiers were repelling attacks by themselves from the direction of Amarah where a huge number of Iranian soldiers were advancing further into the strip of land and converging into a number of armed detachments.

Actually, three months prior I was at the front, but I didn't participate in a real battle. Before that, I was stationed at a number of rear positions in the supply line. I would silently watch the injured soldiers on stretchers and the dead officers, those who would be laid to rest in coffins. I would look in their direction from afar, never approaching them. For long stretches of time I would watch the supply trucks move along in a strict column, and follow the artillery shells that fell on the heavy cement blocks of the army camp's trenches.

The city was sad and distant, as if it had been exiled to the furthermost frontier. It was completely, utterly, empty, save for the trucks spinning out in the mud while crossing its streets. Just a day ago, in this very place, I witnessed a pitiless lineup of wounded bodies on stretchers, and nurses in white scrubs walking in the field clinic—the mobile hospital that would follow the battlefield, remaining at its edges. There were a large number of coffins placed atop each other. At an old, abandoned garden I paused to smoke a cigarette and began watching, with sorrow, the funerary intertwinement of the colossal trees, as they rose to dark heights surrounded by a thick cloud of flies. From time to time columns of soldiers would pass by in their filthy coats in front of barbed wire checkpoints; columns of soldiers who would be killed in hours and placed in these wooden coffins. This is the other image that completes the nightmare.

* * *

The young officer had a rough appearance, a jet-black moustache, and a stern look. He was busying himself with staring at a map laid out on the table. His forbidding expression contained the terrifying possibility to both ignore and condemn. I don't know why he looked at me with such deliberate scorn. His provincial appearance betrayed an affected arrogance and an unjustified resentfulness which I knew I would face many more times here at the front.

He ordered me to join the reserve camp near the hospital . . .

I put my sack on my back, placed my gun on my shoulder and headed towards the truck parked near the headquarters. I threw myself on its cold iron bed and crept towards the right corner, squatting down and pressing my knees up towards the top of my chest. We were more than 20 soldiers, crammed together by the cold iron, absentmindedly staring at each other in silence.

The trucks traveled the long route that connected the rear camps to the combat trenches. They passed a number of encampments, grave, solemn, their many flagstaffs carrying the banners of their legions and regiments. Images of the harsh bombing campaigns, one after another, on the road: ambulances full of the injured passing quickly by, their sirens blaring; supply trucks continuously passing by. On both sides of the military route were bleak stations, packed with injured soldiers, their heads wrapped with white gauze, their broken hands set or walking on crutches; grim cities completely smashed by artillery; muddy trenches, frozen from the cold.

Not one among us—the soldiers in the truck—uttered a sound. In these residual moments of our lives, not a word was spoken. That silence alone was enough to demonstrate the slow penetration of death into each one of us. It was enough to corroborate everything we had seen in the abandoned cities that we were passing by; burnt homes in the form of our own deferred deaths. After those images of ruins, blood, ashes and smoke—nothing. Nothing but silence. The silence of those soldiers, on that morbid and rainy afternoon, heading towards an unknown fate.

* * *

After the last heated battle more of the battalions' troops were killed in the positions at the front and they began to replace them with us. That's why they named our rear encampment a "replacement center."

"A replacement center" that's what the soldiers say to someone they don't know. It's a camp surrounded by barbed wire, stretching over a large area on the rear lines and supply depots. Arriving there, however, was the beginning of the inevitable end. The replacements continued their work because the killing continued. It was death alone that incessantly marched forward, devouring lives. You replace a casualty and, at the same time, feel that your own death is only being postponed. There are plenty who wait for your replacement. You think of nothing except the hope of life . . . an unconquerable hope. In moments of pain you think of preparing to accept death, the way that a cancer patient endures the thought of death after his condition suddenly worsens. Doubtless, most thoughts during wartime are about death, not life. During the harshest moments of war, these two thoughts interchange to the point that you confuse them completely. Yet you cling more to life. Through an imminent death you become more deeply acquainted with life.

What do I do here, between the bodies, dirt and weapons?

You say to yourself that life from afar seems like an extended moment of time. You doubt death, but you never doubt life, yet you feel like that you've just now learnt that. That's the sad thing about it: you won't know the meaning of life except for when you stand in front of the humiliation of war, the hideousness of killing and the passing smiles of soldiers.

* * *

After marching for two days I reached the front. My khaki jacket was completely drenched. The rain was pouring on my face and kept dripping down my chin, and the mud stuck to my shoes until it prevented me from marching comfortably. I was very skinny, pale, and 23 years old. I had graduated from university almost a year earlier and hadn't participated in any battles before. I didn't know what a battle was. All that I knew about them was what I had read in novels by Hemingway, Remarque and Tolstoy.

My strong passion for reading was such that my mother had sewn me a pocket inside my military uniform that could hold at least one or two small books that I would carry with me wherever I went. On the off hours I would sit separate from the other soldiers and sink into my book. I would drown in lines as if I were in another time and place, as if I were living in another world. Not the world I was forced to exist in, something different from it completely.

Reading: this was truly a special privilege. It was an escape from this world into another world. Thus, almost every hour—even at times of intense shelling and during the horrifying terror of attacks that knew no bounds—I would escape through reading. I would go quickly with the events of a book, without stopping, arming myself with the strength of a passion that possessed me, never returning to the time and place that I was living in.

I would perpetually wonder: was the young hero, Proust, wiser when he secluded himself in his room and drowned himself in his books so that he could flee from seeing his grandmother who was suffering in pain?

Far from the putrid smell of dead bodies that would waft towards us from the battlefield and far from the gunpowder that penetrated my inner depths causing me to vomit, at times decimating my insides, to the point that vomiting became a trivial matter, I would secretly isolate myself and read. It was a guaranteed sense of harmony, I could savor the smell of the lines of my book, like the fragrance of a distant lily . . . or the scent of the wood in my library rubbed down with alcohol, or the smell of a stone house drenched in water.

Reading was a real alternative to having to surrender to the degrading world that I was living in. It was a kind of infatuation with escaping from a wretched, fated life—a pleasure, unrestrained by a muddled mind. I existed among the dead, or among those whose deaths were suspended, no doubt, until I would be killed. Yet, I felt myself sitting down like a wild apricot tree growing out of the stones of a wall.

* * *

I got out of the military car and saluted the officer. He then ordered me to enter a semi-dark position. Under the cover of the sounds of explosions and a plethora of images, constantly shifting, the scene was slowly distorting and fading. I could no longer see anything, save for a sort of pale darkness and a soaking wet night because of the rain that covered everything. On that harsh, stormy day the rain would not stop. Everything became water: the sandbags at the door of the position, a soldier carrying his gun, even the words that we exchanged between each other, which, in the end, concealed our wet lips from the water pouring down from our brows to our chins.

I entered with slow steps, my gun in hand and my iron helmet sliding off a little. I didn't bother adjusting it, mainly because my shoulder bag was bearing down on me, too. My enormous shoes were stumbling through the water and mud was weighing me down. Every minute I would run my hand over my books that I placed in the interior pockets that my mother had sewn for me, nervously trying to keep them from getting wet. I was aware of my comical appearance and ashamed of it as well.

At the time I was often preoccupied with my physical appearance. I would pay close attention to such shallow things, because of upbringing and my age. But, what lessened the sorrow that I felt imposed upon me were the smiles I encountered from the older officers, and those who were guarding the front of the position who would greet me in a friendly manner. Their clothes were muddy and dripping. Their khaki helmets trickled water and their young faces were soaked. Until today I wonder just how during this time of fighting they had the time to greet me and present me with a smile that I'll never forget.

I looked around the tight position. Someone was holding a book in his hands, near a small lantern so that he could read in its weak light. That really cheered me up.

The corporal approached the lantern and raised up its glass by the handle. He lit his cigarette and started puffing smoke into the air.

Another person was sitting a bit further away, in the right corner. He was sitting on his knees oiling a rifle in his hands. In this encampment, packed with war materials, arms, papers and books, there was another group of soldiers sleeping, leaning on a wall, wrapped in blankets.

I looked at them. Their legs were pressed up to their stomachs. Their heads and a part of their backs and shoulders were leaning against the wall. I, on the other hand, was tired, scared and very confused. Would there be an attack today?

"No," they said, "maybe tomorrow."

I looked at the corporal with a shy smile and asked him if he would let me sleep with my fellow soldiers who were sleeping against the wall. I was tired, wet, and only wanted to doze off for just a short while. He was a little confused when I pointed over to them.

He gave me a hard look and nodded his head in agreement.

He gave me permission without smiling. So I quickly went to take my belongings off my shoulders, not understanding something that I saw in the eyes of the other soldiers around me, their eyes started to quickly look at one another.

I placed my belongings close to me and turned toward the sleeping group. I approached them, looked at them quickly, and did just as they had done, going to sleep.

My wet clothes were tossed on the ground, my shoes, too. I pulled a bit of the blanket away from the soldier sleeping near me and placed my head and part of my shoulder on the wall. I put my knees close to my stomach, as if I were squatting.

Sleeping like this wasn't comfortable, but I had no other choice. I had to sleep like them in order to pull some of the blankets onto my body. The sleeping soldier's face was close to me looking the other way. His foot was close to mine, outside the blanket, in a black shoe and bright green socks. Slowly but firmly, so that I wouldn't wake him, I pulled some of the blanket onto myself. All that remained in my mind was the bright color of the green socks that the soldier near me was wearing— the one with whom I shared the blanket.

I was so young, learning about life with all its details. Maybe these superficialities had a high value for me at the time, but I make fun of them now.

"How can this soldier wear socks in that color with the pants that he has on?" I said.

That color truly irritated me. It was a bright color and left quite an impression on me.

* * *

I spent the entire night dozing on and off, waking up to the sound of shelling and explosions. I would hear distant cries and yelling. The images of the nightmares of war and death would mix with the sounds of the living soldiers and the sound of the Morse near me. Time and time again, I would drift off in sad and disconcerting dreams, dozing off and then waking up again. What really remained stuck in my head was the image of those green socks that the soldier near me was wearing, the one who wouldn't turn towards me so that I could see his face. He didn't turn over, didn't move, didn't shake, didn't snore, and didn't say a word. He wasn't aware of me at all.

As the night wore on, I was overcome by the curiosity to see the face of this soldier with the bright socks, but he wouldn't budge.

* * *

I opened my eyes in the morning. Light was filling the position. The shelling had just about died down. Soldiers were passing in front of me and speaking to each other. But the soldier with the bright green socks hadn't moved a bit. Not him, or the five others tossed against the wall who were sharing a blanket between themselves. Everything was talking and moving, but these bodies that were face to face with me hadn't moved at all. After a few minutes, and against my will, I stretched out my arm in his direction and shook him a little.

"Brother . . . brother."

Neither sound, nor movement; I pulled back a little, so that we were completely face to face.

It was as if he had just recently fallen asleep. His face was silent. It showed no signs of movement and had gone a little pallid. His eyes were half-open; his mouth slightly agape. His black hair had uncurled onto his forehead. He was twenty years old.

The panic almost killed me. I stood up and screamed out in protest: "Why did you all make me sleep with dead bodies the entire night?"

The corporal said, "I was afraid to tell you that they had died, since you would have been scared and this is your first time at the front."

* * *

I realized at that moment that seeing a dead soldier is more frightening than our own death. We won't ever see our own death. However, seeing a dead person reminds us of our own mortality. It reminds us of the mystery of death, just as the newborn baby's face reminds a woman of the enigma of life.

Will I also end like this—as a cold body? What sanctity will I leave behind in my death for those men?

There's no glory or holy symbol in dying during warfare. The young soldier's face exposed not only the atrocity that was our presence in the war—if this tragedy was related solely to death it wouldn't need all of this commentary—but it's related to a savagery that we want to sanctify.

I would ask myself how could it be that our deaths could be transformed into heroic acts by others, when it was simply the act of dying, and nothing else? How did that terrifying open grave transform into something sacred—religiously and nationally—something that we rise in front of, like a ritual, as if it is a great act, when it is death, and nothing more?

That we die is not what scares me. What scares me is that, during wartime, death transforms into a something holy. And life changes into a corpse, leaning against the wall waiting for the shovel and pickaxe so that it can be buried. Rarely does death during wartime change into knowledge that we can use to condemn war. Rather, death transforms into a great act that prolongs and repeats wars.

While I was pondering the deaths of those young men in this way—without tears or commotion, tossed aside on the muddy earth like piles of garbage—I realized why my fellow soldiers let me sleep with them under the same blanket.

These lifeless faces are completely disconnected from the civilian world you know. These are people who are waiting for their own deaths.

I am not mistaken. They smiled at me only because after a short while I would be like those young men, dead as well. Gradually, with idiocy and patience, my mouth will fall open like any other dead person. I await a grave, shovel and pickaxe.

(A chapter from a novel entitled *Be Quiet, Soldiers*)

My Brother's Blue Eyes

MARJAN RIAHI

Translated by Mohammad Mehdi Khorrami

What I am writing is the story of Ms. Vavi's coming and staying on. Hossein, who is in charge of the storage room, is telling this story in his stuttering speech, and I am writing it down. I was transferred to this section a week ago. Hossein lost the nerves of three fingers in his right hand during the war, and he has just learned how to sign with his left hand. His jaw is not looking good either. He speaks with a lot of difficulty. One cowardly shrapnel has ruined both his face and the way he talks. Many people have difficulty listening to him.

Hossein says that Ms. Vavi came a year ago. She was looking for a job. Young, tall and thin, with a BA degree; all applicants had least one or two of them in a folder under their arm. On top of her application she had written that she was Martyr Vavi's sister. On the day of her interview she had said that when Martyr Vavi had been martyred she was only two years old. This was told to Hossein by the one who interviewed her. I don't know his name. Hossein didn't say anything either.

After only three days, Ms. Vavi had managed to use the company's bus service. The company has limited resources for transporting its employees, but Ms. Vavi took a letter from the head of the administration to the head of transportation attesting that she was a martyr's sister, and the problem was solved. There were one hundred and four other people waiting in line to use the bus service. Hossein apparently sees her in the transportation unit and wants to talk to her, but Ms. Vavi doesn't realize that and leaves. Hossein was looking for a suitable opportunity to have a few words with Ms. Vavi. Hossein was hoping that the opportunity somehow would arise, but it didn't.

Six months after she came, on Martyrs' Day they give her an appreciation plaque and a gold coin, because she was a martyr's sister; everyone in the hall claps for her. After that, everyone recognizes her as Martyr Vavi's sister.

She was supposed to bring a picture of her brother the same day so that it would be published in the company's newsletter. But she didn't. The editor of the newsletter had told this to Hossein. Because in the newsletter they published the pictures of all the martyrs of the company, or martyrs whose family members worked in the company, but in place of Martyr Vavi there was only a picture of a red tulip.

After the meeting, Hossein stops Ms. Vavi to talk to her, but then someone bumps into Ms. Vavi and the fruit juice she had spills on her chador, and again she doesn't realize that Hossein wants to say something to her.

When the ration for Eid provision was being handed out, Ms. Vavi's name was written on the top of the list of the first group of recipients without any regard for alphabetical order. She doesn't go to the storage room to receive her share; she sends her father. With his small black eyes, the old man reads the list of the items a few times; a couple of times he counts the bags of rice, lentils, sugar, and chickens. Since he is Martyr Vavi's father, a few people jump up to help him and carry the huge sack of rations to the door for him. Then one of the company's drivers gives him a ride to his house.

A year later, Ms. Vavi becomes the head of the administration. In her contract, it is written that she will be paid an extra amount because she is Martyr Vavi's sister. Until one day, Ms. Vavi's assistant brings the order for purchasing thirty-one desks to Supplies, and the manager, who is very busy, delegates the purchase to Hossein.

Hossein says Ms. Vavi's desk is very beautiful. It is not a desk that people would replace any time soon. They order the desks, but then Hossein reneges and says that Ms. Vavi should come herself and say exactly what type of desk she wants so people won't criticize him later. The assistant goes, and Ms. Vavi comes herself. Hossein and Ms. Vavi end up alone in the storage room. Bored, Ms. Vavi asks about different types of desks, but Hossein asks her what color her brother's eyes were.

Ms. Vavi starts. First she tries to change the subject; then she collects herself and says her brother's eyes were the same color as hers; dark brown, almost black.

Hossein doesn't say anything. Ms. Vavi, now in a bad mood, wants to leave. When she reaches the door of the storage room, Hossein, in his stuttering speech, says Martyr Vavi's eyes were sky blue, a color that he has never seen in any eyes. Hossein tells me: "You had to see those eyes to realize how beautiful blue can be."

Ms. Vavi is irritated and says: "You think you know my brother better than I? Maybe you are talking about another Martyr Vavi!"

Hossein tells her that they had been in the same platoon, not just the night of the attack; they had fought together for six months, and it was there that he had been hit by a shrapnel in the jaw and the gun's safety pin pierces his hand. More importantly, he tells her that both he and Martyr Vavi were from the same neighborhood.

From the first time Hossein saw Ms. Vavi, he knew that Martyr Vavi had only two brothers and they went abroad a few years after Vavi's martyrdom. They took their mother, too. Hossein knew that Martyr Vavi's callous father had three daughters from his fifth marriage, and Ms. Vavi is the first daughter of this new family.

At first Ms. Vavi begs Hossein not to raise a stink, but then when Hossein only stares at her, she says angrily that her father and Martyr Vavi's father are the same person, and therefore she is Martyr Vavi's sister.

Ms. Vavi never goes back to the storage room. Once, she sends Hossein a few movie tickets, but Hossein sends them back, and then Ms. Vavi pretends that it was all a misunderstanding and she meant to send the tickets to someone else. But when Hossein applies for retirement, she expedites the process. She makes sure to get the necessary signatures herself, and wherever she goes she says that since Hossein is a disabled war veteran, his file should be expedited.

A few days ago, one of IT's employees who has dark blue eyes, one of them a bit lazy, went to Ms. Vavi to correct a mistake in his new contract, and Ms. Vavi told him: "Wow, the color of your eyes is so much like my brother's." I heard this myself, when I was emptying Ms. Vavi's wastepaper basket from under her inlaid desk.

Hossein wants me to cross out these last few sentences. Hossein says: "Don't make trouble for yourself." But I don't cross them out. I am supposed to make thirty-one copies of this and leave one in each one of the thirty-one desks bought for the administration, so that when the employees open the drawers of their new desks they would see this manuscript, and maybe even read it.

2008

APPENDIX C

Two Poems

SINAN ANTOON

Translated by the author from the original Arabic. Both poems were published in *Mawshur Muballal bil-Hurub* (A Prism; Wet with Wars) (Cairo: Mirit Books, 2004).

WARS
When I was torn by war
I took a brush
Immersed in death
And drew a window
On war's wall
I opened it
Searching
For something
But
I saw another war
And a mother
Weaving a shroud
For the dead man
Still in her womb

A PRISONER'S SONG
(for the POWs of the Iraq-Iran War 1980–1988 . . . on both sides)

from the distant fog
after communiqués had withered
and canons stopped spitting

he returned
soaked with the "there"
his silence an umbrella
under our ululation
he passed by us
through us
to his old room
the lute was still there
its strings in their wooden exile
yearned for his rainy fingers
but he never touched it
what language could explain
that eight years
had gnawed
ten fingers

—*The Baghdad Blues* (Harbor Mountain Press, 2006)

A Chapter from *The Pomegranate Alone*

SINAN ANTOON

Translated by Sinan Antoon

The only time I ever saw my father crying was many years later when he heard that my brother Ameer, whom we called Ammoury, had died. Ameer, who was five years my senior, turned from "Doctor" to "Martyr." His framed black-and-white photograph occupied the heart of the main wall in our living room and yet a bigger part of my father's heart which Ammoury had already monopolized. Ameer, you see, was the ideal son who always made my father proud. He always excelled and was the top of his class. At the national baccalaureate exams, his score was 95% and that enabled him to go to medical school to study to become a surgeon. Ameer wanted to fulfill his dream of opening a clinic so he could take on Dad's burden and Dad could retire. Dad insisted that he would keep working until he died. Ameer insisted on helping my Dad at work even on his short breaks from the army during the years of war with Iran before he was killed in the al-Faw battles.

I was reading in my room on the second floor when I heard a car stop in front of the house and doors being shut. Seconds later, I heard the new doorbell ringing. Ameer had bought and installed it himself after the old one had stopped working and I had procrastinated about fixing it. I drew the curtain open and saw a taxi with a flag-draped coffin on top of it. My heart fell into an abyss.

Whenever I saw a taxi driving down the street with a flag-draped coffin on it, I would think for a few seconds about Ammoury never returning home on his feet, but crouched on a car, and I would quickly cast that thought out of my head. Then my mother's wailing pierced my heart like a spear and I rushed to the stairs barefoot. When I reached the front door my mother was already out in the street in her nightgown without her *abaya*. She stood next to the taxi beating her head, looking at the coffin and screaming "Oh my . . . Ammoury . . . Ammoury . . . Ammoury's gone . . . My son is gone."

A uniformed man stood watching the scene next to the door. He asked me to sign the papers confirming receipt of the body. Without looking or reading, I signed two copies with the ballpoint pen he gave me. I handed him the papers and his pen. He returned the pen to his pocket and said, "May God have mercy on him. My condolences." He gave me one of the papers which I folded and put in the pocket of my shirt.

The neighbors had started to come out after hearing my mother's wailing. Some of them stood around the taxi and women rushed to console my mother, to lessen her pain and cry along. The bald taxi driver had untied the ropes which secured the coffin on top of the metal rack. He put them in his trunk and stood waiting. I went to my mother to hug her, but she was hysterical and surrounded by the women who had started beating their heads as well. I thought of how my father and his weak heart would take the news.

The driver started to move the coffin on his own, as if to give us a hint that we had to unload it. I heard a voice saying "Go to Abu Ammoury's place and tell him." I yelled that no one should go and that I will tell him myself after we bring down the coffin. The driver, I, and some of the neighborhood's young men took down the coffin and brought it inside the house. We put it in the living room.

* * *

A silent tear fell on my cheek as I was rushing to deliver the news of Ammoury's death to my father. Ammoury, who used to play soccer with me on the street. Ammoury, who one summer had taught me how to make a paper kite using twigs from palm trees and who had climbed the neighbor's palm tree to retrieve my kite when it got stuck there. Ammoury, with whom I shared a room for twenty years and who used to snore sometimes, but who accused me of fabricating the snoring accusation. Ammoury, who caught me masturbating in the bathroom once when I forgot to lock the door and who apologized, smiled and closed the door quickly. He told me later that it was a natural desire, but said I shouldn't overdo it or let it control all my time. Ammoury, who gave me his blue 24-inch bike when he became taller and bought a 26. Ammoury, who used to race me and would always let me win at the end. Ammoury, who kept my secret and agreed to go to the high school headmaster instead of my father to convince him to allow me back to classes after I had exceeded the absence limit. Ammoury, who genuinely tried to understand my artistic tendencies and my decision to study sculpture and who used to respect art even though it really was not at the top of his list. Ammoury, who wanted me to be an engineer or a doctor like him and who couldn't hide his disappointment when I got 87.7% in the baccalaureate exams. It was enough to enter the Academy of Fine Arts, but that wasn't what he had hoped for his little brother. Ammoury, who used to stand by me at home, defending and explaining my point of view against my parents' criticisms and who used to tell them that I was talented and must choose my own path and be responsible for the consequences of my decisions. Ammoury, who visited the exhibition we had the second year at the academy to encourage me and asked me to explain the idea behind my piece and expressed his admiration and listened attentively. Ammoury, who used to joke with me thinking he was encouraging me, but who actually annoyed me, by saying that my statues will fill Baghdad's squares.

Dr. Ammoury, the handsome, shy one, especially with girls, but who succeeded in charming Wasan, our neighbor, into falling in love with him through his silence and gravitas. My mother rushed to ask for her hand so they would be engaged before his graduation. He had to join the military after graduation, but he died before they got married. Wasan, with her long black hair and beautiful legs who was studying architecture at the University of Baghdad. I felt guilty when I couldn't drive away her face, time and again, from my sexual fantasies and desires. Ammoury, of whom I was jealous a lot, because he was the favorite, pampered, excellent, ideal which I could never approximate. I felt guilty, because I couldn't stop my self, even in this moment, from wondering so selfishly: *Would the news of my own death in this seemingly endless war have left one fourth of the pain and sorrow Ammoury's departure will leave behind?* I wiped my tears and scolded myself for this utter narcissism.

I got to the *mghaysil*, the washhouse. The door was ajar. I crossed the walkway and saw the Qur'anic verse "Every soul shall taste death" in beautiful Diwani script hanging over the door. The yellowish paint on the wall was peeling away in more than one spot because of humidity from the washing. My father was sitting in the left corner of the side room on the wooden chair listening to the radio as he often used to do in a space of time waiting for what death, depending on its mood, would decide to throw at him. Death's traces, its scents, memories, and details were present in every inch of that place. As if death was the real owner and my father merely an employee working for it and not for God, as he liked to think.

Death, ever present in my father's place of work and his days, was about to declare its presence once again, but with a cruelty and force that would tattoo itself on my father's heart and on what was left of his years. The washing table was empty and dry. My father's yellow amber worry beads were clicking in his right hand. Hammoudy must have gone out to buy something and left him alone. My father's eyes greeted me. He must've heard my footsteps. "Hello, Dad."

"Hi there, son. What brings you here?"

I'd not set foot there for more than a year. I tried to steer away from death and my relationship with my father had soured. He must've sensed something in my voice and seen the sadness on my face. There was anxiety in his voice:

"What? Is something wrong with your mother?"

"No, Dad."

"What then?"

I approached him and leaned to embrace him as he sat in his chair. He asked me: "What then? Did something happen to Ammoury?"

The news in the last two days was all about the bloody battles in al-Faw[1] and the heavy casualties suffered there. Two months before, Ammoury's unit was had been transferred from the northern sector to al-Faw. I hesitated for a few long seconds trying to postpone the grave news. Then I told him, as I hugged him and kissed his left cheek without being able to stop my tears: "May you have a long life, Dad. They brought him home just now."

He put his arms around me and repeated in a trembling voice: "Oh, God. Oh, God. There is no power save in God. There is no power save in God. There is no God but God. Only he is immortal." Then he wept like a child. I hugged him tightly and felt we'd exchanged the roles of father and son for a few minutes. I felt that he wanted to stand up, so I loosened my arm. He stood up and wiped his tears with the back of his right hand without letting go of his worry beads. He turned off the radio and put on his jacket. We locked the door and went home together without exchanging a word.

We didn't wash Ammoury. According to tradition, martyrs are not washed. He was buried in his military uniform. I never saw my father cry after that time, but the grief I saw piercing his eyes and voice that day would resurface every now and then on his face, especially when he gazed at Ammoury's photograph which hung on the wall, as if he were silently conversing with him. It's that very same look I saw on my father's face when Ammoury's coffin was being covered with dirt and the gravedigger recited:

> We come from God and to him we return. O God, take his soul up to you and show him your approval. Fill his grave with mercy so that he may never need any other mercy but yours, for he believes in you and your resurrection. This is what God and his messenger promised us. Verily they have told the truth. O God, grant us more faith and peace.

After the funeral was over the black banner stayed for months hanging on a wall at the entrance of our street:

> "Think not of those who die for God as dead,
> but rather alive with their God."

The martyr Doctor Ameer Kazim Hasan, died in the battles to liberate al-Faw on the 17th of April, 1987.

My father had never been chatty and didn't laugh often, but Ammoury's death intensified his silence and dejection, and made him more moody and volatile. My mother was the one who had to withstand the waves of his anger with a mumble or a complaint she would whisper to herself when he yelled: "Enough already" or "Turn the TV down." The TV had become her only solace. I hadn't spent much time at home even before Ammoury's death, but my clashes with my father became more frequent and I tried to avoid him so as to avoid them. More than once when I came back late at night he told me that I treated the house like a hotel.

In August of 1990, almost three and a half years after Ammoury's death, Saddam invaded Kuwait. To secure the eastern front with Iran and withdraw troops from there to Kuwait, he agreed to all the Iranian conditions and relinquished all the demands for which he'd waged the war in the first place. My father punched the table and shouted: "Why did we fight for eight years then and what the hell did Ammoury die for?" As for my mother, she would bury her face in her hands and weep whenever she remembered him. My sister used to console her and hug her and they would drown in each other's sorrow.

NOTES

Wahdaha Shajarat al-Rumman (Beirut: Mu'assasat al-Dirasat al-Arabiyya, 2010).

1 A peninsula on the Iraqi side of the border with Iran which was occupied during the Iran-Iraq War (1980–1988). Fierce and deadly battles were fought in and around it in the late 1980s.

A Letter to the Saad Family

HABIB AHMADZADEH

Translated by Paul Sprachman

The first finder or finders of this letter are kindly requested to deliver its contents in any way possible to the family of "Saad Abd al-Jabbar," a member of the 23rd Battalion of the Special Republican Guard Forces of Iraq; the letter is from the forces under control of the Third Army of Basra.

Esteemed Family of Soldier Saad:

Greetings,

I don't know whether writing and sending this letter is the right thing or proper under the circumstances, but whatever the case it seemed necessary in my view to write the letter and entrust it to your son, and in this unorthodox way have it reach you. The subject of the letter is the mysterious manner in which I became acquainted with your son. Eleven years have passed, and this enigmatic acquaintance has to be explained somehow to you; I feel compelled, then, in order to eliminate any doubt or misunderstanding on your part as regards the lamentable incident, to write you an exact and detailed account of how we met and the circumstances surrounding our meeting.

Right now your son Saad is beside me and no doubt is waiting for me to finish the letter so he can be the bearer of the facts to you.

This is the last time we will see each other, and certainly it will be our last goodbye! I know that it would be best to be brief and get to the point.

The incident began around ten years ago: the morning of 28 September 1981 to be exact. That was the first time I saw your son. During the morning of that day I was returning from the banks of the Karun River to our back lines. Major operations had taken place in the sector the night before. The operations were intended to break the siege of our city. By morning we had fought our way to the area around the river.

This was the first time during the one-year siege of the city that our forces were able to recapture the sector. Delighted to take part in these pivotal operations and wanting to make a record of my participation, I had brought with me an expensive camera, but the intensity of the fighting did not allow me to use it.

Until this moment everything that could have happened took place as they did in other operations; with the leaden skies of pre-dawn, fresh forces took the place of the tired fighters and everyone but me took advantage of the cover of night to return. I had the urge to tour the newly liberated areas to see what befell the region. Having gone around the minefield, I came upon the road made with packed sand that the Iraqis had constructed to join up with the asphalt road. I followed the sand road until it came to the intersection of the two roads. I was now face to face with a causeway that I had hoped to reach for a year so I could use it to go on leave.

The road still hadn't been cleared of mines, booby traps, and barbed wire; nevertheless it was a freeway to me.

As I walked along the road, I remember clearly that the sun was rising. I let out several loud cries and, without paying attention to the surroundings, started to prance around, happily waving my weapon up and down. I was overjoyed. At that time I was sixteen, about two years younger than your son was at the time.

This marked the beginning of the actual incident. I didn't know what had hit me, but for a moment I turned and was suddenly stunned, and, automatically assuming a defensive position, I dived quickly to the ground. I must admit was terrified; the whole time I was on the asphalt road, an Iraqi soldier was sitting watching me from behind, and I had absolutely no idea.

In an incredibly short time I scrambled behind the shoulder of the road and released the safety on the weapon. All the while I was wondering why he hadn't taken aim at me from behind. This was the context for the consolation thought that he was totally alone having been abandoned in the newly liberated territory and now wanted to surrender.

The sum of these thoughts gave me the nerve to try to get behind him. After hesitating briefly, I ran to the other side of the hill and was about to shout "Hands up!" in Persian. Now that you have the letter, of course, everything to an extent will be obvious.

That's right: I came face to face with your son's corpse, which had been put on the ground in a kneeling position; his neck and both wrists had been tied from behind to the crossroad sign with the kind of telephone wire they use in the desert. Blood had pooled under his feet.

It was at this point the weapon went limp in my hands; as I got closer I noticed that he or they had tied your son up so that the wounds on his neck and wrists made a horrible sight. After the shock of seeing him like that wore off, I began to hear the sounds of exploding shells and mortar rounds that were coming every moment toward our sector.

I looked at his innocent face; his eyes were wide open and startled. I don't know why it occurred to me to take a picture of your son's face, but I took it. Maybe it was just because I wanted to use the camera. As I was putting the camera back in my pack, the sound of explosions became more distinct and so did the barking of the stray dogs behind the Baathist lines; these dogs generally would whine every night before the operations. This reminded me what would happen to your son's corpse if it remained out there.

I looked into your son's open eyes, and, to escape the urgings of my conscience, I said to him, "I know, but I swear to God if I had a shovel I would definitely bury you." Just like any other person who uses a big excuse to avoid doing something.

Then I got going trying to escape the explosions, which were increasing by the minute. Would you believe it, but I hadn't gone a hundred meters when I saw a large shovel buried up to the handle sticking out of a pile of dirt next to a bunker! I stood still for a moment deeply undecided, but, having made an irrevocable promise to your son, I had no choice. Despite all the unpleasantness, I managed to pull the shovel out and went back to him. Showing him the shovel, I said, "Here's the shovel," and I began to dig in front of him. I dug so close to him that after a bit a stream of blood appeared in the hole. I would keep one eye on your son and one eye on the stream of blood, as I dug and moved the shovel around lest it leave bloodstains on the heels of my boots. I also would talk to your son, but to keep this letter short I can't set down everything we spoke in it; besides the subjects are without doubt not worthy of your attention.

Briefly then: when the job was nearly over, it occurred to me to wonder, given my short life as gravedigger, whether I had oriented the hole properly, that is according to the direction of prayer or not. But suddenly there was this immense explosion and the next thing I knew I was in the grave along with your son Saad on top of me. I must admit that I was so scared that it beggars description. Here I was in a sector with nobody from our side in it, in a grave face to face with the corpse. I used all my might to push aside your son and climb out of the grave. I realized that the situation came about as a result of an explosion that occurred behind your son. When I looked closer I noticed that there was a stream of fresh blood flowing down his overcoat, and this made me realize he had taken several pieces of shrapnel in the head; he was positioned precisely between me and the explosion or, said in a better way, between me and death.

It was at this point that my interest in your son increased several times over. I quickly finished digging the grave and was about to put Saad in it, when I figured that I shouldn't allow his face to touch the ground; so I took his long coat off and covered his head with it. As I was doing this, I noticed four spent cartridges inserted into his teeth, but there was no time to waste. Having wrapped his head in the coat, I found his ID card and a letter in his pocket. There was nothing else in the pocket. I untied his hands and began to shovel dirt on him. But as I shoveled it occurred to me that this alien being, who was far from his family, would be buried in a grave over which no one would recite the Qor'an; but there was nothing I could do but shovel earth on him.

Anyway, having marked the grave with that same signpost, I got away as fast as I could. Later on, during my first leave away from the front, I had his picture developed and put it in my photo album. From time to time, when leafing through the album, I would think of him as the corpse that saved my life, and despite the fact that I knew his name was Saad from the ID card, I still thought of him as an Iraqi soldier.

Years passed and the whole incident became only a memory in my mind until there was a minor incident. I became acquainted with some fellow countrymen whose job it was to exchange the bodies of Iraqi soldiers for those of our own dead. They exchanged the bodies on the border between the two countries. I brought up the subject of Saad with them, and today was the day we had arranged for me to show them his grave.

When we were at the sight [sic], I realized that one shouldn't rely too much on the signpost to find the grave, but the place where the two roads crossed would be of some help. After two excavations, we managed to dig your son up; possibly in the same condition that you will observe him in when this letter reaches you. But the real reason why I am writing you this letter, in fact, has nothing to do with these matters, but relates to the secret discovery that we made when we were digging him up.

When the fellows who were digging him up unwrapped the overcoat around his head, they looked at one another knowingly and said, "Another deserter!"

"What's the problem?" I asked.

Their experience in finding bodies told them, when the overcoat came off, that Saad was a deserter because the Iraqis would first execute deserters, then clamp their jaws shut with four bullets in their teeth to serve as a warning to others. After I explained the way in which Saad had been kneeling on the ground to them, they said that before execution, he had definitely been shot in the knees. An examination of his knees confirmed the truth, which his clothing and flesh had kept hidden from me for eleven years. I know that these facts are brutal and upsetting, especially since they concern your child. But my emotional and psychological state is no less than yours. During the last eleven years, time and time again I have traveled that road out of the city, and even when passing the crossroads it never crossed my mind to say a prayer for your son, for which I hope God will forgive me.

Because I never had thought I would be writing this letter, I used the back of the forms describing the particulars of the body. If I had been prepared, I would have included another letter and the picture that I had taken of your son's body. Perhaps what one of the disinterment fellows said is right: that it is better to let the truth remain buried under the ground; that way I would not be the cause of so much pain and discomfort to you. There is also the added risk that the letter might fall into the wrong hands, which would prevent you even from taking possession of your son's body. But as you will see I have used this unorthodox method of sending you the letter and thereby decreased to an extent the chances of detection.

I have written my address at the bottom of the letter so that you can contact me in any way you see fit, and I can send you the picture of Saad and his last letter. I don't know how you feel about my hiding the letter in the broken bone of your son's leg. But this method of concealment perhaps might cause the original owners not notice it, and the letter and Saad will be buried together, preventing the truth from reaching you, his respected family.

Am I still grappling with myself about why I am writing this? It's only in these last lines that I will be able to express why. Ten years ago the thought of writing such a letter would never have crossed my mind; but now that I have a child of my own, I can see that it is the absolute right of every family to know how their child spent his last minutes on earth.

The time for saying my last goodbyes to your son Saad have come. I know that in the future whenever I leave the city and pass the crossroads, as I stare at his empty grave my heart again will feel that anguish, the familiar pain of an eleven-year acquaintance, which has but a few hours to go.

The fellows are complaining again about how long this letter is taking. I entrust you and Saad to that same God who caused me to take a different path that day, who allowed me to see Saad and find a shovel, and now to uncover an eleven-year-old secret. And, maybe, that same God will allow this letter to reach you.

SELECT BIBLIOGRAPHY

IRAN

Abecassis, Michaël. "Iranian War Cinema: Between Reality and Fiction" *Iranian Studies,* 44, Issue 3 (2011), 387–394.

Ahmadzadeh, Habib. *Dastan-ha-ye Shahr-e Jangi.* Tehran: Sureh-ye Mehr, 2007.

Ahmadzadeh, Habib. *Shatranj ba Mashin-e Qiyamat.* Tehran: Sureh-ye Mehr, 2008.

Ahmadzadeh, Habib and Sprachman, Paul (trans.). *Chess with the Doomsday Machine: A Novel.* Costa Mesa, CA: Mazda Publishers, 2008.

Ahmadzadeh, Habib and Sprachman, Paul (trans.). *A City under Siege: Tales of the Iran-Iraq War.* Costa Mesa, CA: Mazda Publishers, 2010.

Akbari, Ali, and Samadi, Mohammad Ali. *Ketab-e Ahangaran: Khaterat va nowheh-ha-ye Hajj Sadeq-e Ahangaran,* Tehran: Entesharat-e Ya Zahra, 2012.

Bani 'Ameri, Ḥasan. *Gonjeshk-ha Behesht ra Nemifahmand.* Tehran: Nilufar, 2006.

Baygi, Ibrahim Hasan. *Guzidah-i Dah Sal Dastan-Nivisi dar Inqilab-i Islami,* Tehran: Howzeh-yi Honari, 1989.

Brown, Ian. *Khomeini's Forgotten Sons: The Story of Iran's Boy Soldiers.* London: Grey Seal, 1990.

Bureau de la littérature et de l'art de la résistance. *Guerre et mémoire: table ronde sur la littérature de guerre (6–7 décembre 1999), mémoires de guerre, combattants iraniens (conflit Iran-Irak), combattants français (Première Guerre mondiale).* Institut français de recherche en Iran: Faculté des sciences sociales de l'Université de Téhéran, 2002.

Chelkowski, Peter, and Dabashi, Hamid. *Staging a Revolution, The Art of Persuasion in the Islamic Republic of Iran.* New York: New York University Press, 1999.

Dehqan, Ahmad. *Safar Beh Gara-ye 270 Darajah.* Tehran: Nigah-e Imruz, 2001.

Dehqan, Ahmad. *Man Qatel-e Pesaretan Hastam.* Tehran: Nashr-e Ofoq, 2004.

Dehqan, Ahmad and Sprachman, Paul (trans.). *Journey to Heading 270 Degrees.* Costa Mesa, CA: Mazda Publishers, 2006.

Fahimi, Mehdi. *Farhang-e Jabheh: shu'ar-ha va rajaz-ha.* Tehran: Mu'avvanat-e Farhang va Tablighat-e Jang, Sitad-e Farmandeh-ha-ye Kul-e Qova, 1991.

Farasat, Qasem-'Ali. *Nakhl-ha-ye bi Sar.* Tehran: Amir Kabir, 1988.

Faridani, H. *The Imposed War.* Tehran: Ministry of Islamic Guidance, 1983.

Fasih, Esma'il. *Suraya dar Ighma.* Tehran: Kaviyan, 1985.

Fasih, Esma'il. *Sorraya in a Coma.* London: Zed Books, 1985.

Fasih, Esma'il. *Zamestan-e Shast o Dow.* Tehran: Nashr-e Now, 1987.

Ghaffarzadegan, Davud. *Fal-e Khun*. Tehran: Intisharat-e Qadyanai, 1996.

Ghaffarzadegan, Davud. *Zakhmha*. Tehran: Howzeh-ye Honari, 1996.

Ghaffarzadegan, Davud and Ghanoonparvar, M. R. (trans.). *Fortune Told in Blood*. Austin: Center for Middle Eastern Studies, the University of Texas at Austin, 2008.

Ghanoonparvar, M. R. "Postrevolutionary Trends in Persian Fiction and Film." *Radical History Review* 2009, 105 (2009): 156–62.

Gholami, Ahmad. *Fe'lan Esm Nadarad*. Tehran: Ofoq, 2001.

Gholami, Ahmad. *Kafsh-ha-ye Shaytan ra Napush*. Tehran: Chashmeh: 2004.

Gieling, Saskia Maria. *Religion and War in Revolutionary Iran*. London and New York: I.B. Tauris, 1999.

Hanif, Muhammad. *Jang az sih Didgah: Naqd va Barrasi-yi bist Ruman va Dastan-e Jang*. Tehran: Sarir, 2007.

Hasanzadeh, Farhad. *Hayat-e Khalvat*. Tehran: Entesharat Qoqnus, 2003.

Hoseyni, Zahra. *Da: Khaterat-e Sayyedeh Hoseyni Zahra.*, Tehran: Sureh-ye Mehr, 2009.

The Imposed War: Defence vs. Aggression. 5 vols. Tehran: War Information Headquarters, 1987.

Karimabadi, Mehrzad. "Manifesto of Martyrdom: Similarities and Differences between Avini's Ravaayat-e Fath [Chronicles of Victory] and more Traditional Manifestos." *Iranian Studies* 44, Issue 3 (May 2011), pp. 381–86.

Kazemi, Asghar. *Dasteh-ye Yek: Baz-revai-yi khaterat-e shab-e 'amaliyat* (24/11/1364, Jade-ye Fao—Um al-Qasr). Tehran: Sureh-ye Mehr, 2007.

Khosrokhavar, Farhad. *L'islamisme et la mort : Le martyre révolutionnaire en Iran*. Paris: Harmattan, 1995.

Khosronejad, Pedram. *Iranian Sacred Defence Cinema: Religion, Martyrdom and National Identity*. Canon Pyon, UK: Sean Kingston Publishing, 2012.

Khosronejad, Pedram. *War in Iranian Cinema: Religion, Martyrdom and National Identity*. London: I.B. Tauris, 2012.

Mahmud, Ahmad. *Zamin-e sukhteh*. Tehran: Entesharat-e Mu'in, 1982.

Makarami-Niya, Ali. *Barrasi-ye Shi'r Defa'-e Moqaddas*. Tehran: Tarafand, 2005.

Makhmalbaf, Muhsin, *Bagh-e Bolur*. Tehran: Nashr-e Nay, 1997.

Mandanipur, Shahriyar, *Del-e Deldadegi*. Tehran: Zaryab, 1998.

Mortazaiyan Abkenar, Hoseyn. *Aqrab ru-ye Pelleh-ha-ye Rah-ahan-e Andimeshk, ya, az in Qatar Khun michikeh, Qurban!*. Tehran: Nashr-e Nay, 2006.

Nazar-Nezhad, Mohammad Hasan. *Baba Nazar: Khaterat-e Shafahi-ye Shahid Mohammad Nazar-Nezhad*. Tehran: Sureh-ye Mehr, 2011.

Nazemi, Nader. "Sacrifice and Authorship: A Compendium of the Wills of Iranian War Martyrs." *Iranian Studies* 30, 3 (1997), pp. 263–71.

Potter, Lawrence G. and Sick, Gary. *Iran, Iraq, and the Legacies of War*. New York: Palgrave Macmillan, 2004.

Rabihavi, Qazi. *Az In Makan*. Tehran: Mu'assaseh-ye Entisharati-yi Mina, 1990.

Rahguzar, Riza. *Khuda Hafez Baradar: majmu'eh-ye dastan*. Tehran: Barg, 1989.

Rahguzar, Riza. *Nim negahi beh hasht Sal Qesseh-ye Jang*. Tehran: Howzeh-ye Honari, 1991.

Rahguzar, Riza. "Postrevolutionary Persian Literature." *Radical History Review* 2009 (105), pp. 145–50.

Rahmani, Zabihollah. "Filmsazi baray-e defa'-e moghaddas tofigh ast: Goft-o gu ba Abolqasem Talebi, filmsaz va rooznameh negar." *Soureh*, no. 40, Azar 1387 (2008), p. 45.

Rahmani, Zabihollah, and Sprachman, Paul (trans. and intro.). *One Woman's War: The Memoirs of Sayyedeh Zahra Hoseyni*. Costa Mesa, CA: Mazda Publishers, 2014.

Varzi, Roxanne. *Warring Souls: Youth, Media, and Martyrdom in Post-Revolutionary Iran*. Raleigh: Duke University Press, 2006.

Vatanabadi, Shouleh. "Stories beyond History: Translations beyond Nations." *Critique* 18:2 (2009), pp. 177–83.

"Website of Iranian Oral History." Tehran: Resistance Culture and Literature Research Center, 2011; oral-history.ir/.

IRAQ

'Abbas, Lu'ay Hamza. *'Ala Darraja fi al-Layl*. Amman: Azmina, 1997.

'Abbud, Salam. *Thaqafat al-'Unf fi al-'Iraq*. Cologne, Germany: al-Jamal, 2002.

'Abd Allah, Ibtisam. *Bakhur: qissas*. Baghdad: Dar al-Shu'un al-Thaqafiya al-'Amma, 1998.

'Abd al-Wahid, 'Abd al-Razzaq. *Fi Lahib Qadisiyya*. Baghdad: Wizarat al-Thaqafa, 1982.

'Abd al-Wahid, 'Abd al-Razzaq. *Salaman ya miyah al-'ard*. Baghdad: Wizarat al-Thaqafa, 1986.

'Abd al-Wahid, 'Abd al-Razzaq. *Ya Sayyid al-mushriqin, ya watani*. Baghdad, 1987.

Antun, Sinan. *Wahduha Shajarat al-Ruman*. Beirut: al-Mu'ssasa al-'Arabiyya lil-Dirasat wa al-Nashr, 2010.

Antun, Sinan. (trans. by author). *The Corpse Washer*. New Haven, CT: Yale University Press, 2013.

al-'Azzawi, Fadil. *Rajul Yarmi Ahjaran fi Bi'r*. London: Riyad al-Reyes, 1990.

al-'Azzawi, Fadil. *al-'Amal al-Shi'riyya*. Cologne: Manshurat al-Jamal, 2007.

Ba'ath Regional Command Council, Iraq Memory Foundation Archive, Hoover Institution. Hitherto (BRCC) 01–3665–0001–0006 to 0053.

Baram, Amatzia. *Culture, History and Ideology in Ba'thist Iraq, 1968–89*. New York: St. Martin's Press, 1991.

Blasim, Hasan. *Majnun Sahat al-Hurriya: qisas qasira*. Beirut: al-Mu'assasa al-'Arabiyya lil-Dirasat wa-al-Nashr, 2012.

Cooke, Miriam. *Women and the War Story*. Berkeley: University of California Press, 1996.

Dulaymi, Lutfiyya. *Budhur al-Nar*. Baghdad: Dar al-Shu'un al-Thaqafiyya al-'Amma, 1988.

Hillawi, Janan Jasim. *Layl al-Bilad*. Beirut: Dar al-Adab, 2002.

Hillawi, Janan Jasim. *Qissas al-Hub, Qissas al-Harb*. Uddevalla, Sweden: Dar al-Manfa, 1998.

Hamudi, Basim 'Abd al-Hamid (ed.). *Diwan al-Aqlam*. Baghdad: Dar al-Shu'un al-Thaqafiya al-'Amma, 1986.

al-Khafaji, Muhsin. al-'Awda ila Shajarat al-Hana', Baghdad: Wizarat al-Thaqafa, 1983.

Khidr, Abbas. *Al-Khakiyya: Min Awraq al-Jarima al-Thaqafiyya fi al-'Iraq*. Cologne: Manshurat al-Jamal, 2005.

Khoury, Dina Rizk. *Iraq in Wartime: Soldiering, Martyrdom, and Remembrance*. Cambridge: Cambridge University Press, 2013.

Khudayri, Batul. *Kam Baddat al-Sama' Qaribatan*. Amman: al-Mu'assasa al-'Arabiya lil-Dirasat wa-al-Nashr, 1999.

Khudayyir, Muhammad. *Basrayatha: Surat al-Madina*. Damascus: Dar al-Mada, 1996.

Khudayyir, Muhammad. Trans. William Hutchins. *Basrayatha: Story of a City*. New York: Verso, 2008.

Khudayyir, Muhammad. *Ru'iya al-Kharif*. Amman: Mu'assasat 'Abd al-Hamid Shuman, 1995.

Maysilun, Hadi. *al-'Alam Nagisan Wahid*. Ammān: Dar Usama lil-Nashr wa-al-Tawzi', 1999.

Mazlum, Muhammad. *Haṭab Ibrahim ow Jil al-Badawi: Shi'r al-Thamaninat wa-Ajiyal al-Dawla al-'Iraqiyya*. Damascus: al-Takwin lil-Ta'liif wa-al-Tarjama wa-al-Nashr, 2007.

Milich, Stephan. "The Positioning from Baathist Intellectuals and Writers Before and After 2003: The Case of the Iraqi Poet Abd al-Razzaq Abd al-Wahid." *Middle East Journal of Culture and Communication* 4 (2011), p. 301.

Milich, Stephan et al., eds. *Conflicting Narratives: War, Trauma and Memory in Iraqi Culture*. Wiesbaden: Reichert Verlag, 2012.

Mohsen, Fatima. "Cultural Authoritarianism." *Iraq since the Gulf War: Prospects for Democracy*, ed. Fran Hazelton. Atlantic Highlands, NJ: Zed Books, 1994. 7–19.

al-Musawi, Muhsin Jasim. *al-Mar'i wa-al-Mutakhayyil: Adab al-Harb al-Qissasi fi al-'Iraq: Dirasa wa-Mukhtarat*. Baghdad: Dar al-Shu'un al-Thaqafiyya al-'Amma, 1986.

Nasir, 'Abd al-Sattar. *Qissas fi Thiyab al-Ma'rika*. Baghdad: Wizarat al-Thaqafa, 1982.

Nasir, 'Abd al-Sattar. *al-Matar taht al-Shams*. Baghdad: Wizarat al-Thaqafa, 1986.

Nasir, 'Abd al-Sattar. *al-Shahid 1777*. Baghdad: Wizarat al-Thaqafa, 1988.

Qadisiyyat Saddam: Qissas Taht Lahib al-Nar (vols. 1–10). Baghdad: Dar al-Shu'un al-Thaqafiyya, 1981–1990.

Qazwini, Iqbal. *Mumarrat al-Sukun*. Amman: Dar Azmina, 2006.

Qazwini, Iqbal, and al-Kholy, Azza. Nowaira Amira (trans.). *Zubaida's Window: An Iraqi Novel of Exile*. New York: Feminist Press at CUNY, 2008.

Quigley, John., "Iran and Iraq and the Obligations to Release and Repatriate Prisoners of War After the Close of Hostilities." *American University International Law Review* 5, 1 (1989), pp. 73–86.

al-Ramli, Muhsin. *al-Fatit al-Mub'athar*. Cairo: Markaz al-Hadara al-'Arabiyya, 2000.

al-Ramli, Muhsin, and Hanoosh, Yasmeen. *Scattered Crumbs*. Fayetteville: University of Arkansas Press, 2003.

Rhode, Achim. *Facing Dictatorship: State-Society Relations in Ba'thist Iraq*. London: Routledge, 2010.

Rhode, Achim. "Opportunities for Masculinity and Love: Cultural Production in Ba'thist Iraq during the 1980s." In *Islamic Masculinities*, Ouzgane, Lahouchine (ed.). London: Zed Press, 2006, 148–201.

al-Saqr, Mahdi 'Isa. *Imra'at al-Gha'ib*. Damascus: Dar al-Mada, 2004.

Talib, Alya. *al-Mamarrat*. Baghdad: Wizarat al-Thaqafa, 1988.

Tramotini, Leslie. "Poetry Post-Sayyab." In *Poetry and History: The Value of Poetry in Reconstructing Arab History*, Ramzi Ba'labakki, Salih Sa'id Agha, and Tarif Khalidi, ed. Beirut: American University of Beirut Press, 2011.

Wali, Nijm. *Ṣurat Yusif*. Casablanca and Beirut: al-Markaz al-Thaqafi al-'Arabi, 2005.

Wali, Nijm. *al-Harb fi Hay al-Tarab*. Budapest: Sahara, 1993.

Mardin Aminpour was born in the Iranian Kurdistan. He pursued higher education in Tehran, where he obtained a bachelor's degree in English Language and Literature at Tehran University. Subsequently, he received a Fulbright scholarship in 2007 to teach Persian at the University of Texas at Austin, where he is currently working toward a doctoral degree in Middle Eastern Studies. His research is focused on Kurdish identity politics in the Hashemite Iraq (1921–1958).

Michael Beard is Chester Fritz Professor of English at the University of North Dakota. He earned a doctorate from Indiana University in Comparative Literature. His primary interests in research are in Persian and Arabic literature in international contexts. His book *The Blind Owl as a Western Novel* (1990) is a study of genre and the possibility of multicultural identity, using the Iranian writer Sadeq Hedayat (1903–51) as an example. He translates frequently, usually in collaboration with Adnan Haydar. Their translation of a collection of poems, *Aghânî Mihyâr al-Dimishqî* (1961) by the Arab poet Adonis (Ali Ahmed Said), appeared in 2008 under the title *Mihyar of Damascus, His Songs*. It won the Lois Roth Award for translation (2008–09). He works as co-editor of the series Middle East Literature in Translation for Syracuse University Press and associate editor of the journal *Middle Eastern Literatures*.

Peter Chelkowski studied Oriental Philology at the Jagiellonian University and Theater Arts at the School of Drama in the city of Cracow. Later, when he moved to England, he attended the School of Oriental and African Studies (SOAS), where he studied Islamic Middle East History and Culture. Later still, he went to Iran and studied Persian Literature with several distinguished professors and scholars at the University of Tehran. These experiences and his education in various countries with diverse languages and cultures contribute to and are reflected in his teaching and writings. He is currently Professor Emeritus of Middle Eastern and Islamic Studies at New York University. His interests include Islamic and Iranian Studies in general, Islamic Mysticism, Popular Beliefs and Rituals, Persian Language and Literature, and the Performing Arts. Chelkowski's major publications include *Mirror of the Invisible World* (1975); *Ta'ziyeh: Ritual and Drama in Iran* (New York, NYU Press, 1979); and *Staging a Revolution: The Art of Persuasion in the Islamic Republic of Iran*, co-authored with H. Dabashi (1999).

Farzaneh Farahzad began her career as translator and interpreter, received her PhD in Teaching English as a Foreign Language, and has been teaching translation practice and theory ever since. She is Professor of Translation Studies at Allameh Tabataba'i University in Tehran, author of several textbooks for the translator training program in Iran, and has written many articles in Persian and English in translation studies. She has been actively engaged in curriculum development for the undergraduate translator training programs and the graduate and PhD programs in translation studies in Iran. She is editor-in-chief of the *Iranian Translation Studies Journal*, and series editor of a collection of books in Persian in Translation Studies. She has actively contributed to the introduction and promotion of Translation Studies in Iran as an academic discipline.

M. R. Ghanoonparvar is Professor Emeritus of Persian and Comparative Literature at the University of Texas at Austin. He has published widely on Persian literature and culture in both English and Persian and is the author of *Prophets of Doom: Literature as a Socio-Political Phenomenon in Modern Iran* (1984), *In a Persian Mirror: Images of the West and Westerners in Iranian Fiction* (1993), *Translating the Garden* (2001), *Reading Chubak* (2005), *Persian Cuisine: Traditional, Regional and Modern Foods* (2006), and *The Neighbor Says: Letters of Nima Yushij and the Philosophy of Modern Persian Poetry* (2009). His translations include Jalal Al-e Ahmad's *By the Pen*, Sadeq Chubak's *The Patient Stone*, Simin Daneshvar's *Savushun*, Ahmad Kasravi's *On Islam and Shi'ism*, Sadeq Hedayat's *The Myth of Creation*, Davud Ghaffarzadegan's *Fortune Told in Blood*, Mohammad Reza Bayrami's *The Tales of Sabalan* and *Eagles of Hill 60*, and Bahram Beyza'i's *Memoirs of the Actor in a Supporting Role*.

His edited volumes include *Iranian Drama: An Anthology*, *In Transition: Essays on Culture and Identity in Middle Eastern Societies*, Gholamhoseyn Sa'edi's *Othello in Wonderland* and *Mirror-Polishing Storytellers*, and Moniru Ravanipur's *Satan Stones* and *Kanizu*. He was the recipient of the 2008 Lois Roth Prize for Literary Translation. His forthcoming books include *Dining at the Safavid Court*, *Iranian Films and Persian Fiction* and *Literary Diseases in Persian Literature*.

Arta Khakpour studied modern Persian literature at NYU's Department of Middle Eastern and Islamic Studies, where he defended his dissertation, "Each Into a World of His Own: Mimesis, Modernist Fiction, and the Iranian Avant-Garde." His research examines the role of literary magazines and salons in developing modernist fiction in post-Reza Shah Iran, focusing particularly upon their theoretical and literary interventions in the evolution of anti-realist narrative techniques. His articles are featured in the journals *Iranian Studies* and *Middle East Literatures*, and in 2013, he worked as the archive consultant for Asia Society's award-winning Iran Modern exhibition.

Mohammad Mehdi Khorrami is Professor of Persian Language and Literature at New York University. His research field is contemporary Persian fiction. His latest book, *Literary Subterfuge and Contemporary Persian Fiction: Who Writes Iran?* (2014), focuses on identifying classical and modern rhetorical and aesthetic dynamisms and their functions in forming literary discourses. His publications include *Modern Reflections of Classical Traditions in Persian Fiction* (2003), *Sohrab's Wars: Counter-Discourses of Contemporary Persian Fiction* (translator and editor, 2008), *A Feast in the Mirror: A Collection of Short Stories by Iranian Women* (co-editor and co-translator, 2000), and *Another Sea, Another Shore: Persian Stories of Migration* (co-editor and co-translator, 2003). He is founder and co-director of the Association for the Study of Persian Literature (www.persian-literature.org).

Dina Rizk Khoury is Professor of History and International Affairs at George Washington University. She writes on Ottoman and modern Iraq. She has published two books: *State and Provincial Society in the Ottoman Empire: Mosul 1519–1834* (1997, 2002) and *Iraq in Wartime:*

Soldiering, Martyrdom Remembrance (2013). She has also published articles on urban popular politics in Ottoman Baghdad and more recently on the securitization and militarization of social life and urban spaces in modern Iraq.

Amir Moosavi has completed his PhD through the Department of Middle Eastern and Islamic Studies at New York University. His dissertation, entitled "Dust that Never Settled: Ideology, Ambivalence and Disenchantment in Arabic and Persian Fiction of the Iran-Iraq War (1980–2003)," treats representations of the Iran-Iraq War in Arabic and Persian literary texts written between 1980 and 2003, using the period as a starting point for the comparative study of literary and cultural production between Arabic- and Persian-speaking worlds. He is interested in modern prose fiction from the eastern Arab world and Iran, with a focus on cultural representations and aesthetics of war and violent pasts. He holds a Bachelor of Arts in History from the University of Wisconsin-Madison and a Master of Arts in Near Eastern Studies from NYU. He has taught language and literature courses at NYU, Bard College, Hunter College (CUNY), and the Cooper Union. His publications include an article entitled "How to Write Death: Resignifying Martyrdom in Two Novels of the Iran-Iraq War," in the 2015 edition of *ALIF: Journal of Comparative Poetics* and multiple book reviews.

Kamran Rastegar is Associate Professor of Arabic and Comparative Literature at Tufts University. He is the author of the books *Surviving Images: Cinema, War and Cultural Memory in the Middle East* (2015) and *Literary Modernity Between the Middle East and Europe* (2007), and he edited the special issue *Authoring the Nahda: Writing the Arabic Nineteenth Century* for the journal *Middle Eastern Literatures* 16:3, 2013.

Marjan Riahi was born in Isfahan. She studied Business Management at the University of Tehran and Professional Scriptwriting at the Center for Islamic Filmmaking and Drama at Tarbiat Modarres University. Her short story collections have been published in Iran, the United States, and Turkey. Her filmmaking experience includes directorial credits for documentaries as well as short films. In addition, she has written and directed more than a dozen plays, most of them intended for an adolescent or young adult audience. Riahi has also served as a writing consultant for several major films. Two of her works have failed to obtain a publishing permit from the Ministry of Culture and Islamic Guidance: the first, entitled *Letter*, is a collection of three short stories and the second is a novel entitled *A Little Before the Beginning.*

Ella Habiba Shohat is Professor of Cultural Studies who has lectured and written extensively on issues pertaining to Eurocentrism, Orientalism, Postcolonialism, transnationalism, and diasporic cultures. More specifically, since the 1980s she has developed critical approaches to the study of Arab Jews/Sephardim/Mizrahim. Her work has been translated into diverse languages, including: Arabic, Hebrew, Turkish, French, Spanish, Portuguese, German, Polish, Dutch, and Italian. Shohat has also served on the editorial board of several journals, including: *Social Text, Middle East Critique, Meridians, Interventions,* and *Middle East Journal of Culture and Communication.* She is a recipient of fellowships, including: the Rockefeller Foundation Bellagio Center, 1999; the University of California "Regents Lecturer," UC Davis, 1997; the Society for the Humanities at Cornell University (1991–1992), where she also taught at the School of Criticism and Theory (2006). In 2010, she was awarded a Fulbright research/lectureship at the University of São Paulo, Brazil, working on the cultural intersections between the Middle East and Latin America. Recently, together with Sinan Antoon, she was awarded the NYU Humanities Initiative fellowship for developing the course "Narrating Iraq: Between Nation and Diaspora." She is Affiliated Faculty with the Comparative Literature Department; the Gender and Sexuality Studies Program, Department of Social & Cultural Analysis; the Center for Latin American & Caribbean Studies; Media, Culture & Communication and the Visual Culture Program (Steinhardt); and also Affiliated Faculty, NYU–Abu Dhabi.

Shouleh Vatanabadi teaches Global Cultures in the Global Liberal Studies Program at NYU. She has been a member of NYU fulltime faculty since 1991. Her areas of specialization include: Cultural Studies, Middle East Studies, Iranian and Turkish Studies, Women's Studies, Transnational and Postcolonial Studies. Her current work focuses on the intersections of cultural studies and the politics of translation of the Middle East and the global South-North and South-South cultural flows. She is the co-editor and translator of the award-winning book, *A Feast in the Mirror: Stories by Contemporary Iranian Women* (2000) and *Another Sea, another Shore: Persian Stories of Migration* (2004). Among her recent articles are "Stories beyond Histories, Translations Beyond Nations" in *Critique: Critical Middle Eastern Studies* 18 (2): 2009, and "Translating the Transnational" in *Cultural Studies* (special Issue: Trans-nationalism and Cultural Studies), Vol. 23 (5 & 6): 2009, "Uneven Bridge of Translation: Turkey in between East and West," in *The Cultural Politics of the Middle East in the Americas*, Ella Shohat and Evelyn Alsultani, ed. Ann Arbor: University of Michigan Press, 2013.

INDEX